IMAGES OF INFORMATION

SAGE FOCUS EDITIONS

IMAGES OF INFORMATION

Still Photography in the Social Sciences

Jon Wagner, Editor

Preface by Howard S. Becker

 **SAGE Publications**   **Beverly Hills/London**

For information address:

SAGE PUBLICATIONS, INC.
275 South Beverly Drive
Beverly Hills, California 90212

SAGE PUBLICATIONS LTD
28 Banner Street
London EC1Y 8QE, England

Printed in the United States of America

Library of Congress Cataloging in Publication Data

Wagner, Jon.
  Images of information.

  (Sage focus editions)
  Includes bibliographical references.
    1. Photography in the social sciences. 2. Social science research. 3. Social sciences—Study and teaching. I. Title. II. Series.
H62.W22   300′.7′8   79-16894
ISBN 0-8039-1088-6
ISBN 0-8039-1089-4 pbk.

SECOND PRINTING, 1982

CONTENTS

PREFACE

Howard S. Becker

I was arrogant enough to think (though I never said it to Jon Wagner) that I wouldn't learn much new from this book. After all, I had been making photographs for eight or nine years, sociology for a lot longer than that, and had written, thought, lectured and taught about the inter-relationships between the two. Well, I've been wrong before, though it hasn't often been such a pleasure. I learned a lot I didn't know before as I read the articles and photographs in this book. Anyone who goes through it is bound to get the same measure of instruction and pleasure from it.

Visual social science isn't something brand new, as Stasz usefully reminds us in her article, but it might as well be. It is only in the last eight or ten years that a sufficient number of people have had a joint interest in the two fields to create the critical mass for some real progress to be made. One advantage of a field which has just reached that state is that there has not been time for standard procedures and paradigms to get established. As a result, people come into the work with a variety of backgrounds, training, and experience, of necessity make a great variety of experiments (almost anything you do is an experiment at this stage), and the ratio of novel ideas, procedures, and results to the total volume of work produced is very high. The complementary disadvantage is that it is all very confusing, so that it is at present a field for people who can tolerate disorder.

Wagner and his associates are so aware of the lessons to be learned that there is little left for a preface-writer to comment on. A few things are so striking, however, that I will run the risk of repeating what is said by others later on in the book.

The authors show us the serious, manifold difficulties faced by anyone who tries to use photographs in their social science work, the very difficulties which lead other social scientists to be skeptical of the results. But, in every case, it is easy to see that the difficulty is not unique to photographic work. On the contrary, visual materials simply make obvious the difficulties we have with every variety of data. Do we worry because the photographic frame, putting a line around much that is of interest to us, excludes everything else? We should, just as we should worry that a questionnaire finds out something about what it asks about, and tells us nothing about the rest. Do we worry about the way the relation between the photographer and the people being photographed affects the material we get? We should, just as we should try to understand the effect of the relationship between investigator and the people investigated in participant observation or experiments. Worrying over the difficulties of photographic work can revitalize our thinking about problems of method and epistemology, problems always in danger of being so ritualized that they lose contact with the day-to-day work of social science.

Academic social scientists habitually complain that their teaching interferes with their research, the implication being that the two have little in common. The papers in this book, on the contrary, show the intimate relation between the two. Almost every chapter in the section on research could, with little modification, be transferred to the section on teaching, and vice versa. When a field is developing so rapidly, students become what they should always be in principle: coworkers and codiscoverers. Teaching, you discover and try out methods of getting and working with data. Doing research, you discover new ways of teaching students about the visual aspect of society. When Harper shows us how to see the meaning of the details in some of his photographs of migrant workers, we discover both how to learn about society and how to teach our students to learn in that way. Krieger uses his experience with photographs as teaching tools to explore some knotty problems, of immense importance to working social scientists, about the relations between truth, clarity, and notions of the good. Lifchez' ingenious use of scale photographic manikins as a device to teach architecture students to pay attention to the social dimension of design immediately sparks notions of how such materials might be used in experimental and interview studies.

This is a book for people presently using photographic materials in their teaching and research. Even if they are as arrogant as I was, they will learn some new things. It is also a book for people who want to know what this talk of "visual social science" is all about. They will find both examples—in sufficient detail to stimulate their own experiments —and general discussions which make clear the theoretical and methodological bases for developing forms of practice in visual social science.

—Howard S. Becker

ACKNOWLEDGMENTS

This book has come and gone and come again for me several times in the last ten years, and it is not an easy matter to thank all those who have helped it along. My most immediate appreciation is for the contributors, all of whom have participated with such good spirits and encouragement in the final business of bringing it to press. I also thank the editorial, production and marketing staff members with whom I worked at SAGE Publications—all of whom took the time to see this book for what it could be at a time when there was little to show for it. I have enjoyed their interest and faith as well as their technical counsel.

Parts of the manuscript were given a careful and responsive reading by several of the contributors, and both Howard Becker and Clarice Stasz have been invaluable to me for their critical encouragement and editorial advice. I would also like to thank Daniele Spellman and Teresa Harlan for their assistance in typing and correcting much of the manuscript.

My own interest in photography is indebted to other social scientists as well as to situations in which I was able to work on many of the themes discussed in the book. In the first instance, I must mention the work of John Collier (1967) and Howard Becker (1975), without which my own thought on these matters would be much less informed than it is. Between them they have staked out a rather large area to explore and have tirelessly and unselfishly encouraged others to have a go at it.

In the second instance, I am grateful for the opportunity, many years ago, to combine photography and social science teaching at Columbia College (Chicago, Illinois). The photography department in general— Jim Newberry, Harold Allen, and Charlie Traub in particular—were my first photography teachers; they were all excellent at what they did and interested as well in social science. Some time later I was fortunate to work with Suzanne Keller on her extended study of Twin Rivers. In this capacity I designed and executed a series of social scientific and photographic research projects, and I thank her again for the four years of our working association. More recently, as director of the Field Studies Program at Berkeley, I have been encouraged to examine the relationship among field research, field teaching, and field learning, and many of my own ideas about photography have emerged within this context.

I would like to underline the manner in which this book is a collective product. This is so not only because chapters have been written by several people, but also because as authors we have benefited a great deal from our formal and informal association. A growing and vital culture of inquiry around social science and visual imagery is the real, phenomenal context in which our work has emerged, and for that we are all most grateful.

It is to this collective context that the book is dedicated, to that and to Lynne Hollingsworth, who, long before she became my wife, regretfully observed that my involvement with photography seemed to have ended before my involvement with her began. We have both been pleased to find that she was wrong, though it was largely through her fresh appreciation of old images that I found my way back to cameras and photographs. For her regrets of long ago, and for the renewing example of her own vision, I thank her.

ABOUT THE COVER . . . .

The image on the cover cuts two ways, as do many of those in the rest of the book. On the one hand it is "art," or something like it, and makes sense to us in terms of form, shading, and line. But who can resist asking, "Where can you get gas for 25.9?" a question about information which stands independently of aesthetic issues and concerns. Or does it?

—J.W.

INTRODUCTION 1
Information in and about Photographs

Jon Wagner

If I were to make a photograph of you, one which showed you seated casually in a familiar chair, your legs crossed and your eyes looking clearly into the lens, would it be the "real you" I photographed? And if you were wearing the clothes you have on now, your hair just as it is and your shoes as well, your teeth brushed neither more nor less than they are as you read this, would that be an accurate picture of who and what you are?

Or should I include your friends within the frame, seated around you, casually, in their familiar chairs, in the clothes they might be wearing at this moment, their teeth brushed neither more nor less? Should I have them bring in their friends as well, with familiar chairs and eyes looking clearly into the lens? And should I have them come many times? Today, tomorrow, a week from now and a year ago? Should I follow you to visit them in their homes? Should I photograph as well the places where you go when you leave your chair and your home, the settings in which you work and play, worship, socialize, shop and sin? And should I stop at that, or should I go on and make photographs of the people you admire—are they part of you as well?— and the things you want to have? What about the neighborhoods in which you have lived and the schools in which you spent years of your life? What about the doctor's offices and banks and gas stations through which you have passed in pain and need? Your moments of joy and abandon, should I see to it that they are within the frame as well? And if I did it all and photographed all there was to be seen of you and of your connections to the world, would it be the real you that I was photographing? Would you identify yourself as the subject of all the images I had made?

Or, if I were to show you a photograph of me, one which showed me seated at my typewriter in my flannel shirt and pleated jeans, would you know something about me? Would you know more if you saw my face, tired and slack from a day's hard work? Would you know even more if such a photograph showed my unfinished room, the light green walls and luxo lamps, the ugly maroon carpet which my predecessor in this house glued to a hardwood floor? Would you know even more if I made the frame large enough to take in the cat which is now asleep on a chair in the dining room or my wife who, from the sounds of things, is taking a shower? How much more would you know, and how much more could I show you through my expanding photograph?

What about my other photographs, the old ones kept in a box or two beneath the desk and others still placed in albums behind plastic sheets? What could you learn from the negatives of my parents' wedding pictures and the color slides I have made of almost every place I've ever been? Would these be useful to you in understanding the meaning of my life and the social worlds in which I participate?

Perhaps, and perhaps not.

Let's say we wanted to understand something of our lives, and we decided to work towards that understanding through photographs. How could we proceed?

We could look at each other's photographs and ask questions of them.

We could take pictures of what we felt to be the important features of our lives.

We could make photographs of each other.

We could talk about the things we found hard to photograph.

We could install automatic cameras to record our routine behavior.

We could arrange the photographs we had into sequences, groups, and categories.

And, we could expand this conversation with and about our photographs to include others important to us for one reason or another.

Through this hypothetical photographic encounter—one which captures some of what we do with cameras in everyday life—we can play at social science. In "capturing the world" we can test our ideas about each other against the photographs and the realities they represent. In "creating visual statements" we manifest our understanding of the interesting and important. Through the photographs we increase our knowledge of each other while at the same time raise questions about how well we understand our own lives. Through both *taking* photographs and *making* photographs we casually participate in scientific inquiry.

There are things to be gained by making our science less casual. By working towards more thoughtful process and more explicit social theory, we can become increasingly sophisticated about the kinds of evidence needed to make an observation about or with our photographs. By expanding our awareness of the frame "behind" the camera—the context in which the photographer is working—we refine our understanding of the social processes involved in making the images themselves. Without denying the rich and varied impact that photographs themselves can have on us, we ask questions about the situations in which we look at them. In collaboration with other social scientists—those who have taken these concerns to be their own—we begin to identify in greater detail the structure of our ignorance and the threads of what we know. And, as we deal collectively with issues such as these, we raise as well important questions about how we learn about the world at all, the nature of our scientific goals, and the methods by which we pursue them.

Taking seriously the camera work in which we are already engaged, we can move from snapshots of friends and scenery to a confrontation with contemporary social science. In doing so, we quickly notice a peculiar state of affairs: The visual images which permeate and organize our daily lives generally lie "outside the frame" of social science inquiry. The "seeing" which is clearly central to our personal way of being is but a peripheral concern of the study of our social order. With respect to visual images, social science itself seems almost to be blind.

Elaboration of photographic exercises about the "real you" and the real me into the ambiguities and contradictions of social science thus leads to a complex set of issues. Not only must we attend to the business of designing appropriate methods for recording what we see, but we must begin to question that seeing itself. We find ourselves working within a dialectical science, the object of which is the study of the species which has itself constructed the science. We find ourselves returning to the variety of life and to questions of how much of it we can hope to understand.

And all this we find within our photographs.

TECHNIQUE AND MEANING

What we find in photographs, however, we find as a result of our willingness to look and our skills in doing so, for photographs are at least as ambiguous as the contexts in which they are examined and viewed. At times they are more so, a characteristic they share with words, gestures, and other systems of representation and symbolization. But not always.

In some contexts the ambiguity is quite low, and the clarity and meaning of photographic images is held to be matter-of-fact. For purposes of official identification, photographs are frequently seen to be less ambiguous than words, a fact to which the FBI posters in post offices readily attest. In the natural sciences as well, photographs have a long and rich tradition of unambiguous service to research. Archaeology, geology, physics, botany, chemistry, and biology have all made extensive use of photography in data collection, experimental manipulations, and comparative analysis. In some fields, such as high energy physics and astronomy, it has been through photographs alone that objects of inquiry—subatomic particles and distant stellar constellations—have been "seen" and their movements charted and measured. Similarly, in the applied sciences of medicine and engineering, photography has become an essential and routine tool for research.

The social sciences, in contrast, exhibit a fundamental lack of consensus about the significance and meaning of photographic images. It is the purpose of this book to examine still photography within that domain.

When we think of using photography in the social sciences, the ambiguity need not arise immediately. There are, for example, a wide range of questions which could be discussed in matter-of-fact terms about application and technique:

How can photographs be used to record human behavior?

What kinds of photographic strategies are most likely to generate interesting data?

In what circumstances are photographic images appropriate stimuli for interviewing respondents?

What kinds of questions about the social order can be explored through photography?

How does the use of photographic equipment constrict or expand the role of the social researcher?

These questions may not be familiar, but their forms should be. They emerge from within areas of social science activity in which there is some consensus about method and practice. These questions focus on the application of photographic techniques to the existing paradigm of research and investigation, and it is one purpose of this book to provide reasonable answers to them.

Social scientists could deal with photographs in a manner only slightly less straightforward in their presentations. Within this context a second set of "technical" questions can be identified:

How can photographs be used to present information to students and colleagues?

What kinds of photographic projects are effective in encouraging students to observe and conceptualize about human behavior?

In what ways can photographs enrich the students' understanding of particular social phenomena?

By what critieria and under what circumstances are photographic assignments and research best evaluated?

What kind of photographic equipment lends itself to particular photographic projects?

Once again, these questions emerge from areas of some consensus about method and practice, and they focus on the application of photographic techniques to the existing paradigm of social science teaching and research. It is a second purpose of this book to provide reasonable answers to these questions as well.

There remains another set of concerns, however, which calls into question the matter-of-factness of these two centers of consensus. If we deal seriously with photographic images we must inevitably encounter a set of issues which are critical not only for the intelligent use of photography by social scientists, but for the discipline of the social sciences itself. It is here that a great deal of ambiguity arises, for these concerns point to fundamental inadequacies of the existing paradigm of social research. So much ambiguity and dissensus emerge out of these less technical questions that some social scientists have probably been scared away from productive and routine use of photography in the more matter-of-fact context characteristic of the natural sciences. This happens when we ask the following:

What is the relationship between a photographic image and the phenomenon it was intended to record?

What relationship exists between the viewer, the photograph and the social situation in which it is viewed?

How do we "make" photographs and how does our understanding of that process contribute to our ability to "read" them?

Within what systems of logic and systematic association do we process and "understand" the photographic image?

With these questions we return to the core, the articulation between social science research and the world it is designed to describe and explain. We are back at the dissensus surrounding what can be said about and what can be said with a set of photographs.

Our canons of good practice suggest that we need to answer these fundamental questions first, before dealing with those of technique and application. It is arrogant and naive, however, either to think that we can answer them, or to think that we don't have to try. In between "good practice" and these two poles of arrogance lies a much less clean and tidy strategy, one that finds us using photographs *as if* we could agree about their significance, while at the same time raising fundamental questions about what they do or what they might mean. It is a dialectical process, one in which we learn something about these "core" issues by taking photographs for more narrowly defined purposes; one in which we learn something about doing research by confronting the ambiguity of what a photograph can imply. It is a process in which we work towards refined understanding, both of the techniques and application, and of the visual language in which they participate. It is a process of many starts and many stops, of insights small and large, confusion, clarity, and confusion once again. It is an adventure into the visual order of human behavior as well as into the processes themselves by which we know about the world, and it is this adventure which this book is designed to examine.

ORGANIZATION OF THE BOOK

C. Wright Mills (1959) has made a useful distinction between the context of "discovery" and the context of "presentation." Within the contemporary practice of social science, these can fall rather neatly into "research" and "teaching," and this book is similarly organized. The advantage of this format is that it reflects the two matter-of-fact contexts in which social scientists can productively use photographs. The disadvantage is that it obscures, at least at one level, the dialectical concerns I raised in the preceding pages. There are two correctives to this latter problem: One is that the following articles do deal individually with issues of photographic ambiguity as they relate to more specific applications in both research and teaching. The second is that for both teaching and research, the book offers explicit discussions of "issues" as well as "applications." A concluding section entitled, "Problems and Prospects" examines some of the more persistent and important of these, and the references at the back of the book should prove useful to those who wish to explore these matters more fully.

RESEARCH/DISCOVERY

In social science alone, there are at least five separate modes of photographic research.

1. Photographs as Interview Stimuli. Social scientists have used photographs to interview respondents about such diverse phenomena as the expression of emotions (Ekman et al., 1972), landscape preference (Greebie, 1975), the My Lai massacre (Thompson et al., 1974), and community design (see my own work in Chapter 6). This kind of research is just beginning to develop as a subfield in its own right, and an interesting and interdisciplinary literature is growing rapidly.

2. Systematic Recording. Both still and motion picture cameras have been used by scientists to record and inventory a wide range of social phenomena, including the play of facial expressions (Ekman et al., 1972), seating patterns along Manhattan streets (Whyte, 1972), accumulation and arrangement of household possessions (Collier, 1967), and pedestrian traffic patterns in airports (Davis and Ayers, 1975). Some of this work draws on a long and valuable tradition of photographic study of animals, insects, birds, and the like. As the techniques of systematic photographic recording become more familiar to social scientists, this line of inquiry will no doubt expand as well, and we can expect to see more work similar in concern to Zube's study of pedestrians and wind (Chapter 5).

3. Content Analysis of Naive Photographs. All photographs contain data in addition to that "intended" by the photographer, and a growing number of studies have taken this as a point of departure. Content analysis of photographs recently has been brought to popular attention through the social historical studies of Michael Lesy (1973; 1976). While Lesy's presentation format is anything but systematic, other social scientists have looked at materials similar to his with greater rigor. Seaford (1971) has studied "smiling" in photographs with respect to geographic region; Cloninger (1974) has examined the "male" and "female" imagery of famous photographers; Thompson and Clarke are currently studying photographic imagery in corporate self-presentations, and Stasz (Chapter 8) has done a careful study of early photographs in the *American Journal of Sociology.*

4. Native Image-Making. Worth and Adair (1972) completed a pioneering piece of research on "native vision" by making the technology of film-making accessible to Navajo Indians. Their subsequent analysis of the "native ways of seeing" suggested a rich mode of social research. In recent years, others have followed their example and examined the visual documents which different groups and individuals are inclined to make once they are familiar with the equipment for doing so. One of the more ambitious of these recent studies is that done by Bellman and Jules-Rosette (1977).

The analysis of "native image-making" brings us up against complex conceptual problems, of course, when we recognize that we are ourselves "natives" of our own culture. Chalfen (1975) in his preliminary work in this area has teased out at least one "native format" in which most of us participate, and dubbed it the "home mode" of visual communication. Musello has elaborated on Chalfen's formulation in his work on family photographs (see Chapter 7), and other visual modes of our native culture await the attention of further research.

5. Narrative Visual Theory. Drawing heavily on the rich traditions of social documentary photography, a number of social scientists have been exploring with a camera the visual coefficients of social organization. Some of these researchers are primarily ethnographers, such as Harper in his study of "tramps" (Chapter 2) and Aron in his work on the Jewish community of the Lower East Side of Manhattan (Chapter 4). Others—such as Ewen in her study of beauty parlors (Chapter 3)—are interested in the connections between people's lives and the social and economic structure of the larger world. In calling such work narrative visual theory, I am indicating that these efforts share a commitment to the narrative organization of photographs in which implicit elements of social theory are clearly ackowledged. Social scientists who take up photography quite frequently take it up in this mode, and a rich variety of such studies has developed, including Becker's study of rock music medicine and Stasz's work on county fairs.

While these different modes of photographic social research require different skills and, at times, different equipment, it is also clear that they are fascinating in their complementarity. We are all "native image makers," and we "interview" each other when looking at photographs together. In addition, we can use photographs generated in one research context in quite another. In my own work with photographic "community study," we interviewed residents about photographs originally taken as part of a systematic inventory of built forms. In addition, we performed a content analysis of photographs taken for "narrative" purposes, generating by so doing a new set of insights into our "native" photographic strategies as well as the visual order of the community we studied (see Chapter 6).

This reflexive and complementary use of photographs may hold the greatest promise for investigating the meanings of social life. As photographic social scientists increase their familiarity with each other's work, a new generation of fruitful collaborations is emerging. Within this expanding climate of attention and inquiry, abstract questions about what a photograph means can be translated into the more concrete question of "what does this photograph mean to whom and in which situations?"

The cutting edge of social research through photography is thus broad, varied and ragged. There are many places for someone to pick it up and take another step forward. On the other hand, it owes immeasurable debts to a century-and-half's worth of photographers who were untrained as social scientists. These craftspeople and artists were fascinated by their equipment and what it could do, and there is a lot to be learned from looking closely at the photographic images they have already produced. It also stands to reason that social research through image-making and analysis is an inevitable development in our own culture. Our visual language has expanded exponentially during the past several decades—both in use and in structure—and it is our immediate heritage to know what we can of the world through it. In all respects, there is much research and analysis underway, and more to come.

TEACHING

Photographs which are used in social science teaching cut two ways. As visual *illustration* they can assist instructors in making a more powerful presentation of their argument and textual material. As visual *stimulation* on the other hand, they can turn a passive student audience into active and critical analysts, each of them striking out through visual associations towards a different object of inquiry. To use photographs and use them well requires that the teacher be aware of both these "contributions" to the classroom, develop techniques for acknowledging them, and work comfortably within their separate domains.

In teaching, as with research, there are several modes in which photographs can be an integral part of social science practice:

1. Illustrated Lectures. Perhaps the most long-standing use of photographs by social scientists is as "visual aids" in lecturing. Within this format, photographs provide a richness of immediate detail about a people, a place, or an historical period which is not otherwise available (see my own discussion in Chapter 13). In addition, through careful selection of images and presentation formats, a skillful lecturer-photographer can provide visual examples of the argument and concepts which make up the content of the lecture.

2. Common Classroom Stimulus. Photographic images can perform another important function for the classroom teacher of social science by ensuring that students "share" the material to be discussed. Reading assignments are quite private in relation to the presentation of photographs in class, and a carefully chosen set of images can provide an excellent common point of departure for classroom discussion.

3. Student Presentations. Photographs can add at least as much to student presentations as they can to those undertaken by the teacher. Students are frequently eager to work with images—perhaps to redress the imbalance of attention to many images out of school and few within—and if they are guided in their efforts, they can produce work that is rigorous as well as entertaining.

4. Student and Class Problem-Solving. A rich and growing body of photographic exercises—some of which are described by Curry and Clarke (Chapter 12)—encourages students to learn about the social order through visual problem-solving. These require students to take their own photographs, arrange or rearrange those taken by others, or identify the details of what cannot be dealt with photographically. Lifchez (Chapter 15) describes a dramatic application of those techniques in teaching social science to architects.

5. Explication of Concepts. By asking students to find or make photographs of the content of a course, a lively and effective means is provided for refining their understanding of underlying concepts. Such translation exercises can work in either direction: as Ellis (Chapter 16) and Krieger (Chapter 17) report students can be asked to generate concepts from the analysis of photographs, as well as to generate photographs which reflect their analysis of the concepts.

6. Student and Class Research Projects. Individual students, groups of students, and students and teachers together can complete a number of interesting and valuable photographic research projects within an academic term (see Cheatwood, Chapter 14). All the modes of social research in which photography can play a central role are amenable to the generation of classroom assignments. *Photo-Interviewing, systematic observation and recording, content analyses of naive photographs, native image-making,* and *narrative visual theory* can all be used as vehicles for students to learn about the social order and, in so doing, learn about the research conventions of the various social sciences.

One of the more remarkable features of photographic exercises for students of social science is the opportunity they provide to do original and interesting research, and this has not been lost on those teachers who are currently using such assignments in their teaching. Two factors important to this process of generating quality research are the students' high level of interest in visual images and the immediacy of visual presentations in the classroom. When students can bring to their classmates and the teacher a set of exciting images—it does not matter whether these were made by the student or found—they know that their presentation will be stimulating even if not illustrative. This changes the business of teaching, of course, and many of us find ourselves trying to calm students down rather than wind them up.

Another remarkable feature of the use of visual images in teaching is that it provides an excellent vehicle for raising all the issues of the discipline. Questions of reliability and validity, the designation of appropriate indicators of social process, criteria of good evidence, the explication of concepts, and the articulation of social theory, all these emerge quickly and effortlessly within thoughtful discussions of photographic assignments or presentations. There is an important sense in which the classroom use of visual images can bring students firsthand into the adventure and contradictions of scientific inquiry, and the lessons they learn through their own photographs are not lessons quickly or easily forgotten.

When students have come to realize that photographs owe something to the preconceptions of the photographer in selecting and framing the subject, and something to the situation in which they are viewed, and something as well to their own preconceptions in looking at them, they have taken a rather large step towards understanding the social construction of the world in which we live. When they experience, in learning all this, that there is something "out there" which contributes to the photograph as well, they have become more sophisticated students of the social order than they might have been through reading alone.

VISUAL LANGUAGE AND SOCIAL SCIENCE

Photography represents no solution to the difficulties and ambiguities of either social science teaching or research. It is new only in part, and its freshness in these contexts is certainly a product of the moment. There are probably some things which can be examined through visual representations, and others which cannot. Photography has no corner on processes of knowing about the world.

For its part, the social science which informs this book is neither doctrinaire nor representative of all which goes by the name. It does derive, however, from two long and fruitful research traditions: the observation of human activity in naturalistic settings; and the analysis of artifacts—in this case, photographs—as social and cultural products. To the extent that these traditions characterize the social sciences in general, work in all the disciplines is examined in this book. There are more sociologists and anthropologists among the authors than there are representatives of other disciplines, but the work as a whole is inclusive rather than exclusive. In its interdisciplinary conception, the book rests on the assumption that visual images are an essential means by which we perceive and order the world, and that they will continue to be so for the foreseeable future. It seems reasonable to examine as closely as we can how that process is organized within ourselves, the social situations in which we act on it, and the cultures in which we participate.

In terms of visual research techniques, this book is narrow in focus, but broad in its implications. Still photography is not the only visual technology used by social scientists, but it is the only one reported on in this book (the one exception is the research described by Zube, in which he used a movie camera to do time-lapse studies of pedestrians, a mode of recording which can be done as well by automated still cameras). This is not to suggest that the work being done with motion pictures and video tape is less interesting or important. The decision not to include these other formats is based on my commitment to show the visual work as well as report on the issues which have emerged around it. Within the format of a book, video tapes and motion pictures get short shrift, for the reader has no access to the visual statements of the contributors which complement their verbal discussions. By focusing on still photography alone, we have been able to present both visual and verbal statements together, an arrangement which is more suggestive of how we work and how we view our work.

There are some social science issues which emerge only through working with motion pictures or video tape, and the visual language of these two other media differs somewhat from that of still photography. On the other hand, each of these three formats can be used to make complex and compelling statements about the social world, and there are many conceptual issues which they share. The approach we have settled on—in which still photographs are examined as one representation of visual language—is a limited but effective means of confronting and expanding our understanding of social science and the social order.

There is no argument made in this book that all photographs are always meaningful. There is, however, one persistent theme which plays upon their general significance and continues to intrigue those of us who work with them: the relationship between language—in this case a visual language—and what we know as "social reality." It is a theme which leads us to question the meaning of what we see, and it is a theme which many of us think ought to be played in and around and through the disciplines of social science. By seeing how it engages us in the examination of photographs, perhaps we can bring it as well to other areas where its dialectical refrain is clearly needed.

I shall play it once more after we have moved through the other business of this book.

PART I

RESEARCH APPLICATIONS

Introduction

As the following seven chapters illustrate, photography is both a "method" of social science research as well as an "area of inquiry." We begin with explorations of life in three field settings: railroad boxcars (Harper); beauty parlors (Ewen); and the Lower East Side of Manhattan (Aron). In each of these studies, photographs were made in an attempt to understand and portray both the setting and the social life characteristic of those who frequent it. In these three chapters, photographs and text are combined to account for what you might see were you to visit such places yourself as well as to identify concepts important to understanding the meaning of activity within their domains.

The fourth selection presents research that is both more narrow in focus and more rigorous than that of the first three. In this chapter Zube takes full advantage of photography as a vehicle for systematic observation and recording, developing as he does a stochastic model of pedestrian movement in windy urban areas. As a "matter-of-fact" use of the medium, this research illustrates the manner in which some observational techniques of the natural sciences can be used to study the human organism in its physical environment.

There is more to human activity than "behavior of the organism," however, (or, the environment is symbolic as well as physical) and the remaining three chapters in this first section explore the meanings which individuals invent (see Sekula 1975) or attribute to photographic images. In my own essay ("Perceiving Community in Twin Rivers") I report on the use of photographs to interview residents about their community. This is almost matter-of-fact, but the content of resident responses suggests several larger issues. Musello explores in greater detail some of the questions we must ask in evaluating the "content" of photographs—in this case, for family photographs—and Stasz directs historical attention to the use of photographs in scholarly social science publication. These last two chapters, taken together, suggest that photographs can play an important role in both popular culture and professional discourse, a matter to which we will return in concluding this volume.

The chapters in this first section thus move from the matter-of-fact use of photographs to describe and record human activity to examination of the complex dynamics characteristic of their presentation and interpretation.

—J. W.

LIFE ON THE ROAD 2

Doug Harper

The skid row man has been the focus of major attention in social science. He embodies, in many ways, a perfect subject for study. His lifestyle is not integrated into the mainstream. His use of alcohol seems to be abnormal or diseased. He sleeps in the open, or as a ward to the state in a mission; and his filthy clothes, messed hair, and offensive odor mark him as a likely object of public disdain, scorn, or pity. As a "deviant" his lifestyle has been considered in terms of "role-failure"— failure to integrate successfully into socially sanctioned places in the social order. Representative studies demonstrate this point well. Bahr (1973A, 1973B) conceptualized the skid row man as "disaffiliated," and alienated, and other studies are similar. Although her theoretical perspectives and methodology make her more sensitive to insiders' cultural definitions of their situation, Jacqueline Wiseman (1970) presents the various institutions with which skid row men deal as "stations of the lost," and Donald Bogue (1963) suggests that the skid row man lives in a cultural vacuum, in semiisolation, without a well-integrated or organized community—without an identity derived and maintained through peers (1963: 169-170).

Most of the research which supports these generalizations has been dependent on the "social survey" as a primary source of data. What we learn from surveys, however, we have learned through an asymmetrical social encounter, one which formalizes the roles of both professional and informant. Such encounters have a reality of their own, one which reflects the contrived and socially loaded interactive settings in which they take place.

Another way to proceed is for the researcher to enter, as much as possible, the world of those researched. This requires a different set of skills than those associated with survey research. The "inside observer" may have to learn a specialized language, eat unfamiliar food in strange settings, and engage in forms of social interaction for which the researcher's professional training has been wholly inadequate. By succeeding at becoming more of an "insider," however, the researcher

AUTHOR'S NOTE: Parts of this essay were first presented to the Session on Visual Sociology at the American Sociological Association annual meetings, San Francisco, 1978.

gets much closer to the subjects of his or her study and is presented with a richer variety of interaction settings in which information can be revealed and recorded. In the study of so-called deviant groups— of which homeless men represent a classic example—working within the world of the informant can bring the researcher to unforeseen hazards as well as rich data. It is a difficult way to proceed, but in my own work with homeless men it has generated data clearly at odds with generalizations based on the survey alone.

RESEARCH THROUGH IMMERSION

The research I conducted on "homeless men" combined photography, participant observation, and informal interviewing. The project began as a photographic essay on the life of the skid row man, and my motivation initially was to make "good photographs" of the most desperate looking individuals I could find on the streets of Boston's skid row. Initially, my main research strategies were intended primarily to protect my extensive and expensive photographic paraphernalia in settings where it was likely to be stolen. After a year of such "picture taking" I had a number of good photographs, but I knew little more than I had before I'd begun about the lives of the men I photographed.

The second phase of my research led me to undertake a two-week stay on skid row in order to make a different kind of contact with the culture I had been photographing. I went to the skid row in the winter, and presented myself with the outside trappings of a skid row man. I took neither money nor camera, and while I recognized the ethical issues involved in appearing as something I was not, I decided that in this case the potential learning justified the means.

Changing my role and thus my participation in the life caused me to reevaluate all I had gained in "folk knowledge" about the life on the road. The world looked different from the inside looking out, and after this experience I felt I had begun to pay my dues as a field worker. I gained confidence in my ability to learn from members of a culture in their own setting, and while the personal risks were great, the information gained was multidimensional and rich. As the emphasis of my project shifted and narrowed to an investigation of the western tramp in his settings of freight migrations, hobo jungles, and fruit harvests, I became resolved to adapt my photographic method to the intensive field experience. As I entered the cultural settings of the tramp I did so with substantially less photographic equipment which I used with a restraint I had not practiced before. The quality of the relationships I sought to establish with my informants became more important than making visual documents, and thus photographing began to follow rather than precede my interaction with those with whom I travelled.

I made three field trips before I finally established a strong contact with a single informant. We met in a Minneapolis freight yard and "buddied up" a thousand miles down the road to spend over a month winding through the West together. He led me through encounters with tramps he'd known for as long as I had been alive, and as companion to this seasoned tramp, it quickly became obvious to me that photographing the settings we shared with others along the road was out of the question. It simply was not possible to photograph and remain in my companion's company.

There was, indeed, another issue. As I became more and more integrated into the lifestyle, I realized that it was more attractive to me to experience the life of my informants than it was to produce documents about it. I passed up photographs I desperately wanted when the act of photographing would be alien, disruptive, and totally out of context with what I had become. I did this work without a research grant, and the few dollars that I took along each time I rode the freights was the limit of my monetary resources. Even though I knew I would stay only briefly in the life, I entered it completely when I entered it at all.

There were photographs which I did take, however, and they made a special contribution to what I learned about the men I studied. In addition to providing me with a rich document of much of what I saw, my experience in "making" these photographs has served to educate and inform the way I now "see" the tramps and others like them.

For example, if we consider a few representative portraits of the homeless man (photos 1, 2, 3) our familiar interpretation suggests destitution, dereliction, and severe personal disorganization, the same "themes" which have guided traditional social science research in this area. Through immersion in the tramps' world, however, I was forced to suspend these interpretations. The density of my interaction with homeless men and the shared understandings which that entailed, combined with my first-hand experience of making visual images of tramps, has taught me a great deal about the relationship between how we "image" this deviant group and how they image themselves. In so doing, I came upon a set of concrete data which clearly contradict the conventional "portraits"—both visual and verbal—of homeless men.

From the images I made of tramps, therefore, I learned something about our conventions for interpreting "social documentary photographs." What has become equally clear to me as I show these photo-

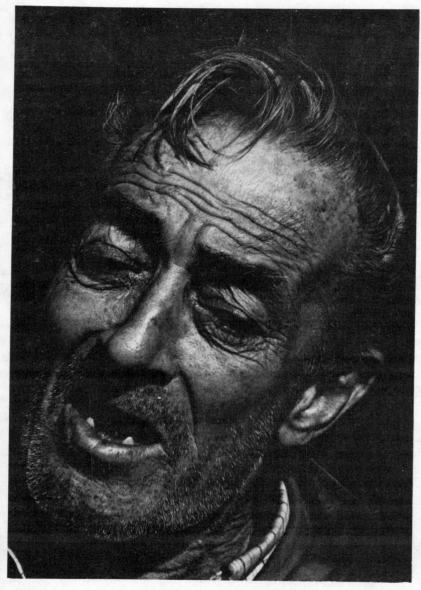

Photo 1

Photo 2

Photo 3

graphs to other social scientists, however, is that the images I made also provide specific illustrations of elements of tramp reality, elements which are at best only partially understood by those outside the culture.

TRAMP SELF-IMAGE

The theme of independence is dominant in tramps' self-expression. They see themselves as the last on the American landscape who control their own destiny, and it is, they maintain, their exclusion from the malaise of materialism which is the key to their freedom. A tramp seasoned with over a quarter century on the road commented:

> It ain't what you *got*, it's how you live. Like those people we watched going along the highway in their big fancy trailers. Would you live like that? They're afraid to sleep on the ground. They couldn't do what we've been doing! They'd turn their noses up at the perfectly good food we've been eating and they've got to cover their heads up. They live for those things and they can't live without them.

He later elaborated:

> see, I'm *free*hearted. I don't have no attachments, not to men and not to things. When I got something, I'll give it to you. You don't have to steal it—I'll *give* it to you. . . . Nope, you don't have to steal from me.
>
> Like those guys came up this morning? If I'd had something the first thing I'd asked them: "Well, come on, let's eat. Here's the coffee pot— help yourself. . . . You hungry? Here's something to eat. . . ." See, that's the way I am, I can't see another guy go without.

This theme is based at least partly on their association with groups they see having occupied the same role historically:

> We get angry too easily, but we're a different breed. Did you ever read about the people that explored? Like Lewis and Clark? The mountain men, that's what I think this tramp is about. We're a generation too late. If you gave us a longrifle, a pair of buckskins and a pair of moccasins a hundred, er, a hundred fifty years ago, we'd be right at home. Not the heroes, don't get me wrong. Just the explorers. Go out by ourself all winter long, live with a squaw maybe, and trap and hunt. Then we'd be in our element. Because we can make do and make things on our own. . . and we ain't one bit afraid to work.

But the tramp's view of himself is not derived solely from a romantic view of the past, nor an idealized view of the present. As an individual dependent on his own wits for his survival, he has a storehouse of information and skills. His skills and knowledge take him to available food and lead him to the use of the most mundane of normally discarded objects. The following example is characteristic:

> The tramp had come across some young tramps who complained that they were out of food. "Why, I looked at them people like they were *stupid*," he said. "That whole flat out there was covered with nothing but wild mustard. All you had to do—they had a five gallon bucket—was to wash them up, put them in the bucket, add salt and cook it. And you got *greens*. Some of the best greens you can eat! Just like spinach—same thing. So I gave them a little square of salt and says: 'There, go get yourself some of those wild mustard leaves and boil them up.' 'Ahhh, that's no good!' they answered. 'Go try it!' I says. So they went out and got armfuls—you know, then pressed them down and boiled them, and almost filled that five gallon bucket. Why, they ate that and they was goin' out to get some more!"

The tramp maintains himself on the fringes of American society in complicated and creative ways, as this single illustration shows. His life is guided by strategies that guide him through his "own" settings—hobo jungles, freight train migrations, and stints on skid row, and yet even as he interacts with the society as a worker, his independence is at the forefront of his concern. Tramps work hard but they leave their jobs when they see their independence threatened. What *most* workers accept on the job because they can't afford to quit, tramps reject as an affront to their independence. The stories abound in the places tramps get together; this comment summarizes the general attitude:

> "But you been leaving a lot of good jobs," I said, "what makes you leave?"
>
> "I get tired of the *man*. . . ." The tramp leaned close to make sure I caught his words. "I work hard for a man but after a while he thinks he *owns* me! He starts puttin' more and more work on me with the same pay. I say to hell with that—that's when I leave."

DRINKING AND DEPENDENCE

Losing control, and thus independence, during periods of heavy drinking usually on a skid row, is seen by tramps as an episode in a cycle of life events. Photographs of the homeless man on skid row (2, 3, 4, 5) communicate all of the familiar elements that are associated with the public image of the derelict: shabby personal appearance, the setting of door stoops and alleys in dirty parts of the city, the behavior of drinking in public in the kind of aggressive manner in order to become inebriated, and the image of the individual incapacitated—passed out or asleep—in public view. Yet, while tramps recognize their drinking sessions as setbacks in their search for a life without attachments,

Photo 4

Photo 5

they also exhibit a high level of self-awareness and self-acceptance in facing their drinking behavior. The following conversation shows well the sense of irony, acceptance, and humor that characterizes these attitudes:

> "Well, I helped with all the thinnin' and all the proppin'," Blackie said, "an' I worked in the summer apples, drivin' tractor. Five hundred and eighty-four dollars after I paid for all my gracharies out of the grachary store. Bars of candy and tobaccee I bought. Lasted three days in Brewster."
>
> Carl said: "Shit, I was makin' *God*damn good money in Minneapolis. Showed him a checkstub—earned a hundred seventy-nine dollars in one week. Hundred twenty-three the week before."
>
> Blackie interrupted: "I get so dees-gusted with myself. Goddamn it I don't know what to do . . . I can have a hundred dollars this mornin' . . ."
>
> Carl interrupted, "You won't have a dime tomorrow . . . I know, I know, I'm the same way . . . well, when *he* saw me I was drinking a quart of Grand Canadian, wasn't I?"
>
> "Year," I answered, "that you were."
>
> "That's pitiful," Blackie said seriously. "You ought to be ashamed of yourself. But who's kidding who—it's the same with me." He looked the other tramp straight in the eye and bent forward to emphasize his point: "Several times lately I found myself wondering'—just what in hell's going to become of me!" They laughed and laughed until their eyes watered—I thought Blackie was going to roll on the ground.

DIFFERENT KINDS OF TRAMPS

While the drunk is considered as an episode, the setting of the drunk, usually skid rows of American cities, must be understood as a scene in which a complicated system of social stratification is played out. This contrasts with the view—signalled by the images of the skid row— of a homogeneous population desperately existing without social norms or clear patterns of social interaction. This public (and sociological) misconception was recognized by a tramp in the following conversation:

> "My friend used to drive me up and down Hennepin Avenue to show me about a side of life I'd never seen," I said.
>
> "He didn't know what he was talking' about," the tramp interrupted. "He *saw* that—that's all—the bums lined up along the streets. They think that's it—that all the guys that ride up and down the road are just like those guys on Hennepin, which is just not true!"

"I'm beginning to learn that," I said . . . "you are one of the hardest working son of a . . . guns,"

"*Bitches*,"—the tramp corrected me. "One of the hardest working son
of a *bitches* you ever saw. And I could take you to Minneapolis and show
you fifty guys just like me."

The social stratification on skid row is complicated—the man one
sees may be, in the tramps' definition of their culture, a wino, a hobo,
or a tramp. It should be noted that while these definitions are only
relatively consistent within the culture there appears the consistent
theme that the wino—the man who cannot get off skid row—has suc-
cumbed to the alcohol which they all use. There is a very fine line,
however, between the different groups. Some of the skid row populations, in parts of the country where the homeless man no longer
functions as an important labor force, are perhaps almost permanent.
Yet, in other skid rows the tramp or hobo mingles with a population
of permanent alcoholics as they drink up the money which has been
accumulated during periods of work. The tramp or the hobo drinks
with the permanent skid row man yet he distinguishes his life from
the others on the basis of his ability to leave the booze *and* the skid row
when the binge is over.

The tramp said: "If you can't stop a drunk then you turn into a bum."
[He said he'd never stoop so low as to bum a bottle.] "because then you're
dependent on somebody else. Any time you start dependin' on that
bottle . . . you're an alcoholic. You lost your packsack, your bedroll,
your gear . . . you lose everything you got. Then all you got is the clothes
on your back and you become a *bum*."

SKID ROW

The stratification of the cultural group takes place in a setting which
can be thought of as an ecology. Typical institutions—such as the
barber college, the mission and the skid row bar, revolve directly
around the needs and the uses of the homeless man. These institutions
are vulnerable to the types of city renovation which are now common,
thus the relationship of the individual to his institutions is susceptible
to change from the outside. The social dimensions of the ecology of
the skid row area include not only homeless men drinking together,
spending time together in missions, bars, and public areas, but also
groups who come into the setting to use it for their own purposes.
Among these groups are the police (Spradley, 1970), labor contractors
who recruit skid row men for specific jobs, and men who peddle nar-

cotics or prostitutes by day, and rob the resources of the skid row man at night. A tramp put it this way:

> "Used to be this was our part of town. Now them blacks are movin' in and they pick us clean. They watch while we head out to the bank to cash our social security . . . then they way-lay us. Used to be they'd wait until it was dark. . . now they get us in the light of day."
>
> "Don't the police give you some protection?"
>
> "Are you out of your mind? Do you think I'm goin' to start singin' with that metal at my throat? You think the cops give a shit about an old bum gettin' his pockets picked or his throat slashed?"

Photograph 4 conveys much of this information. The image provides a partial inventory of skid row institutions: the mission, the barber college, and the pawn shop, but the photograph also suggests, with the juxtaposition of the posture of the individuals, the relationship between the skid row men and an outside population. The black men are dressed in clean, stylish clothes and they control the space of the sidewalk. Their interaction seems casual yet appears to dominate the space. The homeless man, face marked by scars and contorted in displeasure moves away, displaced and threatened. And when we see this photograph in the context of the conversation cited above, we begin to understand the way in which the tramp is a victim of particular predators who share the space in an exploitative manner.

GEAR, BEHAVIOR AND STATUS

The differentiation within the culture is evident in different settings as well: the hobo jungle, the freight train and the freight yard, and the labor camp. In these settings there are cultural definitions for many sets of behavior. Included is the issue of carrying gear which will facilitate the tramp's adaptation to his environment, and wearing clothes that signal particular status. The tramp in photograph 6 fits all of his possessions into a small airline bag yet it included salt and pepper shakers with lids, a knife with a can opener, and a water bottle. The tramp in photograph 7 adds a plastic sheet to keep his sleeping bag clean. The collection of individuals inside the boxcar in photographs 8, 9 show differences in appearance, as well as behavior that are important in determining, to the actors, issues of status.

> We were talking about our afternoon ride up the Okanogan River. "I noticed today in the boxcar everybody shied away from that drunk with the bottle," I said.

Photo 6

Photo 7

Photo 8

Photo 9

"Not everybody shied away," Carl replied. "It was your tramps that wouldn't touch him. He tried to offer *me* a cigarette—he offered us a drink—but we didn't take it. He knew it, too—he knew he was wrong—but he found his buddies quick enough, you saw that, didn't you?" The tramp asked me if I had noticed the difference between those men who had been drinking and those who hadn't. I told him I had not.

"Then you weren't looking very carefully," he said. "The bum, the riff-raff, was wearing clothes that looked like he'd pulled them out of a Salvation Army barrel. The tramp had workingman's clothes—they might have been a little worn, or a little dirty, but that was his uniform. And that tramp was wearing' his boots—didn't you see that? He had on his hat, and he had his boots, and he had his gear tied up by his side. The bum was dirty and filthy, he didn't have no hat, and was wearin' those three-quarter height shoes with white socks fallin' over his ankles."

"Proper riding behavior" is illustrated in photograph 9 where we observe the rider maintaining his control by keeping his feet inside the car and staying away from open doors in the often lurching, jolting ride.

Conversational support for these visual themes runs throughout tramp conversation. Tramps initiate newcomers (such as the author) by instructing them, for example, in the proper techniques of riding in a boxcar:

"When you see something like that (the train had snapped forward) you *duck*," the tramp said. "God, I've seen a man get his head cut off! He was stickin' it out and *looking*, you know—door open about this much and it slammed shut, and . . . there it goes! That's it! Christ, what a bloody mess! Hands, same thing. I've seen em bust off their feet—sittin', hanging them out of the door and, WHAM! Those switches, or those close bridges I showed you. You can't see them coming. *Never* sit with your feet hangin' out the side of the car. Never! Even standing here like we are, if that thing jerks—out you go!"

DATA AND IMAGE:
A RECONSIDERATION OF THE TRAMP

Tramps present an image to the world that we usually overlook. Reconsidering photograph 1—which we easily interpret as a dramatic portrait of "desperation"—we might note that the individual has elaborately combed his hair. His beard, while highlighted on his face, is evenly long, indicating that he has in fact shaved within the past couple of days. Both of these visual cues show that he has presented his face to the world in a manner which he has determined. These visual details

Photo 10

Photo 11

are neither irrelevant nor superficial. They suggest an individual who has composed and maintained his presentation of self.

The tramps took their appearance seriously enough to go through elaborate procedures to shave (photograph 10). Tramps carried mirrors and razors among their scant possessions. If they did not have water available, they dry-shaved, and if they didn't have razors, they used sharp edges of broken bottles. A shaved face was simply an important aspect of the normal view of self, as illustrated in this conversation:

> We'd been on a freight trip for three days. At our first stop of any consequence the tramp had scoured the landscape for a can to heat water in. As he shaved, he commented, "God, that feels good. I'll betcha you hardly recognized me!" And after he finished shaving he said, "Here, you shave, or you go up the river alone. Ain't no excuse to look like hell when we got hot water and a razor."

Hair length was similarly important. Some tramps wore it long, but they kept it trimmed at barber colleges and usually under a hat. Short hair added to an image of self as a worker, and one who is responsible for one's self.

> A tramp stated, "They know me—I work hard for them. And I usually keep my hair cut pretty short, but *now* I'm short—I only got a few pennies to buy beans till I get something going. But you hear me loud and clear—I'll get up there and get a few weeks' work in, and if we happen to have one wet morning, you know, if it rains at night and we can't get our work in, then I'll go in town and get all this brushpile knocked off."

In reviewing the photographs, we can look as well for more subtle information about the life of tramps. Posture (5, 7) and facial expression (1, 4, 11) can be considered as an index of psychological makeup. I believe that it is not inappropriate to consider the control of space or the presentation of self through body postures as indications of a type of personal control, or to look at facial expressions as informal "records" of how a life has been lived. These analyses are suggestive but indicate a direction for further research.

ETHICS AND INFORMATION

My involvement with tramps and my efforts to photograph their world has generated information which contradicts existing stereotypes held by both professionals and lay persons about the nature of their lives. Themes of positive self-image appear in statements tramps make about strategies for piloting themselves through their own cultural milieu, as well as in statements they make about the relation of their culture to the society in which it symbiotically exists. Tramps see themselves as "successful," independent, and relatively optimistic about their futures. They maintain a wry detachment about their "success" (their ability to remain independent) and their "failures" (temporary or permanent dependence, usually to alcohol) and they show a fine understanding of the peculiar relationship of their culture to the society. The tramps and derelicts I came to know and photograph are nobody's fools. They give outsiders what they are generally looking for in order to gain what they desire themselves, be it a free bed or a bowl of soup, a paid reward, or just to be left alone.

One of the first questions people usually ask when looking at my photographs is: "What did these people think of being photographed?" It is a question usually passed over or ignored by photographers, but I believe it is an important one that deserves an answer.

When I record someone's apparent desperation on film as an outsider, I have exploited their condition for whatever ends I've chosen. I justified this in my early work—as many social scientists have justified their "portrayals" of poverty—through my hope that the public or academic record would be an initiator of social change. I've subsequently come to believe, however, that one's motives, even when altruistic in some sense, cannot be used to explain away means which are essentially exploitative.

The "means" refers to the way we make photographs. If our photographs come from momentary encounters with strangers, I think we can be faulted as perpetrators of superficial human interaction, the product of which can be considered exploitative as well as culturally uninformed. I am suggesting, for example, that the method of work chosen by W. Eugene Smith in *Minamata* represents a certain ideal—Smith lived and suffered with his subjects and thus gained an ethical "right" to make visual records. In much the same way we gain the ethical right to tell a story or create an analysis when our knowledge has been formed by genuine involvement with the subjects we wish to portray.

After I had immersed myself in the world of tramps and traveled with them for several trips along the rails, I had become less an outsider and less a stranger. In some sense I began to feel that I had the ethical right to tell their story, for it had become in part my own. As I put in my hours of participant field work, I moved a bit closer to seeing tramps as "us" and not as "them."

At times, my camera was the sole reminder of that other world— the one where people studied tramps rather than became them. It was an important kind of reminder, and it worked in both directions. While I was with the homeless men, it called my attention to the larger purpose of understanding their life. After I left their world the camera reminded me—through the photographs made with it—of the tramp's world which I had shared. Through taking and making photographs, it has kept me in touch with both of the worlds within which I worked.

THE BEAUTY RITUAL   3

Phyllis Ewen

The beauty ritual is a fact of life for most American women, yet it has been hidden from view. Usually described from the outside as self-indulgent narcissism or from the inside with apologies and self-deprecation, it is considered an example of the weakness or gullibility of women. As a cultural phenomenon worthy of social inquiry, it has been largely ignored. When beauty work has been thoughtfully examined, the focus has frequently been on the men who participate in it (see, Shroder, 1973), even though 90% of the workers in this field are women (Howe, 1977). A women's ritual, it has been passed over in favor of the examination of the culture of male work, wrestling or bars. Recently, women have begun to take their own history seriously and have begun to explore aspects of their culture; the culture of everyday life. It is within this context that I have been photographing and studying women in beauty parlors over the past few years.

Like other exchanges which were formerly a part of the relationships within the family or the community, hairdressing has become in the last sixty years a commercial transaction. However, it retains a deep psychological meaning because it involves touching and care. It is commercialized mothering. Having one's hair done provides an opportunity to retreat into a space in which feminine modes of interaction predominate; it is a time to rest, away from the pressures of a male-dominated society. It is ironic that the concerns we share about our appearance, a major source of anxiety and preoccupation, can bring us together with other women. At the beauty parlor, where we make our images, bonds between women—generally separated by the patterns of nuclear family life and work discipline—are reasserted.

My "research" has always been closely connected to my own image-making, photography being my work and my pleasure, and the themes that emerged in my study came first from my interaction with my photographs. What began as a portrait series has evolved into an essay on sisterhood: I began by feeling that I was looking at something outside myself and came to learn that I was part of it.

AUTHOR'S NOTE: Many people contributed to the ideas in this chapter. I am especially grateful to Margaret Cerullo, Jim Campen, Anna Dunwell, Michele Clark, and Jasminka Gojkovic.

FEMALE APPEARANCE AND THE BEAUTY RITUAL

I always say, when you have your hair done and you got on a nice pair of shoes, you're all dressed up [Betty Kelly].

Our fate, we are taught, is our own individual responsibility, closely bound with how others see us. We are constantly being looked at and spend an enormous amount of time and preparation covering our social vulnerability and political powerlessness. In F. Scott Fitzgerald's short story (1959), "Bernice Bobs Her Hair," Bernice's cousin explains to her why she has had little social success:

You have no ease of manner. Why? Because you're never sure about your personal appearance. When a girl feels that she's perfectly groomed and dressed, she can forget that part of her. That's charm. The more parts of yourself you can afford to forget, the more charm you have.

Like Bernice, we are also taught that to feel confident we must look "in order" and we feel exposed when we don't. In general, we don't groom ourselves to be exotic or to call attention to differences. Special cases make the public display of uniqueness desirable, but usually being different makes one isolated and vulnerable. Rather, we dress and wear our hair like our friends and those with whom we identify. Within these limits, we select our images from a range of options.

Fitzgerald, in this story, is documenting the period—the 1920s—in which the choice among options was becoming a new part of women's "work." Women, who had been the producers of goods within the home, were in the first part of the twentieth century becoming consumers of goods sold on the market. They were also buying images; images which promised new opportunities and possibilities. Advertising and fashion photography began to influence the perceptions women had of themselves and to give form to the longing for glamour, sexuality, beauty, and class.

The appearance and rapid spread of beauty parlors in the 1920s reflected new needs created by the changing structure of women's daily lives under industrials capitalism. A government study done in the 1930s noted that although few women used commercial beauty establishments in 1920, by the thirties these services "had a place in the time and budget of women of all groups and ages" (Erickson, 1935). By 1930 beauty parlors were found in private homes and apartments as well as near the places where women worked: in department stores, office buildings, hotels, and storefronts.

A ninety-year-old spinster recalled that she first started going to a beauty parlor to have her hair "marcelled" (curled with an iron) in the 1920s when she was living with her brother and his wife and working in a Lynn, Massachusetts department store. Growing up on a farm in Maine she "didn't know anything about style, you just were who you were." Later, living in the city as a single woman and working outside the home, she had the need, as well as the opportunity, to think about and experiment with her appearance.

This double-edged choice is still our lot: we feel it as creative self-expression and at the same time as a requirement for survival. Appearance is layered with many meanings which we have learned to intuit and to use. We have learned that, because we are constantly being looked at, our appearance influences how people treat us and makes a public statement about how we feel about ourselves. We put on a "face" to be noticed or to distance, to excite reaction or to protect ourselves from harm. Hair, like clothing and gesture, is a cultural statement: at the same time an indication of social position and an expression of individual identity. We recognize social class, age, and race in a hairstyle. We intuit sexuality and personal style. Because we have been made to feel personally responsible for how we look, our apperance is entangled with issues of identity.

Young women experiment with whom they want to be and what kind of impression to make. Demands on them can be conflicting: finding a sexual image that feels right, conning employers into thinking they're older, keeping parental approval. One teenager I interviewed had surreptitiously bleached the front of her hair after hearing a friend refer to her as "uncool," only to be ridiculed by her parents. Another blamed her social isolation on the fact that her dark curly hair wouldn't take the popular Dorothy Hamill "wedge" cut—"you have to be a blonde." Groups of friends often adopt a particular style as a sign of their belonging together, and it is painful to be separated when one's physical characteristics don't conform. Yet, several young women have talked to me about the fun they have experimenting and creating a self-image that expresses themselves. "Feeling special" can be creatively announced through a new hairstyle.

Elderly women, in contrast, have often settled on a particular style and use the beauty ritual as a mediation between themselves and death —it is a sign of self-respect. At a time when society deems them no longer useful or sexually attractive, it is a way of retaining dignity. "I want to grow old by due process, not out of self-neglect." Letting oneself go, giving up the fight, is the enemy,

> Call it false pride. My mother used to take me down now and then if she thought I was caring too much about my appearance. But when I see old people with their hair stringy and their clothes all dirty, I say to myself,

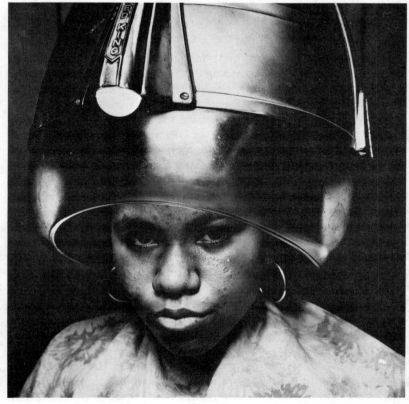

'I hope I never get to the point where I don't care.' When you get older it's hard to look anywhere as attractive as you did when you were young. You get old and wrinkled and fat and all those things that go with old age. Keeping your hair looking nice helps. It's my one extravagance [Veda Achorn, retired schoolteacher].

We must even take responsibility for growing old, it seems. Elderly women are regular customers at neighborhood beauty shops where hairdressers hold together styling with spray and lacquer. A great-grandmother living in a subsidized apartment in the city goes weekly accompanied by her neighbors. She compared the "lift" she gets at the hairdresser's to the comfort of a visit to her GP. Nursing homes often house, as the one concession to personal dignity, a beauty parlor.

The need to feel in order is especially strong among Black women in America, the most vulnerable group in our population. African hair has been something one must hide or disguise to be even minimally accepted in a culture that has defined beauty—and presentability—as white. An artist I spoke with remembers that when she wore her hair "natural" in the late sixties, she was often passed over in stores or not waited on in restaurants. To let people know she exists takes an elaborate self-presentation, and creating an appropriate self-image is as important as making her large woven sculptures. For many Black women, hair becomes an obsession: it is covered under a brightly colored turban, pressed straight and covered with pomade, or given expensive and time-consuming straightening perms. One woman recalls that from the age of eleven she had been sent by her mother to have her hair pressed straight in a basement beauty shop in Harlem. She was afraid of becoming a "nappy-headed hussy" with unkempt frizzy hair; afraid to let her appearance be a reminder to herself and to others of poverty, of Blackness, of a history of slavery.

The need all women share to take care with their appearance gets transformed through an ideology of individual responsibility into a personal effort. In talking with many women—of different ages, races and classes—I found that each had a highly developed explanation and rationale for her choice of a hairstyle. The range of options we choose from may be given to us from sources outside ourselves, but we mediate these choices and give them personal meaning. Except for younger women, most I interviewed denied being influenced by "fashion," rather said that they chose a hairstyle they thought suitable to their age, face type, station in life, or personal philosophy.

The beauty parlor allows women to share the burden of choice with another, but passivity regarding one's appearance can be experienced as

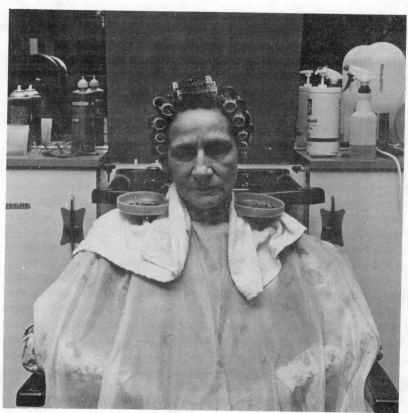

a loss of control. Hairdressers are felt to hold a lot of power; they are the "experts" who know how to make our images better than we do, or in some cases to destroy them through incompetence or misogyny. In neighborhood beauty shops hairdressers and customers often come from the same social class and share expectations about aesthetics, relationships, and lifestyles. In this situation it is easier to trust the outcomes. When customers and hairdressers come from different social worlds, a process of negotiation begins about control, style, and touching.

Because appearance is so intimately connected to a woman's sense of self, it can be frightening to give over control to a hairdresser, even when it is felt as necessary. One's appearance might be ruined for a period of time and with this, one's ability to navigate the outside world is threatened. I watched a teenager weep as the hairdo she had asked a hairdresser to copy from a magazine took shape on her head: inappropriate and incongruent. In this neighborhood shop, in the North End of Boston, the usual laughter and recipe-sharing stopped as the older women empathized with the girl's pain and the beautician's helplessness.

The touch of a particular hairdresser can make a customer anxious or put-off. It can feel distant, too rough, or not deliberate enough. The degree of control that a hairdresser will take in deciding style has to be established. Many women shop around changing beauticians frequently until they find the right person with whom to set up a regular relationship. The loyalty, when it develops, is to a particular hairdresser rather than to the shop. Hairdressers take a "following" with them from one shop to another.

The other side of vulnerability is trust. When the search for a hairdresser is successful and the relationship continues over time, a great deal of intimacy can develop. Many female hairdressers I talked with elaborated on the connection between physical caring, image-making, and emotional nurturing. "We are poorly paid psychiatrists." At the beauty shop, a woman can let her guard down, be seen without a "front" and give in to a state of comfortable receptivity.

Some women choose to leave known surroundings and to have their hair done where they can retain some anonymity. They may prefer to confide in a beautician who is a stranger to the rest of their lives.

And for many the beauty parlor releases fantasies and daydreams. It's a "secret" time when it's all right not to be who you are in real life. It can be a time to feel frivolous; a way of entering a forbidden world. A young teacher shared a fantasy about her hairdressers.

My outside friends are down-to-earth and practical. I have to be serious. But at the salon, the people are sophisticated and fashionable. Their lives, I think, are different from mine. They stay up really late and drink and dance a lot and then drag themselves to work the next morning. For me, it's kind of fun to be involved in their world for an hour or two.

A housewife in Oakland, California confessed that although she subscribed to *McCALLS* at home, her secret pleasure at the beauty shop is reading the movie magazines and catching up on the lives and loves of Cher and Jackie Onassis. And for working class women it's a way of buying for a few hours a week time with a "personal servant," the luxury possessed by the wealthy, now made available through the beauty parlor—the democratic marketplace.

The beauty ritual provides time separated from the flow of everyday life. We spend this time without our "image" in order to have it re-created or remade. It is time during which we are not being looked at; precious time to relax. Into this private space, I intruded with my camera.

IMAGES OF IMAGE-MAKING

You should call this series, "The Other Side—*l'altra facia*—of Beauty." Some of these women are old, but were once young and beautiful. Now people pass them by. Yet, you are making pictures saying that they are beautiful, that they shouldn't feel bad [Angelo, a friend of Rosetta's, while visiting her beauty shop].

Four years ago I began making formal portraits of women in beauty shops—in curlers, with soapy hair, under dryers. Because I was catching them in a state of "undress," I wanted to give them the opportunity to "dress" for the camera and asked them to pause for a moment from what they were doing, to look up from a magazine, to compose themselves and confront the camera directly. I wanted my own presence at the encounter to be a central fact of the image. These photographs, still some of my favorites, were comments on photographic portrait conventions (a small selection is included in this volume). As I lived with these images, studied them, shared them with other people, I began to see new things and to ask further questions. This led me to take different kinds of photographs as well as to spend time in beauty shops without my camera to see what I could not see with it.

The formal portraits set in bizarre surroundings made the images appear to me as religious icons, making the ceremonial aspects of the beauty

process more obvious. Through photographing, I could get outside my subjective experience of the beauty parlor, that of a participant in the beauty ritual, and see it anew. When entering a beauty shop, a customer is stripped of the trappings of an outside identity: street clothes are either covered or replaced by a dressing gown or a bib. I often felt this as a transition to a state of vulnerability in which I would be out of control. But in the photographic images, these gowns and other objects of beauty technology become anthropological artifacts. Plastic bibs patterned with *kitsch,* cotton dressing jackets, and covering sheets become *ceremonial robes;* rollers, pincurls, perm-rods, henna mud packs, shiny foil wings, hairdryers become *ritual headdresses.* Blow-dryers, curling irons, combs and brushes are *ceremonial tools* and the lotions, *anointing oils.* The photographs record strange and wonderful costumes that mark the specialness of the rite. These costumes of preparation help to separate the beauty process from the rhythms and appearances of everyday life and make it a *beauty ritual.*

My vision, and hence my understanding, was actually changed by my experiences with these first portraits. After living for some time with the photographic image of a particular woman, I would be startled on seeing her again in reality. The photograph had become more real to me than the live woman. In each case, as I visited a woman in her home to interview her, I would be struck by how "unreal" she looked to me. Her clothes appeared to be a deliberate costuming and her hairdo as an addition to her head. Gender as well, in the photographs often ambiguous, appeared to be part of her created appearance, not an innate quality. I began to see the image she had created for herself as a "creation," to actually *see* the distinction between the presentation and the self. Thinking about these experiences helped me complete the circle and see my own photographs as another kind of image-making.

I began to explore the relationship between my own "beauty photographs" and those that the advertising world brings to us. In some of my photographs I juxtaposed conventional media presentations of beauty with women whose lives are revealed in their faces—l'altra facia of beauty. In making photographs I wanted to pay attention to the women I met, who transcended the stereotypic vacuous images of beauty, but I realized that we have so internalized these images of decontextualized glamour that we often see as "ugly" the lines and wrinkles of lived experience. Beauty in media images is for the spectator; the "beautiful woman," is there to be seen, passive; she doesn't do anything. The women in my photographs, representative of those who frequent small beauty parlors, work hard and rest infrequently. I tried to capture their

dignity as well as their fatigue. In many cases their strengths come through, but in others the conventional "beauty" on the wall, selling images and products, overwhelms.

When preparing to exhibit the series for the first time, I began to think about the context within which people would be viewing the photographs and about the personal baggage they would bring to them. I was caught between my impulses as a photographer to trust the images, letting people use their own abilities to make connections and explanations, and my desires as a teacher to persuade viewers of my meaning. Although we are inundated with images daily, we are not well trained in reading them, nor in using them to explain and interpret social reality. The media exploit images out of context to sell, and we have developed in response a self-protective distrust of images. I understood that people would be bringing to my photographs histories of pain and confusion about beauty and that I had some responsilitity to mediate. I decided to accompany the exhibit with a short statement as a possible tone of approach to the photographs. The text was not an explanation of the photographs, but a piece which provided some background, talked about what was not explicit in them and reinforced certain aspects of my vision.

The continuation of text and pictures allows some of the direction that words can give as well as the opportunity to construct one's own explanation that a visual presentation can offer. This is a complicated phenomena and it received some attention in Susan Sontag's discussion of the relationship between photography and knowing (1977). In her essay, Sontag argues, ultimately, for the supremacy of words as a language of knowing: "Only that which narrates can make us understand." In contrast, photographs allow us to engage only in "deduction, speculation, and fantasy." While we must be careful in making grandiose counterclaims for photographs, I find Sontag's conception of "understanding" to be overly narrow and uninformed by the importance of deduction, speculation, and fantasy in forming our own knowledge of the social world. As active viewers, we do derive and create explanations from interacting with visual images: reflections and symbols for social reality.

In my own work, the words grew as did the series of images and it has recently become a book-length photographic essay with a complementary, but separate text about the importance of women's community spaces (i.e., beauty parlors) and of cleansing rituals.

I continue to learn from people's responses to the series. The words I have written allow some to relax their defenses and to see the photographs in a fresh way. To the thoughts and descriptions, people either agree, argue, or gain "understanding." To the photographs, responses are often spontaneous and personal. The photographs generate "stories." People talk about the women in the photographs as if they know them and then about their own mothers. They talk about their men, their dreams, and about their day-to-day rhythms and their own beauty experiences. Men have told me that they feel threatened by the intimacy in some of the photographs or that a beauty parlor looks like Mars. Men and women have thought the photographs poignant, affectionate, bizarre, or ugly. Many talk about dignity and self-respect, or elaborate on American consumer culture. But almost everybody has a story.

My photographs show comfortable women—women at ease with themselves and the process. This is largely due to the atmosphere of the beauty parlors. But my intentions as a photographer, are, of course, also important. Women understood me to be sympathetic to them. In every case, the women photographed agreed to cooperate. Often we talked, laughed and joked about what we each were doing and the way in which we were meeting. My paraphernalia—tripod, strobelight, umbrella—often rivalled theirs. At first I was surprised, but came to accept how readily women agreed to let me photograph them. Very few customers refused, even though I was photographing them when they were not "presentable." And very few hairdressers felt that their business activities would be interrupted by my presence, perhaps because the social nature of the establishment is as important as business in the places I chose to study. At times I was made uneasy by the trust people had in the camera, an instrument which can be used quite cruelly. Usually their trust made me take special care. Certain ground rules applied from the start: I would never take a picture of anyone without their knowing it (later I required releases from all subjects), and I would give prints to the beauticians to distribute. When buying a new camera, I chose one with a loud shutter sound so that I could never sneak a shot. The prints I distributed—and eventually a portfolio I took around with me—helped me gain acceptance and confidences and stirred interest in what I was doing. This helped me feel that I wasn't the only one asking questions. By choosing to shoot in a certain way and to share my perceptions with my subjects as I progressed, I clearly limited the kind of photographs I could get and the statement I would make. I chose not to show things that I couldn't get while remaining clearly visible and present to those whom I was photographing.

Taking pictures in beauty shops has been a way of participating by complementing the nurturing that is going on, but it has also been an intrusion. Inasmuch as I have, as a photographer, paid respectful attention to my subjects, the photographic process became another aspect of the "care-taking" that is intrinsic to the beauty process. But insofar as the camera's presence transgressed on an intimacy between beautician and client or interrupted a reverie, it was antagonistic. At all times, I was both *of* the place and *looking at* it; the camera both made connections and created distance. And as the photographs are not merely gifts to the women in them, but have been exhibited and published, they make public a private ritual.

A DISAPPEARING COMMUNITY 4

Bill Aron

The Lower East Side of New York City is an important landmark in the life of the American Jew. It was, in its time, the source of a variety of Jewish cultural institutions—yeshivot, synagogues, Yiddish newspapers and theaters, as well as the restaurants and coffee houses depicted in the stories of Isaac Bashevis Singer. The Lower East Side was one of the principal areas of settlement for Jews as they immigrated to this country; by the turn of the century, it contained the largest Jewish community in the world. Today it is but a symbol of a rich past that is about to disappear.

In its heyday, East Broadway was a kind of Jewish promenade where a revered generations of artists, entertainers, politicians, businessmen and intelligentsia flourished. The neighborhood was bustling and vibrant, full of immigrants from many lands working to attain the American dream, or, at least, hoping that their children would. The whole range of Jewish life could be found, from the pious Hassidim to the socialist Bundists, from artists and scholars to entrepeneurs. For many Jews, however, the Lower East Side was only a stopping place. Financial success was usually followed by a move from the old neighborhood. Irving Berlin, Eddie Cantor, Jimmy Durante, Jacob Javits, and David Sarnoff are but a few of those who came out of the Lower East Side. They started here, and when they began to "make it," they left.

The neighborhood which remains bears testimony to the struggle of that first generation of Jewish immigrants. Hundred-year-old tenements still stand with their shabby ornaments and fire escapes. Practically every doorway shows the signs of a former mezuzah. On nearly every block stands the remains of at least one synagogue, many of them only shells of their former selves. In Seward Park, where once thousands of Jewish workers celebrated May Day, old men and women hawk used clothing. Across the street from the park stands the Forward Building, once the home of a large Yiddish daily newspaper. Pushcarts with knishes and kosher food can still be found. People still come from all over the city to buy religious articles, stopping off for a supply of Gus' extra sour pickles before returning home.

But these are only meager remnants; the Jews who remain on the Lower East Side today are, for the most part, poor, afraid, and alone.

Congregation Anshei Slonim, the oldest synagogue in New York, served worshippers for 125 years. Several years ago the synagogue was vandalized repeatedly; shortly thereafter the synagogue was forced to close its doors permanently. Seward Park is left to gangs and derelicts after sunset. The Forward building has been sold, and is now an oriental church; the newspaper has moved uptown, as has the Folksbiene Theater, the last of the Yiddish Playhouses. Many of the yeshivot and synagogues have closed or been converted to churches. The Jewish grocer, butcher, baker, and tailor have all but disappeared, leaving only token traces of a way of life that once was. The tenements are being razed due to urban renewal, and their small street level shops, so intrinsic to the neighborhood's character, are going out of business. The once populous Jewish community is but a fraction of its former size. New waves of immigrants, predominantly Puerto Rican and Chinese, have replaced their Jewish predecessors. The population trends are evident in the following statistics:

Table 1: Population Estimates* for the Lower East Side

Category	1963	1967	1975	Change: 1963-75
Jewish	70,000	60,000	50,000	−29.6%
Over 65	9,000	9,500	10,000	+11.1%
Total Growth	200,305	244,390	289,950	+30.4%

*From the New York Department of City Planning.

While the Jewish population has declined by about one-third since 1963, the total population in the area has grown by approximately the same amount. All the ethnic groups resent and fear each other. Each conflict situation tends to escalate, each case of assault, and burglary increases in scope with the telling. Those in the projects and cooperatives fear to go out after dark. Businesses and shops close early and are gated.

Perhaps most poignant is the plight of the elderly. Between 5,000 and 7,500 members of the community have been classified by various social agencies as "Jewish elderly poor." Whatever their exact numbers, most of the Jewish elderly on the Lower East Side are alone and cut off from family and friends, who have either died out, or have moved and forgotten them. The neighborhood, which was once a reasonable facsimile of a European *Shtetl*, is now virtually a foreign country. The old people's English is poor, they are hard of hearing, and their health is failing. The bureaucratic intricacies of social service agencies, such as welfare, social security, and the like, defeat them; clerks who cannot understand their English or who cannot make themselves heard often send these elderly to the end of yet another line as a way of dismissing them. Their tenements are as filthy and as decayed as the streets are dangerous. The Puerto Ricans and Chinese, whose communities are expanding rapidly, feel, with some justification, that they need more territory. The old Jews, however, refuse to move. For better or worse, they are wedded to their neighborhood and are determined to stay. For them, there is no solution. In ten years they will be gone and with them will disappear the last vestiges of the Jewish shtetl.

PERSONAL INVOLVEMENT

I first began photographing on the Lower East Side for personal reasons. I had heard the names of Lower East Side streets—Delancy, East Broadway, Canal, Essex, and so on—since early childhood. But because I did not live in New York, I never had the occasion to visit there. When I moved to New York in 1974, I took the opportunity to visit the Lower East Side in order to give substance to the stories I had heard. I was particularly moved by the sense of history that exists there, but also somewhat horrified by the poverty and deterioration in the old Jewish immigrant section. My impression was that the Jewish Lower East Side is at the end of its history; much of what I saw looked like it would disappear in ten years, or less.

I felt that I wanted to make a record of what remained of the Jewish community on the Lower East Side before it was gone. After I had made the decision to do a photographic study, I was also influenced by my training as a sociologist; I wanted to put together a portrait of what a community looks like at the end of its history, but use a camera instead of a questionnaire or interviews. I became interested in questions of social welfare, ethnic relations, aging, and social change.

Because I believe that both artists and academicians should do something in return for their subjects, I began working for Project Ezra, an independent nonprofit organization that works with the Jewish elderly poor on the Lower East Side. Through working with Project Ezra and photographing old people and fading institutions, I was forced to confront personal questions about the meaning of life and death, and the ties that bind generations together. I was also confronted by a sociological paradox: The immigrant Jewish community on the Lower East Side is dying a natural death; the children and grandchildren of the immigrants have moved on to Brooklyn, Queens, New Jersey, and beyond. It is only right that the other ethnic groups in the area should covet this once-Jewish territory; their populations are

Photo 1

Photo 2

    The Lower East Side is an old Jewish neighborhood and on every block there are signs of both its heritage and its age. The first photograph is of the oldest synagogue building in New York City. Built in 1849 by Anshei Chesed, its present name is Anshei Slonim. For the first time in a century, in 1973, the building was in such disrepair that High Holy Day (the New Year and the Day of Atonement) services could not be held. A combination of deterioration and vandalism finally caused the synagogue to close its doors permanently in 1974. There are some twenty synagogues on the Lower East Side which are still being used. Some of them are well attended, but some barely achieve a *minyan,* the quorum of ten men needed to say the full prayers.

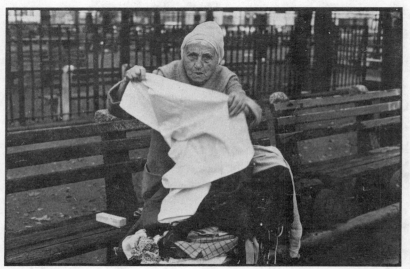

Photo 3

Whenever possible, I try to give the people I photograph copies of their prints. Mrs. S. came to this country from Poland when she was a child. She has no living relatives and now resides in a "senior citizen's residence." The first time I brought her a photograph of herself, she tore it up saying it was a terrible photograph. She went to a drawer in her room and brought out two photographs of herself which were taken about 30 years ago. "Here," she said, "you want to see a nice photograph?" The next several visits were difficult for both of us. We talked about her life, but also about mine. She would occasionally look sad and say, "I used to be something once; now I am old and am nothing."

Gradually, a familiarity developed between us. At first she questioned

Photo 4

my interest, but slowly she came to appreciate that "a young Jew should be interested in my life." For my part, I was learning about a way of life that I would not otherwise know and, more importantly, I was helped, albeit indirectly, to face up to my own mortality.

The Lower East Side has a significant socialist tradition. Seward Park (where photo 4 was taken), and across the street from it, the Forward Building, are important symbols of that tradition. Supporters of socialist causes and the workers who helped build the union movement in the country would often hold their demonstrations in Seward Park. Today the park is mainly used by elderly who, in an effort to earn a few extra pennies, hawk used clothing and other similar wares.

Photo 5

My head is always turned by Hassidim because they seem to me to have just stepped out another century. Rabbi R. saw me photograph him as he crossed Canal and Essex streets to buy lulavim and etrogim for

expanding rapidly. The transformation of the Lower East Side is an entirely natural process, in sociological terms. Yet the human cost, in terms of dislocation and disruption of the lives of individuals, cannot help but sadden even the most dispassionate observer.

It is in relation to these matters of feeling that we find the principle strength of photography as a sociological method, for the photograph can give the viewer an emotional connection with—as well as an intellectual understanding of—the scene depicted. Photographs at their best do not simply make assertions; rather the viewer interacts with them in order to arrive at conclusions, an observation made by Dewey about art in general (1957) and discussed in relation to photography by Becker (1978a). In our interacting sensitivity to their detail and meaning, photographs can help us to see, feel, and understand in ways that words alone cannot.

Succoth. He made no attempt to stop me from photographing, so I continued to do so while he was bargaining for lulavim and etrogim. After a while, one of the men with him started yelling at me to go photograph someone else. Rabbi R. cut him off gruffly saying something in Yiddish. I surmised that I could continue. I later took his address to send him copies of the photographs. After he received the photographs, he called to thank me and to invite me to his house during Hanukkah. My visit with his family was delightful; everyone was extremely open and warm, giving me the opportunity to ask everything I have always wanted to know about Hassidism. I photographed their Hanukkah celebration and learned that Rabbi R. was also a Rebbe and a member of the Bobover community. When I said, in answer to a question of his, that I had never been to a Hassidic wedding, he exclaimed: "Boy have I a wedding for you." Fairly soon after my visit, I received an invitation to the wedding of the daughter of the esteemed Bobover Rebbe.

Photo 5 is of the Bobover Rebbe, his granddaughter, the groom (on the Rebbe's right), and several members of the community close to the Rebbe. During the entertainment, after the ceremony, this little girl broke away from the women's section and came running to her grandfather, who was, of course, delighted.

PEDESTRIANS AND WIND 5

Ervin Zube

Tall buildings and building complexes can create high-speed turbulent winds in ground level, the pedestrian environment of sidewalks, plazas and park areas. Wind-tunnel experiments have determined that tall buildings can cause ground-level wind speeds that are two to three times faster than ambient speeds. Winds are either deflected downward from the top of the building to produce enhanced wind speeds at lower levels or accelerated by the shape of buildings or building complexes which focus the air flow. There has been, however, little attention paid to the effects of these wind conditions on pedestrian behavior (Push-karev and Zupan, 1975). Obviously, high-speed winds can affect pedestrian behavior and cause great inconvenience to people negotiating doors, steps and walkways, or simply going about their daily activities (photos 1 and 2).

The purpose of this chapter is to describe a study that was undertaken to document some of the effects of high-speed winds on pedestrian activity and to provide information that could ultimately influence urban design policy decisions regarding the location and design of structures in urban areas. An important attribute of the study, which will be emphasized in this description, was the use of time-lapse photography for recording pedestrian behavior.

DESIGN OF THE STUDY

The study was designed as an interdisciplinary endeavor and involved physical scientists, environmental designers and behavioral

AUTHOR'S NOTE: This study was supported by the National Science Foundation under Grants ENG 75-04353 and ENG 76-23713; and conducted by an interdisciplinary team made up of personnel from Weather Dynamics, Inc. of Arlington, Massachusetts and the University of Massachusetts. Principal investigators were the author, I. Ian McLaren, physicist from Weather Dynamics and Stanley M. Moss, psychologist from the university. Howard Cohen and Roman Petyk, psychology and landscape architecture research assistants from the university, contributed, respectively, to the behavioral and design guidelines components of the study. The author acknowledges the important contribution of each team member of the study. The chapter is based on the team report to the National Science Foundation (Cohen et al., 1977).

Photo 1

Pedestrians and wind in
downtown Boston.

Photo 2

scientists. The guidelines which were prepared for urban design de-
cision-making were derived from the analysis of: on-site wind data;
wind-tunnel simulation; and on-site behavioral data.

ON-SITE WIND DATA

On-site behavioral data were collected to quantitatively describe
the characteristics of wind that cause problems for people. Spatial
and temporal variations in wind speed and direction were recorded at
four sites in Boston, Massachusetts, including several sites where it
was known that pedestrians are frequently subjected to high-speed
winds. Measurements were made using a mobile anemometer which
recorded three orthogonal directions of wind flow—along the wind or
longitudinal flow, across the wind or lateral flow and vertical flow.
Thus, measures of gusts and ambient winds speed and duration were
obtained for both horizontal winds and vertical winds (winds deflected
downward from the tops of buildings).

WIND-TUNNEL SIMULATION

A 1:400 scale, three-dimensional model of downtown Boston was used for wind tunnel simulation tests of three of the four study sites. Wind tunnel data for gusts and ambient winds were correlated with on-site data to determine the validity of wind-tunnel simulations for predicting the effects of buildings and building complexes on wind patterns.

ON-SITE BEHAVIORAL DATA

On-site behavioral data were obtained through the use of three methods: systematic observations, questionnaires, and sales receipt data. Observational data were obtained from time-lapse films that were taken simultaneously with the wind data acquisition, providing for the correlation of behavioral measures with physical wind measures. Behavioral measures included: pedestrian density, speed of movement, interpersonal distance, gross body movement and orientation, individual path analysis, circulation patterns, and specific behaviors such as sitting, talking, and eating lunch.

Concurrently with the obtaining of time-lapse films, a survey was administered to random populations drawn from principal office buildings in two of the study sites. The first section of the questionnaire consisted of semantic scales which were used to assess individual perceptions of the four sites, and included the following items: un-inviting—inviting; windy—calm; safe—dangerous; quiet—noisy; cold—hot; comfortable—uncomfortable; bright—dull; protected—exposed; chaotic—ordered; and hostile—friendly. Each site was depicted in the questionnaire by a black and white photograph. The second section consisted of a series of attitudinal statements concerning the effects of wind conditions on behavior, such as the following: "Unpleasant wind conditions occur so infrequently that they rarely bother me," "When there are high winds, I try to avoid them by various means," "Wind conditions bother me only when it is cold or rainy," and "There are times when I enjoy going outside on windy days." The final section recorded behavioral responses to various wind conditions by asking respondents whether they change or postpone their everyday activities, such as running errands, or going outside of their office building for lunch, shopping, and the like because of wind and weather conditions.

As a supplement to observational and questionnaire data, a number of businesses adjacent to the four study sites provided information on the number of cash register transactions per day. This provided an evaluation of one relationship between wind conditions and economic activity. Receipt data were correlated with weather data from National Weather Service local climatological records and with the on-site wind measurements.

STUDY-SITE SELECTION

Four study sites were selected in the city of Boston, which has one of the highest average wind speeds for an urban area in the United States. Criteria for selection included:

- suitability for anticipated wind conditions;
- suitability for location of wind-measuring instrumentation without disrupting pedestrian traffic in the vicinity;
- availability of nearby site for camera crew to obtain observational records; and
- cooperation of owners or managers from buildings adjacent to the test sites.

The four test sites that were finally selected are:

- the sidewalk area adjacent to a 500-foot (152-meter) building where it is generally recognized that unpleasant wind conditions frequently occur;
- the entrance walkway to a 600-foot (183-meter) office building where dangerously fast wind speeds are known to occasionally occur;
- on the public plaza adjoining Boston City Hall; and
- a sitting and strolling area on the Boston Common, a large public park.

ON-SITE COLLECTION

On-site wind and behavioral data were collected for three seasons, winter, spring, and summer and for two conditions in each season, baseline and test (Figure 1). The baseline condition was defined as wind velocities less than or equal to ten miles per hour. Test conditions were defined as wind velocities greater than or equal to twenty miles per hours.

Season	Velocity	
	Baseline < 10 mph	Test > 20 mph
Winter		
Spring		
Summer		

Figure 1: On-site data collection

OBTAINING AND ANALYZING TIME-LAPSE FILMS

Why use time-lapse photography for obtaining observational data? There are several reasons why this technique was selected:

(1) Interference with pedestrian behavior by the research team was minimized.
(2) Recording of pedestrian behavior on film could be synchronized spatially and temporally with the wind data (recorded on magnetic tape), thus allowing for analysis of behavioral variables as they covaried with wind speed, duration, and direction.
(3) Pedestrian behavior was recorded continuously over time (20-minute observation periods) providing more information than could be obtained by methods which only record behavior at a point in time.
(4) The filmed record of pedestrian behavior made possible multiple viewings, and thus facilitated both systematic sequential analysis of selected behaviors and easy checking of reliability.

Camera stations were located in buildings adjacent to each site. Locations were slightly elevated, equivalent to being on the second floor, so as to provide a better view of the study area. The camera location was fixed by measured distance from reference points such as walls and building features in the immediate vicinity. The aiming of the camera so as to replicate the same fields of view in each film session was accomplished by reference to an eight inch by ten inch photograph of the precise study area. The view through the camera view finder was established exactly as defined by the photograph. No effort was made to conceal the camera or the research team. They were, nevertheless, quite inconspicuous.

A Canon Model 814 Auto Zoom Super-8 movie camera with an interval timer and a standard heavy-duty tripod were used to record pedestrian movement. Recordings were made with Kodachrome 40 Type A color film over each of the twenty-minute observation periods at the rate of 1.4 frames/second and were coordinated with the wind-data acquisition through the use of hand signals and short-range portable radios.

Two point perspective grids (thirty inch by forty inch) were prepared for each site on which were depicted buildings and other important site features and structures (Figure 2). Films were projected on prints of these perspective grids for the recording of specific behaviors. Each grid was unique to each site and to film conditions such as camera height, angle and filming distance. Grid cells corresponded with pavement patterns at each site and measured either five feet by five feet (1.52 m by 1.52 m) or four feet by four feet (1.22 m by 1.22 m). Each cell was identified by coordinates.

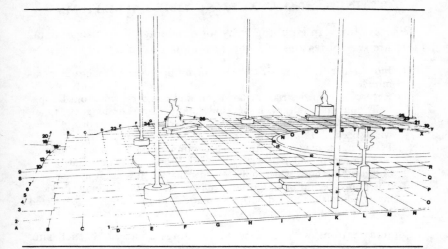

Figure 2: Perspective grid for Boston Common study site

Each on-site session provided twenty minutes of film photographed at the rate of eighty-two frames per minute or approximately 1,600 frames per film. Each film was numerically coded by marking every tenth frame with a pin hole, starting at frame ten and ending at frame 1,600. This coding provided the basis for sequential counts of the entire film as well as a temporal reference guide for the analysis of pedestrian movement and speed (i.e., one minute equals eighty-two frames). Coordination of film image and perspective grid was achieved by matching site feature and building reference points.

Pedestrian paths were analyzed by plotting, frame by frame, the movement of selected subjects. Within each two hundred-frame block, five subjects were randomly selected. The analysis started when the subject's legs entered any one of the peripheral grid cells and terminated when the subject left the perspective grid. As the frames were sequentially advanced, the pedestrian's position was noted, first sequentially by grid cell coordinates and second on the grid itself by a series of points which were connected to define the travel path (Figure 4). This procedure provided both a graphic portrayal of movement patterns and data which are in a form suitable for statistical analysis.

Recording of movement patterns for each subject by grid cell coordinates provides for the use of a conditional probability computer program and the generation of a probability matrix for each cell in

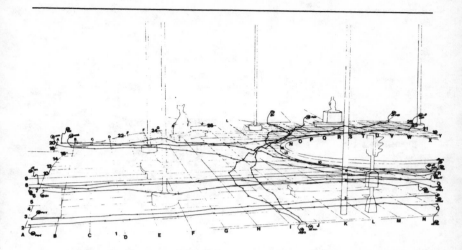

Figure 3: Perspective grid for Boston Common site with drawings of pedestrian paths

the perspective grid. In other words, if a subject is in a specific cell, the computer program determines the probability that on the next step the subject will be located in one of the adjacent cells. From each cell, with the exception of perimeter cells, a subject can move to any of eight adjacent cells. The significance of this procedure is that it provides a way of analyzing multiple paths of multiple subjects and identifying those paths which have the highest probability of being followed under the varying wind and weather conditions on baseline and test days.

Other data obtained from analysis of the film included pedestrian density, behaviors and velocity or speed. Density (Figure 5) was computed by sampling every thirtieth frame of the film for forty consecutive samples. Subject locations were marked on the grid and grid coordinates were noted. Pedestrian behaviors which were recorded were: standing alone, standing in conversation, sitting, assessment of the wind's visible effects on the subjects (i.e., blowing hair and clothes, difficulty in walking, and controlling clothing and packages) and the number of pedestrian platoons (groups of two or more persons walking or standing). Pedestrian velocity was calculated for a sample of twenty subjects for each session by calculating the number of grid cells traversed by each subject (distance) and determining the number of frames that corresponded to this path (time).

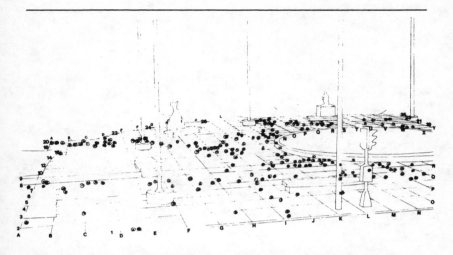

Figure 4: Perspective grid for Boston Common site showing pedestrian
         density

FINDINGS

The data from each site were statistically analyzed comparing wind
speeds (on-site and simulation) and behavioral responses across and
within seasons. Following is a summary of the major findings from
each component of the study including more extensive discussion of
selected data from the film analysis for two of the sites.

ON-SITE WIND DATA

Two of the study sites were urban open spaces and two were adjacent
to high-rise buildings. On-site wind velocity measurements were made
for conditions which ranged from near calm to average speeds in excess
of twenty mph at pedestrian levels. These measurements included wind
gusts over forty mph and once to sixty mph. Average wind speeds near
the high-rise office buildings were significantly greater than those
recorded in the open spaces. Measurements of pedestrian-level wind
gusts near the high-rise buildings were two to two-and-one-half times
the wind speeds recorded two miles east at the U.S. Weather Bureau
Logan Airport Station. Gust speeds in the open spaces were one to
two times the wind speeds recorded at the airport. Analysis of the
U.S. Weather Bureau average hourly wind speed data also indicated
that the highest average wind speeds occur between 8 a.m. and 7 p.m.
with peak speeds occurring between noon and 5 p.m.—periods of
maximum pedestrian activity in downtown areas.

WIND-TUNNEL SIMULATION

Wind-tunnel simulation tests for three of the sites in downtown Boston yielded very good agreement between wind speeds measured in the tunnel and those measured on-site. Gust speeds measured in the wind-tunnel tests agreed closely with those measured on site. Wind-tunnel and on-site data were in agreement to within 10% to 20% for corresponding wind directions. This supports the usefulness of wind-tunnel testing for predicting the wind environment near proposed tall buildings.

ON-SITE BEHAVIORAL DATA

Analysis of the time lapse films and the correlation of these data with on-site wind data indicated that the gustiness of the wind plays an important role in pedestrian behavior and apparent comfort. Even when on-site winds average only six to eight mph, wind gust can be expected to reach fifteen to twenty five mph causing considerable inconvenience and discomfort. When winds average over ten mph, the associated gusts of thirty to forty mph can cause considerable difficulty in such pedestrian behaviors as carrying packages and umbrellas. Furthermore, elderly and infirm pedestrians may occasionally lose their balance. When on-site winds average twenty mph or more, pedestrians are in potential physical danger and movement is limited severely by gusts that frequently exceed forty mph and can reach sixty mph. On the spring test day at one of the high rise building sites, with gusts of thirty and forty mph, pedestrians were observed:

(1) having obvious difficulty maintaining their balance, while running for shelter from the wind (and rain) while entering or leaving the building;
(2) having three umbrellas literally destroyed within one five-minute period;
(3) losing one hat to traffic; and
(4) showing dangerous neglect for personal safety as two pedestrians tried to escape the local wind environment by going against moving traffic in the adjacent street.

Within all seasons for all sites, test days with wind speeds greater than twenty mph resulted in a significant increase in speed of pedestrian movement, significantly less pairings or social groups among pedestrians and significantly lower levels of other types of behavior such as sitting, talking, and eating lunch.

Questionnaire data indicated that perceptions, attitudes, and self-reports on behavior of participants from two office buildings tended to reflect the prevailing wind and weather conditions. They were, however, more sensitive to these conditions in the outdoor spaces

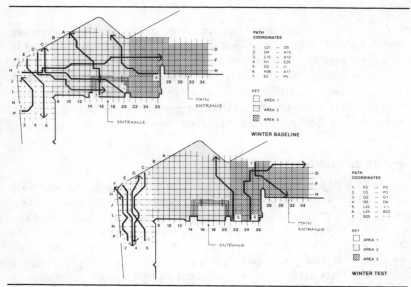

Figure 5: Site A, high probability paths for winter baseline and test
conditions

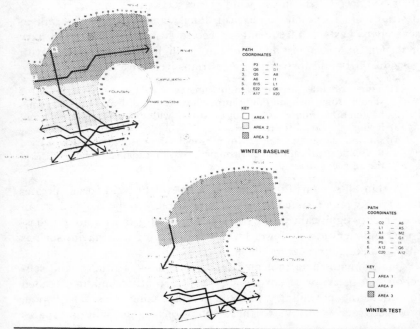

Figure 6: Site D, (Boston Common) high probability paths for winter

Photo 3

Photo 4

Views of sites A (Photo 3) and D (Photo 4) as seen from the adjacent filming locations.

immediately adjacent to the building they worked in, than in the other three study areas. Respondents indicated that they left their office buildings to run errands or to go shopping significantly less on test days than on baseline days. Cash register sales receipt data indicated that there was a significant reduction in the number of sales on test days at one of the sites.

FILM ANALYSIS OF TWO SITES

Figures 5 and 6 depict the seven high probability paths for two of the study sites for winter baseline and test wind conditions. These sites illustrate findings for both open space and high-rise building conditions. Site A is the sidewalk area adjacent to a 500-foot building and Site D is a sitting and strolling area on the Boston Common. Photos 3 and 4 depict the sites as seen from the filming locations.

Analysis of the paths for the winter conditions at Site A indicates that four of the high probability paths are either exit or entrance paths to the building (1, 2, 3, 6) and five of the seven paths cross area 2 on the grid. In general the paths are distributed throughout the study area. In contrast, the analysis for the winter test conditions indicates a more highly structured array of paths and only one traverses area 2. It should also be noted that none of the paths exit or enter at the second entrance area on the left side of the building—the main entrance to a commercial bank. The effects of high wind speeds effectively makes area 2, adjacent to this entrance, unnegotiable for pedestrians.

High probability paths for summer baseline and test conditions are nearly identical to those for the winter. Baseline and test conditions in the spring both yielded patterns of high probability paths that were similar to winter and summer baseline conditions. There was not an apparent difference between spring baseline and test conditions.

Analysis of the high probability paths for Site D on Boston Common indicates a higher concentration of paths in area 1 during test conditions and a more random and diffuse pattern during baseline conditions. Distribution of paths under baseline and test conditions for spring is quite similar to the winter distribution pattern. During the summer, however, paths are distributed in a more random and diffuse pattern throughout the three areas on the grid for both baseline and test conditions. This suggests that the recreational characteristics of the space may be predominant regardless of wind conditions during this season.

Table 1 indicates the different behaviors recorded at the two sites. These data are strongly suggestive of different functional use patterns

Table 1: Behavioral Analysis: Sites A and D

	Winter				Spring				Summer			
	Site A		Site D		Site A		Site D		Site A		Site D	
	Base-line	Test	Base-line	Test	Base-line	Test	Base-line	Test	Base-line	Test	Base-line	Test
Average number of pedestrians[1]	2.88	2.63	4.03	4.88	3.85	3.28	9.75	2.93	3.25	2.95	18.45	13.55
Average walking speed (Ft./Sec.)[1]	2.65	3.65	3.51	3.71	3.15	3.58	2.71	3.41	2.21	2.98	2.61	3.28
Number standing alone	1	1	4	3	1	0	3	4	2	3	2	5
Number standing in groups	2	0	1	2	0	0	9	3	0	0	6	4
Number sitting	0	0	1	0	0	0	7	0	0	0	6	5
Total number in platoons	10	19	34	52	13	19	72	23	20	14	83	90

1. Analysis of variance for average walking speed and pedestrian density indicates significant differences at Site A (p ≤ .05) for walking speed and density by season and at Site D (p ≤ .01) for walking speed and density by season and by session (baseline and test).

of the two sites. Site D is obviously used more intensively and it would appear, from the numbers in groups and platoons, for more social behaviors.

CONCLUSIONS AND RECOMMENDATIONS

The results of this study suggest that some of the heretofore generally accepted procedures for predicting wind speeds at the base of tall buildings (Penwarden and Wise, 1975) may lead to an estimation of severe wind conditions. The results also suggest that recently proposed comfort and safety standards (Isyumov and Davenport, 1975) for acceptable wind speeds and frequencies in various pedestrian areas (i.e., major walkways, arcades, plazas) have been too liberal. Table 2 indicates the suggested pedestrian safety and comfort standards which were developed from this study. Standards are recommended for different kinds of pedestrian areas and for average wind speeds and the frequency with which winds of that frequency should be permitted to occur. These standards are intended to be used for guiding general design decisions on the geographic location of buildings and open spaces in urban areas and for more specific design decisions such as building orientation, location of exits and entrances and the provision of wind screens.

Table 2: Suggested Urban Pedestrian Safety and
Comfort Wind Standards

Activity area	Suggested standards	
	One-hour average wind speed	Permitted occurrence frequency
All pedestrian areas—limit for safety	20 mph (9.1 m/sec)	0.1%
Major walkways, especially principal exit paths for high rise buildings	20 mph (9.1 m/sec)	0.1%
Other pedestrian walkways, including short and arcade shopping areas	14 mph (6.4 m/sec)	5 %
Open plazas and park areas, walking, strolling activities	8 mph	15 %
Open plaza and park sitting areas open-air restuarants	5 mph (2.3 m/sec)	20 %

Greater efforts need to be made in anticipating and ameliorating wind problems generated by high-rise building construction. All proposals for high-rise buildings should be subjected to a preliminary assessment of wind conditions which takes into account existing wind conditions, probable induced winds, building location and form, points of entry, doorway design, and the design and intended use of adjacent outdoor spaces. In those areas where average annual wind speeds exceed twelve mph, wind-tunnel tests should be conducted for all proposed buildings over 200 feet in height. Where average annual wind speeds are eight to ten mph, wind-tunnel tests should be conducted for all proposed buildings over 250 feet in height. The purposes for the wind-tunnel tests are to: locate areas of high induced winds; estimate the frequency and speeds of potential winds that could be generated by the proposed structure; evaluate the suitability of the proposed design from the standpoint of the previously suggested comfort and safety standards; and identify areas near other high-rise buildings where the proposed building would exacerbate existing conditions.

Finally, the methods and procedures used in this study were found to be effective and reliable. In particular, the use of time-lapse photography for systematic observation combined with the questionnaire and sales receipt data was of particular importance for obtaining multiple measures of pedestrian behavior.

6

PERCEIVING
A PLANNED COMMUNITY

Jon Wagner

Our folk models of a community include both physical and social features; to imagine a community is to imagine people living in a built environment. Within professional study, however, we find a peculiar division between the two. On the one hand are those architects and physical planners who have taken the shape and structure of the physical environment to be the essentials of community "places." On the other hand are those social scientists who have focused on the order of social life which characterizes a group of people living in such a place. Recently, there has emerged an awareness of social life among a few architects and planners (Perin, 1970; Cooper, 1975), and it is also encouraging to note that a few social scientists are attending to the physical features in which people construct community life (Suttles, 1972) or lose it (Erikson, 1976).

One of the problems of integrating these two dimensions in community study emerges from an abiding problem in social science practice: How can we investigate the manner in which people perceive their world—for indeed it is within "perceived space" that communities are formed—without structuring their own perceptions within categories of our own? In an interview situation, for example, how can we ask questions without having the questions themselves organize the perceptions of those we interview?

While there is no theoretical solution to this problem, it can be approached practically in community studies through a variety of research designs. Ideally, for example, we might like to accompany residents on a walk around their community, pointing here and there and asking, "What is this and what do you think of it?" Some re-

AUTHOR'S NOTE: Research described in this chapter was supported by a grant from the National Science Foundation (RANN G141311), awarded to Professor Suzanne Keller, Princeton University. I thank both the Foundation and Professor Keller for their support of my work within this larger project of which it was a part. Copies of the complete report on this research are available from National Technical Information Service (NSF/RA-760749). Thanks also to Lynne Hollingsworth who took many of the photographs, did much of the coding, and offered innumerable telling insights about the life she observed in Twin Rivers.

searchers have tried to get at similar information by having residents draw maps of where they live and the surrounding terrain (Gould and White, 1974). Others have tried universal interpretations of physical scenes, and one (Cullen, 1961) has used photographs to illustrate them.

If we want our theories of community to be grounded in resident perceptions, however, we need to find a vehicle for asking these questions without suggesting response categories (i.e., "naming" the phenomenon we are investigating and giving it a meaning of our own). One device which can facilitate this kind of questioning is the photo-interview. As a research strategy lying somewhere in between purely verbal questions and the community tour suggested above, interviewing residents about photographs of their community can generate data about both resident familiarity (Greebie, 1976) and environmental preferences (Zube et al., 1975; Brush and Shafer, 1975).

TWIN RIVERS

About an hour south of New York City, and just a mile or so east of the New Jersey Turnpike, 719 acres of what was formerly a large potato farm have been turned into an interesting and ambiguous housing development. Advertised as a "community," Twin Rivers was a pet project of its builder- developer, Herbert J. Kendall. In it he hoped to provide an alternative to unplanned urban sprawl, and to create an environment which was pedestrian-oriented, visually and socially heterogenous, and, all in all, a pleasant place to live.

The community was designed to house 10,000 to 12,000 residents in 3,000 dwelling units. It was organized into four quadrants, separated from each other by an East-West highway and a North-South "open green spine." As New Jersey's first Planned Unit Development (PUD), Twin River combined a range of residence types (apartments, detached homes, condominiums, and the like) with central shopping, schools, recreation facilities, and adjacent light industry.

People move to Twin Rivers for a variety of reasons, but residents are by and large ex-urbanites—almost half of them from New York City—with middle to moderate incomes. Many come as young families, eager to participate in home ownership and hopeful of finding a comfortable place to rear their young children. In many respects, life in Twin Rivers represents for them an alternative to both unplanned suburban sprawl and the inner city. While reporting general satisfaction with their move into the community, residents also indicate that it leaves much to be desired; some have already left. Several important features of the original plan (churches, a community center, and theaters) have never been built, and both the developer and the administration of the settlement have been the object of resident criticism. Twin Rivers remains for its residents, as well as for those interested in its example, a "community to be," one in which life owes a certain debt to what it might yet become.

THE RESEARCH

As part of a much larger study of the physical and social features of Twin Rivers (see Keller, 1976), we decided to explore resident perceptions of this community-in-the-process-of-becoming through photo-interviewing. A set of seventeen photographs was selected for this purpose, including images of the major housing types; a burned apartment; recycling bins in the shopping center parking lot; an ambiguous warning sign; and a variety of other images which seemed to us to capture some of the essential visual and physical features of the community. A complete set of the seventeen photographs is presented in the next three pages.

Part of the sample for these interviews was drawn from a list of respondents to an earlier part of the study. These included forty adults, stratified by race and age, and twenty-one teenagers. We also included ten additional residents who had been previously interviewed for other purposes, and ten residents who had been winners in a communitywide landscaping and gardening contest, thinking that involvement with their own homes might make them more attentive than most to the visible features of Twin Rivers. The total sample thus included seventy-one Twin Rivers residents.

Deciding what questions to ask about the photographs was difficult. Because a pilot study had suggested that the photographs were much more powerful stimuli than the verbal questions which accompanied them, we tried to keep the questions simple. For each of the first ten photographs we asked three questions: "Do you know what this is?" "Do you know where this is?" and "How can you tell?" For the remaining photographs we added another question, one designed to elicit more projective comments from the interviewee: "What does this photograph say to you?" Our hope was that the questions would generate interesting comments about recognition processes, feelings about the community, and recognition skills as these were developing in the new community. We knew that there were many other things we might have asked, but the experience of the pilot study argued against elaborate questions.

It should be noted that we were eliciting the residents' responses to our photographs and not to the community itself. The relationship

Photo 1

Photo 2

Photo 3

Photo 4

Photo 5

Photo 6

Photo 7

Photo 8

Photo 9

Photo 10

Photo 11

Photo 12

Photo 13

Photo 14

Photo 16

Photo 15

Photo 17

between the photograph and the object it reflects is complex and, at times, ambiguous. Because we were dealing with a population familiar with the community, however, we assumed that they could translate from the image to the community feature it represented. Collier (1967) has reported that such an ability is widespread, and we expected to encounter no difficulty in the interviewee's ability to "read" the photograph. It is true, however, that the same object may be photographed in various ways, and we tried to make photographs which read easily. We avoided dramatic manipulations which would make the photograph "arty" and emphasized in our administration of the questionnaire the subject of the photograph rather than the photograph itself.

We were curious about the process by which individual perceptions would contribute to a more general sense of the community in which Twin Rivers residents lived, and our analysis of the photo-interview responses focused on three main questions: Which features of the community are recognized most easily by which residents? By what process do residents recognize different features of their community? And, what are the residents' feelings or attitudes toward the community features we had photographed?

RECOGNITION

We first coded resident response for correct identification of the subject of the photograph. Some residents could correctly identify what a given item was but not where it was located. For others, the reverse was true. Some knew neither what nor where and some knew both. The code for "Correct Identification," thus included the following five categories:

    1 = correct what and correct where
    2 = correct what and incorrect where
    3 = incorrect what and correct where
    4 = incorrect what and incorrect where
    5 = don't know

Of all seventeen photographs, the one most frequently identified correctly was that of the interior of the pizzeria (photo 12). Everyone to whom this photograph was shown knew what and where it was. This photograph was followed by one of the bus stop (photo 1) for which 88% of the interviewees gave the correct response, that of the recycling bins (photo 11; 86%), and the lake and school in Quad I (photo 17; 80% correct).

What sets these photographs apart from other features of Twin Rivers is that each of them shows a feature of the community which is unique or "one of a kind." These contrast with other elements of the community which are also easy to identify but so numerous that it is

Table 1: Percentage of Respondents (N = 71) Correctly
Identifying Subject of Each Photograph

Photo*	Correct what & where	Correct what & incorrect where	Incorrect what & correct where	Incorrect what & where	Don't know
	%	%	%	%	%
Pizzeria, 12	99				
Inner-court shopping center, 8	91	7			
Bus stop, 1	87	9	3		
Recycling bins, 11	86	6	6	1	
Lake school, Q I, 17	80	14	1	1	1
Townhouse, Q I, 7	75	23		1	
Condominiums, 2	70	9	10	7	3
Playground, Q I, 16	63	34		1	1
Apartment fire, 14	62	21	1	7	7
Townhouse, Q III, 5	61	35		3	
Avon apartments, 4	49	41	4	4	
Detached houses, 3	45	54			
Play at own risk, 13	30	28	10	6	25
Water plant—distant view, 10	28	1	20	25	24
Water plant—close up, 9	13		3	20	63
Lawrence Mews, 6	10	10	1	38	39
Decorated walkway, 15	3	51		20	25

*Photographs listed in order of most correct identifications.

difficult to pinpoint where they are located. For example, all interviewees were able to correctly identify the detached houses (photo 3),
but only 45% knew where these particular houses were located. Similarly, 90% correctly identified the subject of photo 4 as apartment
buildings but only 49% knew that they were located in Quad III. The
recognition of townhouses in Quad I (photo 7) shows a parallel pattern:
98% knew what they were, but only 75% knew where to place them.

Of all housing types, the condominiums were least familiar to the
residents. Only 79% correctly identified what they were, compared to
99% for detached houses, 90% for apartments, 96% for Quad I townhouses and 98% for Quad III townhouses. If residents did correctly
identify the condominiums, however, they were more likely to know
where they were located than was the case for other dwelling types:
80% gave correct *where* answers for the condominiums compared to
45% for detached houses, 53% for apartments, 61% for Quad III townhouses and 75% for Quad I townhouses.

If we look at playgrounds—another community feature which is fairly evenly distributed—we get a similar pattern of response. For the playground in Quad I (photo 16), 97% recognized what it was, but only 63% could say where it was.

These responses suggest a more general model for the correct identification of community features in Twin Rivers. When an element of the visible community is found in many places, it is more likely to be familiar to the residents, but also harder to place. Less widely distributed elements of the community, such as the condominiums, may be somewhat less familiar to residents but those who know *what* it is will also know *where* it is.

The *what* aspects of recognition are encouraged when the element in question is found everywhere, which, paradoxically, makes it harder to place. And, the *where* aspects of recognition are facilitated when the element in question exists in a unique and special place.

THE RECOGNITION PROCESS

Becoming familiar with a strange and new environment is a complicated process, involving cognitive as well as perceptual skills. In our study of their perceptions, we identified at least three different strategies by which residents "recognized" the subject of one of our photographs.

1 = Familiarity (the interviewee recognizes, is familiar with or says he or she "knows" the thing itself)
2 = Context (deduction from surrounding features present in the photograph)
3 = Analysis (deduction from familiar design or details of the thing itself)
4 = Other (including guessing)

We found, first of all, that different strategies were used with different photographs. For example, "familiarity"—by which the respondent says he or she "knows" the item in question—was most frequently used in identifying the pizzeria (62% of such responses), the burned apartment (48%), and the recycling bins (42%). "Context," on the other hand—deducing the subject of the photograph from the nature of its surroundings—was used most frequently in identifying the bus stop (70%), the lake by the school in Quad I (69%), the Quad I townhouses (65%), the "Play at Own Risk" sign (56%), and the Quad I Playground (51%). Still, other features were identified most frequently by a process of "analysis," deduction from some familiar detail or design of the subject of the photograph itself. In this category were the townhouses in Quad III (73% of the responses relying on analysis), the inner court of the shopping center (72%), and Avon Apartments (62%). For the two remaining photographs—the close-up view of the water plant, and

Lawrence Mews—we were unable to discern a "most frequent" recognition process.

When we look at this pattern in the context of our previous description of correct identification, we can see that there is a correlation between identifying a photograph correctly and familiarity with its real-life counterpart, as in the case of the bus stop and pizzeria. The corollary seems also to hold true; those photographs most difficult to identify were of items well removed from personal use or knowledge of the residents. This observation represents no great insight, but it does serve implicitly to confirm the ability of the residents to read the photographs as representations of actual features of the community in which they live.

It is important to note that recognition process varied by photograph, and not by the *subject* of the photograph. For example, both photographs 5 and 7 show townhouses, one from Quad I and the other from Quad III. Most respondents recognized the Quad I townhouses by examining the contextual features, such as the lake which appears in the foreground. In locating the Quad III townhouses, however, the majority of residents relied on a deductive process, one which paid special attention to construction details, window treatment, parking lot design, and the like. When we looked more closely at resident responses to the "How can you tell?" interview question, we found, for example, that three-fourths of the respondents mentioned construction details in conjunction with their identification of the Quad III townhouses, compared with only 1% for the Quad I townhouses. For the latter photograph, three-fifths of the respondents mentioned landscape elements as the criteria which helped them identify the Quad I townhouses.

The comparison of photos 5 and 7 suggests that when strong contextual elements are available—as, for example, the lake in photo 7— they will be used. When they are lacking, however, recognition proceeds by other means. Respondents could have used construction details to identify the townhouses in Quad I but the presence of the lake made this unnecessary, a suggestion that contextual inferences have priority over deductive analysis.

Comparison of responses to these two photographs is only suggestive, but it has important implications for resident perceptions of Twin Rivers. By design, the community is composed of similar and "look alike" residences; the original intent was to build a community which had a distinctive and uniform visual character. To the extent that this has been achieved—and both residents and outsiders seem to agree that it has, for better or worse—residents are frequently forced to ground their knowledge of the community in the analysis of detail. The general lack of dominating landmarks, distinctive landscaping, and dramatic site planning leaves those who live there no alternative. In Twin Rivers a sense of place is frequently derived from the finest grain of the built environment.

LABELING AND NAMING

Residents develop familiar terms of reference to designate their community's key attributes. Through the photo-interviews, we sought to determine whether, given their recent arrival in Twin Rivers, residents agreed on the names used to refer to different aspects of the community. As the structure of these names and references is central to a sense of community, we were curious to determine the extent to which individual perceptions had begun to form collective identities.

In order to investigate this phenomenon, we surveyed resident responses to our three standard questions according to the following code:

    1 = a particular name, e.g., "this is (the)   ."
    2 = a general name—no identifying characteristics
    3 = a class of objects, e.g., "this is one of   " or "some of   ."
    4 = subsidiary, e.g., "this is part of   ."
    5 = association, e.g., "this is like or similar to   ."
    6 = designation by activity involving the item
    7 = other
    8 = no name given

Most residents (71%) referred to the subjects of the photographs by names and agreed on the name they used. For example, the photos of the bus stop (1), the detached houses (3), the recycling bins (11) and the pizzeria (12) were identified by name in over 90% of the cases. Other photos identified by name in over 80% of the cases were: the condominiums (2, 89%); Avon Apartments (4, 85%); Townhouses in Quad I (7, 85%); the burned apartment (14, 80%); the playground in Quad I (16, 83%) and the lake and school in Quad I (17, 89%). These figures support the hypothesis that when residents are familiar with some feature of their community, the follow certain semantic conventions in referring to it. Those who live in Twin Rivers assume a knowledge of their environment in conversation with others, a knowledge which allows them to refer to "*the* bus stop," "*the* recycling bins," "*the* Quad I school," and so on. Obviously, knowing the subject of a photo and naming it are highly intercorrelated.

In reviewing the findings discussed so far, we can derive from response to the photographs three distinctive levels of resident familiarity with their community's physical features. First, there are those elements which residents can easily identify—though they are likely to identify *what* more easily than *where*—and which are referred to by "particular names." These seem to be elements of the community around which residents organize their activities and attitudes and upon which they ground their shared perceptions. A second set of elements are less familiar to residents but are still seen to be part of their community. These might be referred to by a general name or identified as one of a familiar "class of objects." This second set represents the permeable and ambiguous boundary of their perceived community. And third, there are elements which are completely unfamiliar to residents, images which they cannot place or which they have never seen before. These least recognizable aspects do not participate in the shared perceptions of those who live in the community, and Twin Rivers residents have no routine way of referring to them.

The physical environment in which residents live, then, extends well beyond that which they find "familiar"; and it is only by *selecting* features from this larger environment that they construct a set of shared perceptions about their community. This represents a combination of individual and collective processes in which there is not only a variety of perceptions, but also a variety of strategies for organizing and anchoring them in experience of the community's physical environment.

For example, residents could have emphasized "signage" in explaining how they recognized the recycling bins; but they did not, relying instead on "personal use." The townhouses in Quad I could have been recognized through analysis of "construction details" as were those in Quad III, but the presence of a dominant landscape element made context most salient. The detached houses could have been examined with an eye to construction details but residents based their recognition on their own personal knowledge and familiarity. These three patterns —"familiarity-personal use"; "context-landscaping"; and "analysis-construction details"—demonstrate the multiple kinds of information which residents have about Twin Rivers and suggest some of the characteristic strategies they utilize in developing a sense of where they live.

EVALUATIVE RESPONSES TO THE PHOTOGRAPHS

In addition to investigating processes of familiarity and recognition, the photo-interviews were used to elicit evaluative comments from residents about their community. In addition to the three standard questions, residents were asked, for photographs numbered 11 through

17, "What does this photograph say to you?" This question generated both positive and negative responses, as displayed in Table 2.

The photographs most likely to arouse negative comments were those depicting unaesthetic views of the environment, such as the recycling bins and the playground in Quad I; environmental abuse, such as the burned-out apartment in Quad II; or a message of danger or prohibition, such as the "Play At Your Own Risk" sign. One exception to this understandable pattern is provided by the photograph of the decorated walkway which seems neither abused nor unattractive, (in fact it received many positive comments) and yet provoked a fair number of negative comments. When we examined more closely these comments, however, we found that they took the following form: "This photograph shows how bad Twin Rivers is because it shows how some people have made an effort to do something nice with their houses. Most residents have not."

The photograph most frequently generating positive evaluation was of the lake and school in Quad I, followed by the decorated walkway, the recycling bins, and the pizzeria. Positive responses to the lake and school and the decorated walkway are not too surprising for each of these photographs reveals Twin Rivers "at its best." Positive responses to the recycling bins, however, are somewhat puzzling because these were also frequently criticized. Closer examination indicated that the

Table 2: Percentage of Interviewees Who Made Evaluative Comments About the Subjects of the Photographs (N = 71)

Photo number	Subject of photograph	Percentage making negative comments	Percentage making positive comments
1	Bus stop		
2	Condominiums, Quad I	3	6
3	Detached houses, Quad III		4
4	Avon apartments	4	
5	Townhouses, Quad III	6	
6	Lawrence Mews	3	3
7	Townhouses, Quad I	7	6
8	Inner-court shopping center	4	
9	Water plant—close up		
10	Water plant—distant		
11	Recycling bins	61	17
12	Pizzeria	11	14
13	Play at own risk	31	4
14	Apartment fire, Quad II	34	3
15	Decorated walkway	21	26
16	Playground, Quad I	41	13
17	Lake school, Quad I	8	41

negative comments were addressed to the physical appearance of the recycling bins, whereas positive comments reflected approval of the purpose for which they stand.

"BEST," "WORST," AND "MOST TYPICAL" PHOTOS OF TWIN RIVERS

As a final step in administering the photo-interview we asked respondents to select from among all the photographs they had seen, the one which they felt represented the "best," the "worst," and the "most typical" view of Twin Rivers. The actual selections made by residents provide some clues about the way in which they perceive the community, but they also suggest the complexity of their response to it (Table 3).

The first thing to notice about this data, for example, is that response is scattered among many of the photographs. Nine of the seventeen photographs received votes as the best; ten were chosen by one or more residents as the most typical. There is also some overlap between the choices made, and a few photographs received attention as the best, worst, *and* most typical. Only one photograph, the larger view of the water plant, failed to be selected for any of the three categories by any resident.

The best of Twin Rivers, according to most residents, is the photograph of the lake and school in Quad I, and runners-up are the condominiums in Quad I and the playground in Quad I. The condominiums are located in an area where very large and attractive trees have been left standing, but the playground looks almost dismal, the grounds vacant and underdeveloped. Hardly an aesthetic choice, the playground may have represented large and open space, an *idea* attractive to the ex-urbanites moving to this community. The importance of the dwelling to Twin Rivers residents is also suggested by these responses, for all of the various housing types received some votes as the best of the community's features.

Totally in keeping with the large number of critical comments they elicited, the burnt-out apartment and the recycling bins were top contenders for the worst of Twin Rivers. Of greater interest, however, are resident selections of the most typical view of the community. Nearly half selected the view of the townhouses in Quad III for this category. While the bus stop and the playground were also seen as most typical by a large number of respondents, the Quad III townhouses were perceived so with the highest degree of consensus for any of the three choices.

The designation of the Quad III townhouses as the most typical view of Twin Rivers is notable not only because of the obvious importance

Table 3: Percentage of Respondents Selecting Each Photograph as "Best," "Worst," or "Most Typical"

Photo number	Subject of photograph	"Best"	"Worst"	"Most typical"
1	Bus stop	3	4	14
2	Condominiums, Quad I	20		
3	Detached houses, Quad III	7		4
4	Avon apartments		1	
5	Townhouses, Quad III	1	1	47
6	Lawrence Mews	3		
7	Townhouses, Quad I	6		7
8	Inner-court shopping center		9	1
9	Water plant—close up		1	
10	Water plant—distant			
11	Recycling bins		23	6
12	Pizzeria	1	3	1
13	Play at own risk		9	
14	Apartment fire, Quad II		31	
15	Decorated walkway		3	4
16	Playground, Quad I	14	11	13
17	Lake school, Quad I	41		1
	N.A.	4	4	2
	Total	100%	100%	100%

residents have attached to this prevalent dwelling type, but also because something more than that was involved in their choice. After all, the set includes as well a photograph of Quad I townhouses, but few considered it typical. Fully 47% chose the Quad III townhouses as most typical but only 7% chose Quad I townhouses. Why the difference?

A closer look shows that the photo of the Quad III townhouses also includes automobiles and parking facilities while that of the other townhouses does not. Clearly, for Twin Rivers residents the car and the townhouse are closely interconnected, and the two together form their image of what is typical to the community. When we remember that the bus stop was another favorite candidate for typicality, we can infer that housing and transportation figure prominently in the residents' images of Twin Rivers.

Selection of the playground as a most typical view also requires comment. Vacant and barren as it is, the playground nonetheless may symbolize something of the residents' feelings for their community. On the one hand, it may represent an area of open space which they may not have had before, a large play area for their children and themselves. On the other hand it lacks definition, possessing neither the texture of the urban world which residents have left behind nor the pastoral features of a "country landscape" into which they hoped to move. Its typicality may in fact reside in the visual conjunction of these contrasting interpretations.

CONCLUSIONS

It is important to keep in mind that these observations are based on resident responses to photographs of various features of their environment, and not the features themselves. Nevertheless, the photo-interviews offered an interesting setting in which to explore and record residents' perceptions of the community in which they live. Combined with more extensive interviews about other features of their life in Twin Rivers, the information generated from photo-interviews enriched our understanding of the connections between physical features and the shared perceptions characteristic of community life.

The selections which residents made for the best, worst and most typical view of Twin Rivers show that they can look at their environment critically and that the car-townhouse motif is a central visual feature of the community. The ambiguous nature of the development's open space seems highly charged for them as do images of abuse and damage to its physical facilities. Taken together, responses to the photographs show that after no more than a few months—at most a few years—residents are well into the process of building meaning into their environment. While the developer gave life to his hopes and ambitions by putting up houses in a New Jersey potato field, the residents, for their part, build their own hopes and ambitions into the construction site he has since left behind. As they chose to notice and chose to perceive, the residents take crucial steps towards making Twin Rivers their home, or finding ground for leaving it.

FAMILY PHOTOGRAPHY

7

Christopher Musello

In snapshots and family photo albums we can find a fluent and unquestioned use of photography as a tool to meet daily needs and goals. For purposes of analysis this form of photography has been identified as the "home mode" and includes within it the body of still photographs and photographic transparencies produced and accumulated by and for family members within the context of family life. Images of the home mode are made for private—as opposed to public or artistic—use, and they are distinguished from other forms of photography by this context of domestic intimacy rather than by technical or formal qualities of the images themselves. Sociologists, folklorists, communications theorists, and others have approached these photographs as "native" and/or "naive" expressions of experience, relationships, values, beliefs, and so on, and they have asked a variety of questions of them. How are they used to communicate? What aesthetic values guide their production? What is their value as documents, and what can they tell us about daily life, about the social structure of their producer's society, or the culture of those who make and use them?

In this essay I will examine the nature and value of this form of photography as a documentation of family life and suggest some of the functions it serves for family members. Before we tackle questions of function and meaning, however, we need to develop some understanding of how people actually *use* this particular photographic mode. We need to know what family photographers attempt to record, how they go about it, how they evaluate their pictures and the patterns by which their pictures are displayed and viewed. Research in this area is still in its infancy, and my comments are offered not as conclusions, but rather as an indication of what may be learned in studying photographic materials such as these.

STUDYING THE HOME MODE

A friend of mine once showed me a "favorite" photograph of hers (photo 1), which struck me as embodying in an extreme way the fundamental problems that confront anyone attempting to analyze family photographs. A stranger viewing this picture outside of its family con-

Photo 1

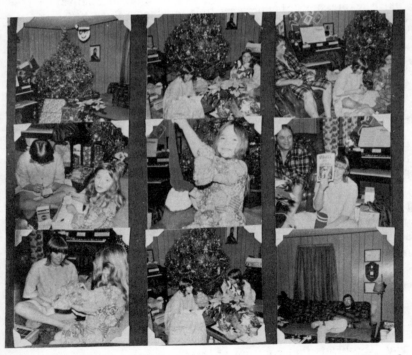

Photo 2

text might at best consider it an impressionistic rendering of color and motion; at worst he might simply think it a mistake. My friend described it this way, (laughing heartily as she told it):

> My sister took this of me as I was taking my horse over a jump, and as she took it she spun with the horse, trying to get real "arty" you know, to catch the horse's motion. Well, everytime I picture my sister whipping around . . . if you knew my sister . . . well, it just cracks me up.

Obviously, if we attempted to study the photograph alone, we would have no way of knowing what events surrounded its being taken, how it was used in following years to tease my friend's sister, and, more generally, the significances which the people who produced and used the image associated with it. These problems emerge in the analysis of even the most skillfully produced photographs, especially when we wish to understand what native significances they encode. Thus, any attempt to "enter" family photography through the photographs alone cannot fully appreciate the meanings associated with the images by their users, nor can it identify the events, activities, and social contexts through which these images are shaped and given value.

In order to understand how families use the medium and the functions it serves for them, we can study family photography ethnographically—as it occurs in everyday life. In this way we can look at photography as a shared or even traditional social process. Photographs can be studied as "social artifacts" and a medium of social behavior, rather than as simply psychological, aesthetic, or technical products (cf. Worth and Adair, 1972; Worth, 1974, and Chalfen, 1975).

Our first objective in this ethnographic approach is to thoroughly describe the activities through which photographs are produced and used, as well as the images themselves. As we examine increasing numbers of families in this way we may begin to see patterns and regularities in the ways in which people use this medium, and come to understand something about the contributions of social and cultural variables to both the products and process of family photography.

In order to provide for such systematic description and analysis of visual media, Richard Chalfen developed what he calls the "sociovidistic framework." Chalfen has applied the framework to the analysis of teenage filmmaking and home movies (Chalfen, 1974a and 1975), and I have subsequently expanded it to account for still photography as well (Musello, 1977). Through this framework the photographic process is broken down into its basic events and components so that each may be carefully described within social contexts. This uniform system of characterization makes possible comparisons between the photography of different social groups, cultures and styles or genres of image-making. In this study, for example, I have used this method to investigate the home mode as a distinct type: family photography. In other contexts the framework can generate a comparable identification of underlying rules and patterns in each aspect of the entire photographic process.

	Participants	Settings	Topics	Message form	Code
Planning					
Shooting: on-camera					
Shooting: behind camera					
Processing					
Editing					
Exhibiting					

Figure 1: The sociovidistic framework adapted

As Figure 1 indicates, photography's basic events and components can be represented as forming a grid through which some 30 relationships are suggested for analysis. The photographic *events* include all those activities involved in producing and using photographs:

Planning Events—activities where decisions are made regarding when to use the camera and what to record;

Shooting Events (behind camera)—all behavior and activities not "on-camera" which structure the use of the camera, including among other things, all techniques and routines in shooting as well as behavior of others which influences the photographer;

Shooting Events (on-camera)—behavior and activities of the camera's subjects which shape the resulting image, including responses such as mugging, posing, and hiding;

Processing Events—all methods and activities through which photographs are developed and/or printed;

Editing Events—all occasions and activities in which people discard, sort, and otherwise organize their photographs;

Exhibition Events—all occasions and means through which photos are displayed; calls for description of all "showing" events as well as all types of display (walls, wallets and albums, for example), and nondisplay (attic chest, drawers, and stored boxes).

By analyzing and characterizing all of these activities a systematic portrait can be formed of how a particular set of people make and use pictures. Analysis of the following *components* can lead to a deeper understanding of the events and the photographs themselves:

Participants—all who participate in the production of the photographs as well as those depicted in them;

Settings—locations depicted in the photographs as well as those in which other photographic events occur;

Topics—subject matter, activities and events represented in the photographs;

Message Form—photographic style, which for these studies is the home mode;

Code—other researchers have demonstrated that distinct photographic codes cannot be isolated (Sekula, 1975), and therefore this category is not applicable to the home mode of family photographs.

Through these components, then, we describe essentially the *who, what, when,* and *where* of the photographs and of the events in which they are made and used.

Initially, the grid helps generate a detailed and uniform *description* of interrelated events and components. Subsequently, however, it suggests sets of relationships which can be productively *analyzed*. At the intersection of "participants" and "exhibition events," for example, we can ask who displays photos and who is allowed to see them; or, at "topics" and "behind camera" shooting events, we could ask what subjects family photographers feel it is important or necessary to record, and what considerations guide their shooting. The framework thus provides both a method for describing the phenomenon and a means for generating research questions. Moreover, as the framework is applied systematically it provides a means to identify rules and patterns, and thus trace social and cultural influences in family photography.

THE NATURE OF FAMILY PHOTOGRAPHY

Sociovidistic analysis of the home mode has to this point suggested that family photography is a largely personal and private process of documentation, incorporating a small yet repeated range of people, subjects, and topics (Musello, 1977). Such analysis is far from trivial, however, for it underlines the importance of social patterns and regularities in the home moder's use of photography. How home moders take pictures, what they take pictures of, and how they use them, for example, seem less dependent upon the capabilities of the camera or on individual decisions than on a social system of conventions and rules. In everyday life, these rules and conventions take the shape of a general orientation towards the place and purpose of family photography and shared ideas about the "right way" to do things.

This is readily seen, for example, in the choice of *components*. The world portrayed in family photo collections consists of a highly select, closed circle of family and friends, seen in a small range of settings in a limited number of activities which are recorded year-after-year. In "recording" these recurring subjects, family photographers consistently focus on the same aspects of their subjects. Christmas, for example, is "documented" through a regular "routine" of secular subjects (photo 2): the decorated Christmas tree with presents; children opening and displaying their presents and so on. Similarly, each of the *events* analyzed through this framework is characterized by a pattern of repeated activities and a shared repertoire of behaviors involving the use of cameras and photographs.

Images of the home mode are thus not simple mechanical records of "real" events, but carefully selected and socially patterned representations of different features of family life. If we are to examine them as "documents" of one sort or another, we must learn to recognize the social processes which have brought them into being and to distinguish these from more personal or idiosyncratic factors.

PHOTOGRAPHY IN DAILY LIFE

As we learn more about the ways in which families *use* photography, we may gain increasing insight into the functions served by this medium and the domestic meaning of its products. Such functions and meanings can be either latent and beyond conscious awareness or manifest and apparent to the users themselves. They may be realized by photographs individually or in the aggregate, and various functions may be served by the actual events of making and/or using the pictures.

COMMUNION

A "communion" function may be served by photographs as they document, reinforce, and in some senses reify relationships, beliefs, and

With your Great-Grandma Super
in Ponca City, Ok.

With Rafiki & Greta in Ft. Worth.

We drove to Fort Worth so your
Great-Grandma & Grandpa Muser
could see you

With cousins Dorris and Ann
in Hearst, Texas

Photo 3

Photo 4

values shared by a group of individuals. This experience and purpose seem implicit in both the contents of family albums and collections, and in the events of sharing and distributing these images through the closed network of family and friends.

The reinforcement of kinship relations and values appears, for example, in the common emphasis on documenting rites of passage such as births, baptisms, graduations and weddings, and the recording of "major" family events. Frequently—as with births (see photo 3) or weddings—home moders will depict the integration of new members into the network of family relations by posing them with a series of relatives. Such strategies seem common to family gatherings, and are traditional in the "routines" of wedding photography. Pictures may similarly serve to depict and affirm bonds of friendship, and they often contribute to the process of creating a group identity for friends and associates (photo 4).

Finally, photographs may contribute explicitly to the maintenance of relationships—through the exchange of pictures themselves or as they stimulate recounting of shared experiences and the reiteration of shared values and bonds. Photos may serve families thus either by graphically *depicting* bonds and relationships or by stimulating and facilitating the *enactment* of these bonds.

INTERACTION

Removing the value of family photography even further from its manifest, iconic, or depicted contents, we can suggest that photography is sometimes used by the home moder primarily as a means to social interaction. The photographs themselves never become irrelevant, but the primary motivations for taking or showing them can lie at times almost totally within the social interaction they engender.

Many people, for example, discussed *picture-taking* itself as a form of entertainment. Surprisingly, joking and provoking others with sudden and unexpected snap shots can comprise a substantial portion of many families' shooting. The process of picture-taking may also signify or communicate other messages to participants. For example, when dad drags the camera out of the closet to take a picture, the *act* itself *signifies* that people involved and/or the event they are engaged in are important to him and "worthy" of being recorded and remembered.

Similarly, *viewing* at times subordinates the documentary significance of particular images to their value as catalysts for social activity. Housewives use their albums as an occassional means to generate light conversation with friends. Wallet photos may be used to initiate conversations with strangers, or as a special form of "introduction," and office photos are often used to create favorable impressions as well as assist in establishing rapport with clients.

As vehicles of communion and social interaction, photographs serve the home moder through more than the mere contents which they depict. Such functions may be latent and beyond the user's awareness, but the contributions of photographs to social relations seem clearly manifest in everyday use, and in these terms alone seem a rich subject for further study.

PRESENTATION OF SELF

As a document of a closed circle of people, the family photo collection is a presentation of identity, personality, and self image. Formally, we should understand that these presentations involve collaboration between subject and photographer to produce each single image. In analyzing family photographs, however, it is often more fruitful to examine the entire collection in an effort to decipher the cumulative portrait it entails and the techniques which produced it.

Perhaps the single highest ideal in home mode portraiture is that of achieving the "most natural" and "complimentary" portrait possible. Given the somewhat contradictory nature of these goals home moders seem to take three broad tacks.

Idealization. These are formal, posed images, often produced by a professional, in which the intent is to obtain a portrait of the person at their "best." They are generally shot in studios or controlled settings which allow maximum control by cameraman and subject (photo 5a, 1 and 2).

"Natural portrayal." Counter to the artifice of the formal images home moders use candid and surprise camera techniques to "capture" people in the contexts of naturally occurring events and activities. These may be posed or candid but in either case the aim is, as before, to produce the best image of that person in an everyday context (photo 5b, 1 and 2).

"Demystification." These first two approaches account for the overwhelming number of portraits in most collections, and the major thrust of home mode portrayal is toward favorable, impressive, and best presentations of family members. Nonetheless, a stable form of photography seems to exist within most families which directly counters this dominant form of presentation. These "alternative" images may be produced knowingly—as a form of self-parody—but generally result from surprise and candid shooting. They include photos of people vomiting, asleep, half nude, strangely dressed, and so on. They may catch the embarrassing or ludicrous, and serve ultimately to demean, tease, or other-

Photo 5a (1)

Photo 5a (2)

Photo 5b (1)

Photo 5b (2)

Photo 5c (1)

Photo 5c (2)

The presentation of self

wise present the person as silly, funny, or in their least ideal image (photo 5c, 1 and 2). They may even provoke a degree of self-reflexivity among home moders. Their contrast to more idealized photographs in the family collection, however, serves primarily to "demystify" and subvert the prevailing image of the family's portraiture.

Family members typically respond to these photographs good-naturedly, and as such the images should not be seen as completely negative or unsympathetic treatments of family subjects. Rather, in the context of the entire family collection, they provide not only amusement but also an additional level of characterization. As such, they contribute depth to the otherwise one-dimensional portrait of happy, healthy, and handsome people in special, significant, or pleasant activities.

These are but a few of the functions of family photography which can be isolated for analysis (Musello, 1977). Taken together, they offer clues about the contexts in which family photographs are produced and used as well as meanings attached to the images themselves by family members. It is important to remember, however, that all family uses of the medium rest on the assumption that it is capable and effective in documenting the events, people, and places of family life.

DOCUMENTATION

To most home moders, family photography is regarded as a "necessary" tool for recording activities and people important to the family's history. As a document, the collection is designed to "capture" and record "appropriate" elements of family life. Such a collection ostensibly permits home moders to recall, reflect on, share, and compare these subjects over time, and rests on the implicit assumption that documenting and recalling such things is of inherent importance.

This family documentation process can be broken down into a number of purposes and activities, the most important being the *retention of memories*. This pervasive orientation to the mode clearly structures its use, and both planning and shooting are typically guided by notions of what family members will want to recall in the future. In viewing, photographs can be used to recall specific information, events, and places or to stimulate a process of general recall by reflecting on or sentimentalizing the past. The relationship of photographs to memory, however, is extremely complex: photos seem deeply implicated in family processes of recall, but more as "keys" to memory than the actual content of memorable occasions and experiences. This is true even though family members think of their collections—to the extent that they are kept up to date—as valid family histories.

The peculiar ability of photography to *document change* is also an important feature of its use in the home mode. The development of homes, projects, pets, and people—especially children—is a subject of marked fascination, and family photographs provide a visual analogue to the sense of time, growth, change, and history that family members experience. Home moders employ a variety of formal and informal means for viewing and displaying such contrasts, including the chronological editing of images such as those from school year books and Christmas cards (photo 6).

We can identify a final aspect of the documentary function as the home mode's use in *family correspondence*. Photographs are used in this way as reminders, "surrogates" or visual reports of people separated by time and space. As such they appear as demonstrations or "evidence" about the condition of people, places, and things which others cannot see.

THE HOME MODE DOCUMENT AS A DOCUMENT

The home mode collection is perceived by families as a "document" of various aspects of family life. It is a document of a particular nature, however, and some of its properties can be briefly discussed.

To begin with, it is a document embued with "evidentiary" value by its users while at the same time requiring direct personal knowledge and recall for its interpretation. The meaning of photographs to family members clearly requires a "filling-in" of information and significance by the viewer (recall Photo 1, for example). The significance of a given picture is often couched in interaction patterns, events, and the way the photo has been viewed or used by others. The document is thus quite dependent for its meaning on the active interpretations of those familiar with it. Furthermore, while people frequently remember the contents of pictures in great detail, supplementary memories of the context and meaning of the images are frequently lost or weakened over time. The significance of family photographs thus evolves and changes as memories of the family members lose their clarity or are forgotten altogether.

This need for intepretation of family photographs is augmented by the home moder's consistent neglect of contextual clues in making the photographs in the first place. With a few exceptions, family events are documented through depictions of people in ambiguous or undecipherable settings (see photos 7a and 7b). For events such as Christmas, Thanksgiving, and birthdays, of course, conventional signs or icons—decorated trees, roast turkeys, and pointed hats—are frequently incorporated, serving thereby to identify the event. In other instances,

Photo 6

Selections from a family Christmas card collection spanning 40 years.

Photo 7a

CHARLES RIVER PICNIC

Photo 7b

Two photographs demonstrating a common failure to incorporate contextual cues: (a) "Vinnie's Confirmation"; (b) "A Charles River Picnic."

verbal clues, including signs and captions, may be included as well. In travel photographs, for example, snapshooters seem to make a conscious effort to capture telling contextual details. In "covering" their own homes, neighbors, and local scenery, however, no such effort is made. Because of their memory-dependent orientation to the medium, family members document home subjects less through representation than through "evocation."

There are other picture-taking customs of family photographers which limit the evidentiary value of home mode documents. Most important among these is the restriction of camera work to a narrow range of settings, topics, and participants. As a result, only a limited repertoire of family experiences is documented. "Special" and "positive" activities are emphasized, as well as artificial or posed interactions. In contrast, everyday experiences and more "negative" features of the family's activities—work, crying babies, arguments, daily customs, and so on— are seriously neglected.

Home mode picture taking is clearly structured at every step by notions about the camera's "proper" use. These customs and conventions in turn shape and delimit the scope and nature of the resulting photo collection. Traditional family patterns of use structure the photo album picture-by-picture as well as encourage broad trends in the documentary collection as a whole. For example, before the arrival of children, couples frequently photograph each other, often on excursions away from the home. When children arrive, however, they become overwhelmingly the subject of highest interest in family photographs. The greatest amount of family picture-taking occurs in the younger years for both child and family (approximately 1 to 6 years), and then declines to a minimal level at which only major family events are recorded. A resurgence often occurs when the children become teenagers and begin to take pictures themselves, with the arrival of grandchildren, or through participation in extended travels. As a result, the document of a family's photographs is inconsistent across time—many families speak sadly and with some embarrassment of large "gaps" in their collections —and reveals a pattern of shifting attention and emphasis.

It is also important to remember that beliefs regarding "appropriate" subjects and participants also shape the family photo collection. Home moders, for example, indicate that their purpose is to document and record the growth and development of the "family." In common practice, however, they aim almost exclusively at the progress of their children. Husbands and wives appear infrequently in these collections, usually posed with children and rarely together. To most couples, the idea of photographing each other purposefully seems irrelevant or embarrassing, a consequence perhaps of their belief that their own changes will reflect "aging" and deterioration rather than positive development. Whatever the cause, the result is that the documentation of adult development is very spotty and unsystematic. For that matter, documentation of children tends to diminish steadily from concentrated attention to the child as an infant to almost nothing as the children approach high school.

As a document of family and personal experience, the family photograph collection is thus a highly select, fragmented, and yet regularized sampling from everyday life. It is a patterned and restricted portrayal of aspects of the general flow of subjects and events. It is designed to give a positive accounting of "important" and "appropriate" family subjects, as defined by convention. As home moders subsequently view the discrete and disembodied images of the collections, these are associated with "real life" events through direct recall and creative interpretation.

The limiations and inadequacies of family photographs as a document of family life, however, should not be thought of as products of neglect or incompetence. These stem not only from the individual intentions of family members but also from shared social values and conventions guiding each aspect of the photograph's production and use.

PHOTOGRAPHY IN SOCIETY

Research on family photography is outlining the patterned nature of the mode in increasing detail. By examining photography as a social process—and the photograph as an artifact of this process—we have begun to identify how shared values and conventions influence and shape the planning and production of images. The photographs that result are not simply mechanical recordings of natural events. Rather, they are the artifacts of numerous decisions which in turn are shaped by the social contexts in which they are made; and to evaluate the document, we must understand the processes which shape it.

The way we organize and view our photos is also guided by beliefs nurtured from childhood about what pictures are proper for public display, those with whom you share your photos and those with whom you do not, and so on. Most of these conventions are implicit and removed from conscious awareness. They play a central role, however, in patterning our use of cameras and pictures; and they ultimately shape the contents of family photo albums.

Family use of the home mode becomes intensely personal when members discuss and interpret their collection of photographs. Pictures are not simply a "text," however, read for the information it encodes. Rather, home moders invest their photographs with a broad range of memories, associations, and responses as they view them, information which far exceeds the particular pictorial references of the images themselves.

All this has important implications for anyone wishing to "decode" photographic documents. To talk about "meaning," for example, we have to understand the document itself as the product of social and cultural dynamics. To understand more about these matters, we need descriptive studies of more families and groups than have been investigated so far. As we identify regularities in their uses of the medium, we can begin to ask questions about the relationship between use and the values, customs, and world view of those who produce and view the images themselves. At the same time, we can direct our attention to analysis and comparison of the home mode within different social and cultural groups.

As a subject of investigation, family photographs call our attention to the connections between the production, use, and meaning of visual imagery. Should we continue to be interested in the general phenomena of photography and the social order, the home mode seems a fruitful place to begin.

THE EARLY HISTORY OF
VISUAL SOCIOLOGY

8

Clarice Stasz

Many visual sociologists date their origins in the genre of documentary photography. Curry and Clarke's (1977: 15) introduction is a good representation of this view:

> Perhaps the best-known documentary images in the United States were the hard-hitting photographs of Jacob A. Riis and Lewis W. Hine. Riis, a reporter, visually depicted impoverished life-styles in New York City's slums in the 1890s, and Hine, who had training in sociology, photographed immigrant laborers and working-class children in the factories and mines of early 20th Century America. It is believed that the images of Riis and Hine, served, in part, to bring about the passage of new labor legislation laws. Later, Walker Evans and Dorothea Lange, among other photographers working with the farm Security Administration, effectively documented the depression years, producing a visual record of over a quarter million photographs that has not been surpassed today for scope and sensitivity.

The other set of forbearers usually linked to visual sociology are anthropologists. In the 1930s, Gregory Bateson and Margaret Mead centered their analysis of culture in Bali upon visual data, both film and stills. Their historic monograph, *Balinese Character,* has never been matched for its subtle blend of photographs within a tightly organized conceptual framework. The text provides a rich interplay of insights as one works from sets of images to words and back again. Visual anthropology has since grown sufficiently to support an organization, the Society for the Anthropology of Visual Communication, whose practitioners have spawned numerous ethnographic films and photo collections. Visual sociologists have relied upon the technical writings of this group to establish their own base.

What most have missed is that sociology itself had a brief encounter with the camera, long before the Farm Security Administration and the Bateson-Mead collaboration. Pull a turn-of-the-century volume of the

AUTHOR'S NOTE: The idea for this essay germinated during a discussion with Howard Becker who, along with Derral Cheatwood and Richard Quinney, provided helpful comments and suggestions.

American Journal of Sociology off the library shelf, blow off the dust, and open it up. You will find something virtually unseen in sociology journals of recent decades—photographs. Between 1896 and 1916 (volumes 2 through 21 of the *Journal*) thirty-one articles used 244 photographs as illustrations and evidence in their discussions. (I omit here articles where a photograph is used to illustrate a mechanical object under discussion, such as Chapin's (1950) tinkertoy model of socioemetric structure, as well as pictures of prominent, usually deceased sociologists.) Often essays with pictures were placed in the lead position. But when Shanas (1945) reviewed the first fifty years of the *Journal,* she made no reference to their presence. She must have been aware of them, because she singled out one such paper (Bushnell, 1901b) for introducing "the first ecological map." Her omission reflects the view now prevalent among sociologists (were one to go by their publications) that visual data have no important role in understanding society. The one exception to this general rule is in textbook publishing—particularly for general interest courses, such as introductory sociology or marriage and the family—but those sociologists showing visual sensitivity in this regard have neglected to apply it to their own professional work.

Thus, it is especially useful to examine the early visual sociology. First, it is a feature of the discipline's history which has gone unnoticed even among those sympathetic to its uses. More important, we must examine why the potential of the method was overlooked or ignored, for this oversight profoundly shaped the way sociologists came to look at the world, as well as their definition of the proper scientific study of it.

EARLY VISUAL SOCIOLOGY

Although one might expect the first uses of photographs to mimic Riis' best-selling series on the Lower East Side, in fact they did not. The first pictorial article was Blackmar's (1897) case study of two impoverished families in Kansas, dubbed the Smoky Pilgrims. His thesis was to demonstrate that the ills of the city were not limited to urban environments. To support his claim, he included nine photographs. Two portray the family groups before their cabins, and seven present closer views of individual members. None of the subjects smile; most look away from the camera; others glare into or stare at it. What is fascinating about these pictures is that the author exaggerated the sense of isolation and depressed state of the people by washing out the background (photo 1). Hence, they are suspended, unsituated in space

Photo 1

Photo 2

or time. This was a most clever manipulation of the image for Black-mar's purposes.

The next illustrated essay to appear, Moore's (1897) "A Day at Hull House," set a format that several others followed. In this case, her point was to present the social welfare center as a place where social order thrived and poverty was vanquished. All the photographs were shot so as to support this view. Three are of rooms, empty of people, furniture pristine and proper in arrangement. Another shows the exterior of the building, as though architecture alone represented the social life within. The four photographs that show children are icono-graphic in pose: a group encircled in a ring game on a balcony; pupil and teacher at the piano, looking one another in the eye with smiles; a well-dressed group seated around a large table and engrossed in reading (photo 2); two children seated against a frence and grinning into the camera lens. Obviously, all the pictures were either staged or selected to depict the positive and healthful functions of the settlement home.

Other articles that used similar presentations were Zueblin's (1898) and American's (1898a) discussions of municipal playgrounds, and Milliken's (1898) and American's (1898b) descriptions of Chicago vaca-tion schools. The photographs for these articles included one new per-suasive device—some sort of "before and after"presentation. Thus, we see a playground before and after the introduction of play equipment. Or we view a stark city street and later a shot of city children romping in a sunlit field. Where Blackmar manipulated his photographs to increase the plausibility of his theoretical claims about the nature of social dis-organization, these writers selectively framed the images of their settings so as to persuade of their social ameliorative power.

Simmons' (1904) discussion of education in the South aptly exem-plifies some of the problems with this technique. One photograph (photo 3) is a stark close-up of a one-room schoolhouse, a virtual log cabin. Underneath, (photo 4) she placed a consolidated school later built in the same district. The building is more ornate and of finer materials. One has to consider, however, how much more appealing this building would have looked were it shot without students, and in such a way as to block out the conifers on its right. The rhetoric of this device, in other words, rests on the addition of elements to the second image that signify humanity and the beauty of nature.

The first essay to approach what many photographers would call "documentary" was Vincent's (1898) study of "A Retarded Frontier," the Cumberlands area of Kentucky. He presented thirteen photographs, including habitations, people at crafts (cottin gin, hand loom, spinning wheel, and so on), industry (grist mill, whip saw), and illegal activity

PUBLIC SCHOOLHOUSE IN MANGUM TOWNSHIP, DURHAM COUNTY, BEFORE
CONSOLIDATION OF DISTRICTS.

Photo 3

NEW PUBLIC SCHOOLHOUSE IN SAME TOWNSHIP AFTER CONSOLIDATION
OF THREE SMALL DISTRICTS.

Photo 4

(a moonshine still). The photographs today make an ironic comment on his title, for the subjects seem most industrious and competent. But seen from the eyes of the new technology of the time, these people may indeed have appeared "retarded" for their refusal to adopt the modern lifestyle. Vincent's images resemble many that have come out of anthropologists' studies of other cultures, that is, pictures of people in the course of their daily activities.

In Moore's (1897) ethnography of the saloon, pictures display the lighter side of what was then considered to be a den of iniquity. (This was, after all, the time of Carrie Nation's hatchet rampages.) Anticipating the functionalist approach to social problems, Moore adroitly supported his view that bars have social value to their participants. We see the bar from the outside—a forbidding building with few windows, then move inside, to face the stern pose of the female bartender. One shot of three men at the bar, though posed, captures a flavor of the atmosphere because the men are laughing. Other shots show the pool room and gym equipment, evidence of sport. Looking at Moore's pictures, it is difficult to believe that alcohol could be the source of social problems, for both the drinker and his family. Of course, this is because Moore did not show fights, inebriates in corners, drunken men beating their wives, families going without food, and so on. But the choice of images flows from his framework—it is not the photographs in themselves that are the source of the inadequacy of the argument.

Others used photographs in a more banal and frivolous manner. McLean's (1903) portraits of sweatshop workers, obtained from a Chicago newspaper, do not provide much flavor of the work setting. Almost all of Van Schelle's (1910) pictures of Merxplas, the largest penal colony in the world at the time, portray buildings, not prisoners or guards. McClintock (1901a) aped Vincent with much less success. His pictures of the Hatfield-McCoy feuding area need lengthy captions, e.g., "Moonshine still cut up by officers, who killed the man running it and mortally wounded his confederate." Some are not technically competent. One, supposedly of a Baptist footwashing service in fact shows a large picket fence which obscures most of what a large crowd in the background is doing (photo 5). Obviously, McClintock did not enjoy the access to subjects Vincent had (or perhaps he was simply very timid with a camera in that gun-happy setting). For these and several other articles (e.g., Monroe, 1898; Commons, 1897, 1898) the photographs are not very informative.

Of all the early studies, one stands out as masterly for its use of visual technique and presentation. In fact, there are several articles, all part of a series on the social aspects of the Chicago stockyards by

A FOOT-WASHING SERVICE OF THE HARDSHELL BAPTISTS ON THE MUD FORK OF ISLAND CREEK.

Photo 5

GENERAL OFFICES, SWIFT & CO., CHICAGO.
(46,918 square feet in area; 685 employés.)

Photo 6

PACKING BUTTERINE.

Photo 7

Photograph by R. R. Earle

BULGARIAN LODGING GROUP ON THE WEST SIDE
Nine men in two rooms

Photo 8

Charles Bushnell (1901a, 1901b, 1902). Here the profuse illustrations are
as useful to an understanding of the subject as the accompanying text
and tables.

The first section of the series dealt with work environments, with
many pictures of slaughtering and the preparation of by-products.
Bushnell had control over the camera (or knew how to direct a photographer) well enough to produce images strikingly different from
any other during these years. For example, one shows a cavernous
office, filled with innumerable workers at unpartitioned desk areas
(photo 6). The caption says "General Offices," explaining that 685
employees fill this vast space of 46,918 feet. But the numbers are unnecessary—at one glance the viewer can imagine much about work in
such a setting: the noise, the poor ventilation, the lack of privacy, the
supervision, the sheer density of personalities in that one enclosed space.
"Packing Butterine," (photo 7) presents to us women in matching
uniforms packing the individual quarters, men off to the side filling large
tubs, and one male supervisor in a white coat. Or another is of the U.S.
Government Meat Inspection Office, in which almost 70 women are
crowded at small tables with microscopes, a male supervisor in the back
of the room, standing as a teacher would while his students took a test.
These photographs provide a sense of the work environment in a glance
that written descriptions and tables fail to convey. Indeed, I think
Bushnell knew this, because by including such pictures he did not have
to discuss certain features of the situations.

His second contribution examined the effects of the meat packing
yards on the community. Here images powerfully document the social
costs. A series of pictures shows the dump with children getting Christmas trees (after the holiday), of men rushing from factory toward the
bars after work, of trash in the streets, of smoke polluting the air. He
also included shots inside the local settlement house, which, unlike
Moore's, show unposed youngsters as active and vital.

His third essay investigated the ways other companies had provided
for the social needs of employees, through dining halls, lounges, rest
rooms, and such. Here Bushnell introduced many pictures from the
Sherwin-Williams paint company and Heinz foods, both considered
advanced at the time for their concern with employee comfort and
sociability, as well as from Swift, the only meat-packing firm he felt
approached the issue adequately. Most of these shots resemble public
relations ads, being of empty rooms of well-arrayed furniture. Nevertheless, they serve an uncanny counterpoint to the text, which damns the
stockyard managements for their neglect of worker needs.

One other extensive application of photographs was the series "Chicago Housing Problems" (Hunt, 1910; Breckenridge and Abbott, 1910, 1911a, 1911b, 1911c; Norton, 1913; Wilson and Smith, 1914; Hughes, 1914; Walker, 1915). These essays analyzed the special problems of various ethnic sectors of the city. The photographs have a direct lineage to Riis, in that they depict interior shots of families or lodgers in small, ill-furnished windowless rooms. The photographer(s) copied Riis' style of moving in close to the subjects, and working with them long enough that poses lacked the stiffness so common to portraits at the time (photo 8). Though the scenes are the same from one essay to another, ethnic influences are present in the dress and room decors, (though it is noteworthy that the only essay in the group that did not have illustrations was the one by Comstock in 1912 on Negro housing). Also, though all are of poor neighborhoods, it is clear that even poverty has its own hierarchy—the room eleven Greek men share lacks the finishings on the walls of other rooms, indeed appears to be almost a stable.

Many of these shots presage the "artistic" documentary work of the Farm Security Administration. That is, they remain memorable as images in themselves, indelible reminders of the daily facts of poverty. One recalls afterwards views of women bending over in the dumps, gathering goods as peasant women once gleaned wheat. (See a related image, photo 9.) Or the haunting presence of a mattress in a pantry, the surrounding shelves almost bare of food (photo 10). Or the four children on a bed that fills a room, an image which stands apart from its caption, "Illegally crowded room in Polish District; one man slept here by day, two adults and four children by nights; the room contains 513 square (sic) feet." Indeed, in many ways the texts of these essays are superfluous. (photo 11).

Overall, two-thirds of the articles employed photographs in a way that contemporary visual sociologists would question. Crassly manipulated prints, iconographic poses, inconsistent before-and-after pictures, portraits out of context, and images based on clumsy technique are among the styles of shooting and presentation considered today to be inappropriate in careful research reporting. They would be good illustrations for that as yet unwritten book every social science student would be required to read before graduation, *How to Lie with Photographs.*

In contrast, the work of Vincent (1898), Bushnell (1901a, 1901b, 1902), and the Chicago housing group employed an approach consistent with contemporary preferences. Although the photographic styles of each were distinct, they shared a set of characteristics that form what

Photograph by R. R. Earle

WOMEN LEAVING THE DUMPS

Photo 9

A PANTRY USED BY AN ITALIAN AS A BEDROOM
The window has been boarded up

Photo 10

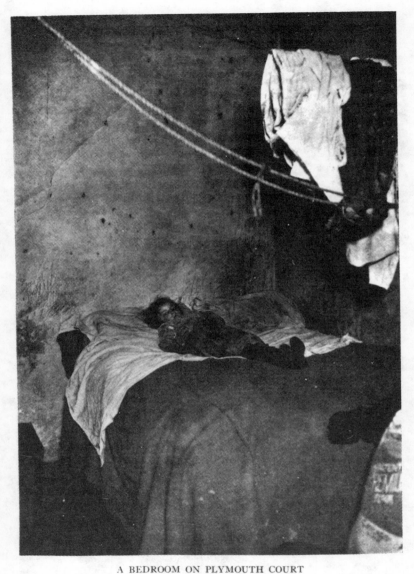

A BEDROOM ON PLYMOUTH COURT

Three children sleep in this room.   The only window opens upon a shaft which is closed at
the top.

Photo 11

Heider (1976) has termed "ethnographicness." Among these qualities are: images informed by ethnography and integrated with printed materials and produced with minimal distortions of behavior as a result of camera presence, basic technical competence, and most important, the framing of activities within a definable context. The latter point means that images include as much as possible whole bodies within the full frame of activity for a particular situation. Thus, these images retain their scientific value today. A social historian of work can deduce much from Bushnell's pictures, or one of ethnicity from the Chicago housing series. For this reason we can conclude that the basis for a visual sociology was present at the time.

INHIBITORS OF THE VISUAL

Photographs disappeared from the *Journal* after the Chicago housing series ended in 1914. In the past few years, however, a number of sociologists have rediscovered the camera. The development of this contemporary visual sociology dates from about 1970, when isolated sociologists around the country simultaneously began to explore the uses of film and photography for research and theory. A network quickly developed which supported the short-lived *Videosociology,* exchanged bibliographies and technical advice, and gave workshops, roundtables, and panel sessions at both regional and national conventions. Articles produced by members of the network have not, however, appeared in journals or outlets known to mainstream sociologists (see Curry and Clarke, 1977, for one bibliography), though several have published photo essays in *Society*. A gallery exhibit, *6 Sociologists,* has travelled around the country from 1975 to 1978. The vitality of these present efforts and the contributions of the earlier era suggest that the intervening years suffered the loss of a valuable research tool. It is as if sociologists had suddenly stopped using card sorters, hand calculators, computers, or any of a number of technical aids for half a century, only to take them up again.

To identify what happened is probably impossible at this time. Something as simple as an unrecorded editorial decision was possibly involved. For example, paper shortages greatly hampered publishers in 1915 and well after World War I. In all but the last two Chicago housing series the photographs are printed singly on glossy sheets, with no material on the backside. In the last two cases, however, they are printed much smaller in multiples on a page backed with printed matter. This change in layout may have represented economy measures; perhaps the glossy paper used for illustrations was no longer readily available or too costly to use.

Such practical possibilities aside, the data at hand offer other clues. Several factors are apparent in the form of the *Journal* at the time that may have served as inhibitors against the continuing publication of visual material. (And with a publishing outlet unavailable, the likelihood that pictures would be taken as matter of course was decreased.)

Looking at the distribution of visual articles over the years, we find a curious gap. Twenty articles appear between 1896 and 1904; none between 1905 and 1909; and ten more between 1910 and 1915. All but one of the last group are from the Chicago housing series. Thus, editorial policy seems to have shifted in 1905.

This in fact happened. At that time, Albion Small, the editor, made explicit changes in both the physical format and tone of the *Journal*. Reviewing his first decade's experiences, he recalled how:

> The most serious pitfall in the path of the enterprise was not the absence of a demand, but the presence of an unintelligent and misguided demand. . . . A large fraction of the earlier subscribers to this *Journal* were evidently of the genus rainbow-chaser. They wanted a springboard that would land them in Utopia [1905: 1].

Confounding this problem:

> Sociology was in fact nothing more than wistful advertisement of a hiatus in knowledge. . . . Sociology was a science without a problem, a method, or a message [1905: 2].

Small was determined to correct this problem, and repeatedly in this and subsequent statements over the years insisted that sociology was "a pure science," that the "attitude of the sociologists toward their problems is precisely that of chemist, of physicist, or of physiologist toward his." (1905: 4).

As for social amelioration, Small argued that its "relations to pure sociology [are] closely analogous with those of public hygiene to biology" (1905: 9). In 1907, he emphasized that the discipline must move "out of amateurishness, not to say quackery, and advance toward responsible scientific procedure." (1907: 637).

What Small defined as "responsible" or "scientific" is evident in the shift in content that occurred at that time. Space devoted to statistical studies of population and methodology, as well as theoretical discussions of social psychology, suddenly multiplied, pushing out papers on social reform (Shanas, 1945).

The change in tone was also influenced by the origin of the American Sociological Society in 1906, whose officers became advisory editors of the *Journal*. This gave Small a cadre of fellow gatekeepers generally sympathetic with his view of the direction the discipline should take. Ward, Sumner, and Giddings were not known for their impassioned commitment to social reform in the manner of, say, Jane Addams, a frequent early contributor. Thus, part of the disappearance of the visual may be linked to the victory of the pure over applied sociologists in control of the discipline, for most illustrated articles dealt with amelioration directly or by implication.

Furthermore, the visual sociologists were different from contributors overall in at least two ways. First, they were more likely to be female. While in the first twenty-one volumes of the *Journal* an average of 12% of the authors were women, this was true for fully 50% of the visually oriented group. (These tabulations are based upon articles only, not book reviews, committee reports, or responses to papers; and gender was identified through first names.) Perhaps an association between females and photography contaminated the editors' view of the technique, causing it to be devalued or seen as frivolous. This would follow from the cultural tendency in Western society to ignore innovations made by women until powerful men take them up. But none of the men associated with visual sociology at the time had the status in the discipline to buck those pressing for causal analysis, high-level generalizations, and statistical reports.

Visual sociologists were also unlike contributors overall in terms of work affiliation. If we consider to be "academically affiliated" all those who listed by their name a four-year college or university, we find that in the first decade of the *Journal*, fully half of the authors were not. Like nonacademic sociologists today, some of these people worked in research for government bodies, such as the Office of the Census. Yet, most held administrative offices in action agencies, such as settlement homes, consumer organizations, religious temperance groups, and charity bureaus. After the 1905 shift in editorial policy, only one-third of the contributors held such nonacademic positions. Of the visual authors overall, less than a third held regular sociology department affiliations. Forty percent were in nonacademic jobs. All of those remaining, writers for the Chicago housing series, were affiliated with the University of Chicago School of Civics and Philanthropy, forerunner of the Social Work School. So again, the connection between visual technique and social reform is evident.

One important question is why Small even ran the housing series pictures. Certainly the institutional tie was important, in that the *Journal* was also housed at the University of Chicago. Also, the research had been sponsored by the Russell Sage Foundation at the request of the Chief Sanitary Inspector of Chicago. Its director, Edith Abbott, was a prominent and influential intellectual figure in the city and university at the time. These social connections aside, on other grounds Small could have had little difficulty accepting the reports, which were filled with the tables and maps he thought to be essential to respectable research.

But for all other cases after 1905, Small and other editors had many reasons to omit visual evidence. Photographs intrude upon a research report, force a confrontation with reality. There is no denying the struggles of the poor in the Chicago housing series, no disguise of the poetry of poverty in tables, graphs, and jargon. The pictures scream "We are real! We live!"—tugging on sentiments and emotions. What a potential embarrassment for a young field struggling to prove its value as a "rational" discipline, a "pure" science.

Furthermore, these men were possibly swayed by the fact that the camera was not then, as it has become, an instrument of their role models, the chemists, physicists, and physiologists. It was primarily a tool for journalists of the muck-raking press, or a plaything for families to record their lives for their private histories. It was too mundane for scientific use, as Small himself once intimated in metaphor:

> Only here and there a person has discovered the difference between this sort of explanation [causal analysis] and *mere photographing of wide fields of unexplained events by means of essentially descriptive formulation* [1905: 8, emphasis added].

That the camera could serve science does not seem to have occurred to any sociologists. One senses that few of those who used photographs had any clear recognition that they were doing something special. While the foundations of methodology were being set in these early years, none of the visual people came forward—as is happening today—to discuss the application of visual techniques for either data collection or theorizing. Only Bushnell showed cognizance of the variety of applications of pictures as evidence. For many others, the images seemed an afterthought, a clever addition to their papers. Several saw their crass rhetorical potential, notably Blackmar and Moore.

Only one writer (Fairchild, 1899) explicitly discussed the camera as a tool, but in this case it was less for research than another use:

> I take my camera, and hunt for important episodes of child life in homes and schools and streets and playgrounds. If fighting is to be discussed, I must be on hand when some fight takes place, and I must press the bulb of my camera just at the right time when the fight is significant. If a girl goes to help an old lady replace parcels which the wind has scattered from her market basket, I much catch her in the act of doing this kindness.

... From these negatives are made slides, and thus is provided visual instruction in ethics.

Fairchild did some simple tabulations based upon his work with these materials, but never saw a connection between the camera and his "natural method" of observation. (It is noteworthy too that even this elementary and inadequate description of method was rare in those days, regardless of the type of research.)

Other inhibitors concern the nature of photography at the time. Technology was rather crude. Indoor shots often required explosive charges which could cause injuries and frightened subjects. The better cameras, of a bellows variety, were large and ungainly to operate. Certainly candid shots were much more difficult than today, and the versatile choice of lenses and films was unavailable. Yet, we know extraordinary photographers who have used simple, clumsy equipment to produce powerful results—Riis and Hine being obvious examples. So the technique alone could not have been a major limitation on the development of a visual methodology.

More important, photography as a means of visual expression was not well-developed. Eugene Atget (see Abbott, 1975) had not yet shot shop windows and steps in Paris. Dorothea Lange (1969) had not documented the labor of migrant workers in California. Weegee (1945) had not broken barriers by shooting corpses on urban street corners. Robert Frank (1969) had not glimpsed people in disarming moments at play. Harry Callahan (1967) had not shot shoppers unaware, his camera held by his side. Gary Winograd (1979) had not slipped through the zoo, glimpsing the interaction between humans and animals.

In other words, at the turn of the century people did not "see" with the camera as we do today. Thus, the vast majority of shots were "stock" —posed and predictable and unilluminating. Stock shots in themselves are not useless (witness Bushnell's factory dining rooms) provided they are selected as most appropriate to one's intention, not entered by default. Given the limited range of poses and frames, photography may have seemed too decorative to be of use to those committed to the development of sociology as a respectable scientific discipline.

Whatever the reasons, the camera disappeared from the ethnographer's hands, and the pages once glossy with reflections of the physical substance of social life became coarse-surfaced beds for discursive analyses and tables. The human shape disappeared from the journals—no eye peered out to confront one in turn. Thus, several years later when Park and others sent their students out to document the neighborhoods, subcultures, and underlife of Chicago, they did not tell them to take cameras. Recording techniques relied on pen and paper, and readers of the reports must visualize these settings and situations in their mind's eye.

Had sociology embraced the camera, it would certainly be a different field today, because visual data are less amenable than other forms to positivistic schema. Indeed, the great challenge for visual sociologists now is to establish a method, a set of rules for using and understanding images that are not simple adaptations of categorize-and-count techniques. In a discipline that is so verbal and quantitative, so devoid of visual awareness or reasoning, this solution is not likely to come easily. Thus, it will be interesting to see whether the current group of visual sociologists can have more impact than their ancestors. They have the advantage of expanded technique and style on their behalf; however, something on the level of an intellectual revolution will be needed to convince their colleagues, who locate knowledge in words and numbers, that visual materials are not, as Small and others may have concluded, mere "quackery."

PART II

ISSUES IN RESEARCH

Introduction

In the three chapters which follow, attention is given to some of the methodological issues frequently raised about the use of photography in social science research. Shanklin, for example, describes the importance of the researcher's social role in making and understanding photographs of social scientific value. In the chapter following, I describe several techniques for avoiding error in both making and interpreting photographs. In the final chapter of this section, Collier examines the complexities of moving from the particular photographic image to statements, both visual and verbal, about social and cultural processes.

The issues explored in these three chapters are central to other modes of research as well as to that in which photography plays a major part. Because research conventions for visual imagery are relatively unformed, however, the issues seem particularly salient in studies which rely on photographs to record or present information. This salience makes possible rather clear formulations of some of the complexities and subtleties of social research in general, and there are things to be learned about social science from a good, hard look at photographic work.

—J.W.

WHEN A GOOD SOCIAL ROLE IS WORTH A THOUSAND PICTURES

9

Eugenia Shanklin

Conventional wisdom tells us that a good picture is worth a thousand or ten thousand words, but too often the necessary emphasis on "good" is omitted. A picture can be worthless or worse, misleading. In the social sciences, the worth of a photograph depends very much on the social roles that researcher-photographers establish for themselves and on their ability to become part of the ongoing scene, and not an intrusive or disruptive element within it.

In this regard, photography in the social sciences is considerably more difficult than in other fields. A naturalist who wants to photograph animals in a natural state hopes, like the social scientist, not to intrude on the scene. Unlike the social scientist, however, the naturalist can build a blind to disguise his presence or take advantage of natural cover. Social scientists have to create a different kind of blind. They do not aim for "invisibility" but for unobtrusiveness, for acceptance as part of the ongoing social scene. For the social scientist, the establishment of social roles is a major task, and one that demands considerable ingenuity and flexibility. I shall take as example the "extreme case" of anthropological photography and draw on my own fieldwork experiences to illustrate three phases through which a researcher-photographer is likely to pass.

THE TOURIST

In the village in Ireland where I lived and did anthropological field work, cattle and sheep were sold once a month at a fair. Farmers came into town, tied their sheep to the nearest stationary object, and gathered in small groups while buyers made the rounds, examining the sheep, asking prices, looking for bargains. The fairs were colorful spectacles and to a tourist must have looked quite "primitive." Fair day is also a time when children are out of school, when everyone comes to town to learn the latest gossip, when the rural girls wear their best dresses—a jolly time, mostly, for all concerned. The pubs and the fairs are the places where one is most likely to hear what the Irish call "good crack" (witty conversation, repartee).

On one fair day, I recall, I was standing with a group of farmers who were talking among themselves when a large, shiny car drove up slowly. Sheep and people milled about in the middle of the street and the driver of the car watched with exasperation as children drove more sheep in his path. Finally, seeing that his progress would be impeded for some time, he began to look around him and then got out of his car and started taking pictures. The lively conversations ceased; everyone concentrated on whatever task was at hand and there was near silence while the tourist took his snapshots. He then returned to his car and made his way slowly out of the village, whereupon conversations resumed and people ceased their "busy work."

This took place after I had been thirteen months in the region and it reminded me of my participation in the tourist's role a year earlier. At this later date, however, I shared the feelings of local people about this stranger, and I knew how they must have felt about me a year earlier. I was annoyed at the tourist's casual intrusion—even at this very public event—and I was careful to avoid eye contact with him while he was there. He probably felt that he was "invisible," that his presence caused no changes in the ongoing activities, and that no one in the village had even noticed his presence, for in no way was he openly acknowledged.

He was, however, neither invisible nor unobtrusive, for there was a definite and dramatic reaction to his presence. As an outsider he could not have known that, for he had little idea of what the normal actions were. I have often mused about this minute event and wondered how his pictures came out, what he said to the people back home as he showed his pictures of the strange village where sheep had the right of way and no one talked. However good his photographs may have been technically, they were worthless from the standpoint of a researcher-photographer because they induced in their subjects artificial, stilted postures that bore little relation to the actual events of the day—the gossiping, the flirting, the buying and selling, and the witty remarks.

I had another reaction to the tourist, one that surprised me greatly. Rather than being sympathetic, I was greatly annoyed with him for treating people I knew as individuals as if they were "natives." I was tempted to shout, "That isn't a native; that's Wee Johnny you're taking a picture of." But invisibility works both ways; the tourist was not interested in the people he was dealing with and wanted nothing more than a photographic record of what, to him, was a curiosity. The local people, knowing his object and his indifference to them as individuals, responded by seeming to ignore his presence.

Being a "tourist" and feeling invisible present a problem to the social researcher, for those individuals who first acknowledge the presence of such a stranger are often those with whom the researcher least wants to be friendly. Marginal or deviant people often approach outsiders, hoping to gain a measure of social approval that their peers, neighbors, and kin will not grant because they are different from the rest of the group.

I faced these problems in beginning field work. The town drunk, an entertaining, charming man, and the village nuisance, a senile old woman, were the first to acknowledge my presence. To them I was not invisible, but rather a prospective acquaintance and source either of drinks or attention. The temptation to be friendly with such people was very great. When most other people turned away and seemed very busy—as we all had done to the tourist at the fair—I began to feel like a nonperson; and it was comforting to have someone recognize me and remember my name. I was aware, however, that my own status in the eyes of the local people could be damaged irreparably by close association with these marginal people. I met their overtures politely and distantly, then turned away to find those people who did not have time to talk to me, who did not especially welcome my acquaintance, but whose knowledge and insights would eventually form the basis of my study. Because I arrived with my camera in hand and carried it with me everywhere, the offers of the local "lunatic fringe" to my tourist presence consisted of suggesting that they show me spectacular views and unique scenery.

THE GUEST

I chose, however, to find my own viewing sites and unique scenes and began visiting farmers in the surrounding countryside, thereby assuming a new role, that of "guest," a role the Irish respect and honor greatly. Losing my status as a tourist and my sense of being invisible was the first step toward assuming appropriately unobtrusive roles: it necessitated speaking to people who did not "see" me and expressing an interest in their concerns and activities.

Americans socialized in an anonymous urban setting have some difficulty grasping the dynamics of what anthropologists call face-to-face societies, where everyone knows everyone else. In such societies, social roles and expectations are learned early and outsiders must create roles for themselves or play those roles already in the local repertoire. The process of learning appropriate roles is a long one of continual trial and error, and is much harder for an adult (with expectations learned in another society) than for an untutored child.

So it was with being a guest. While my new role was certainly more pleasant than being an "invisible tourist," it was also more constraining. At this stage I was learning what attributes and possibilities the Irish had assigned to me and what social roles were forbidden. As a guest I recounted the aims of my study endlessly and was listened to with patient disbelief. Several people came independently to the conclusion that I was the new chicken inspector and therefore conducted me on guided tours of their chicken pens. Not knowing their expectations and having still less knowledge about chicken inspections I murmured as admiringly as I could when ferocious overfed hens were thrust at me. Wherever possible (and always less than gracefully), I declined to hold one, and many of my early photographs are of puzzled housewives holding angry hens. Collier (1967) notes that cameras can be an aid to interacting with people one is studying, but I doubt that he envisioned the use of the camera as a way of warding off chickens.

If being an invisible tourist was painful, being a guest had both mental and physical strains attached. As a guest I was told all the old stories—half mythical, half poetic accounts of individuals long dead or of great events of the pre-Christian era. As a guest I was given endless cups of tea and bits of current gossip but no information of value to my study. Initially afraid to refuse hospitality, I gained about thirty pounds. I later came to count among my best "informants" those who would allow me to refuse cream cakes and biscuits.

But being a guest did give me access to more and more varied settings than those I could frequent as a tourist, and early on I decided that the only solution to the distancing problem set up by my camera was to carry it with me wherever I went. My informants were not comfortable with it, but they came to regard it, like my fondness for cream cakes, as a part of my identity. Accepting the camera as part of my identity, however, did not mean that they encouraged me to use it. No one wanted this guest to photograph their homes or their livestock or themselves. They pointed out—in veiled fashion—that such documentation could be used as evidence of their wealth by a tax collector. If being taken for a chicken inspector had been discomfiting, being taken for a tax collector would have been devastating; and I had to take steps to show that my intentions with my camera were honest and aboveboard.

PARTICIPANT AND NEIGHBOR

To move beyond the role of guest and the very limited photographic welcome it entailed, I began to carefully examine the ways in which photographs were used and displayed in Irish homes. I noticed, for example, that cameras were used by honeymoon couples to record their wedding trip. And ill-focused pictures of the Ring of Killarney were not uncommon items in the homes of those who had married within the last decade. Cameras also recorded special events but not commonplace ones. Because of this the baby pictures so common in the United States were conspicuously absent from homes. Photographs that I was shown were of adult members of the family, people often long deceased, or emigrated. And they included formal studio-posed portraits of brides or of individuals who had emigrated to America.

Within this growing understanding of the manner in which photographs were already used by my informants, I began photographing children. I must have taken snapshots of several hundred of them, all of which I duly gave to the parents. One women told me tearfully that she had no pictures at all of her brood of ten, and was pleased indeed to have some "snaps" of the children before they left home. Another family years later told me that, while they appreciated the "grand snaps" of the children, what they most treasured were the photos of the aged grandfather, who had since died. He was a senile old man over whom the children played as if he were part of the furniture, and I had photographed him along with the children in precisely that role—as if he were a chair. Just as I had to learn something about patterns of social interaction in order to become more a member of the culture I studied, so too I had to learn something about their use of photographs in order to integrate my own picture taking into the roles to which I had been assigned.

Eventually, I was able to photograph adults, houses, livestock, and whatever I chose. Building on those photographic activities most familiar to my informants, I was able to expand the use of my camera to embrace my own research agenda. My informants were most comfortable when they were photographed while engaged in some activity or another, and because this was the kind of photograph I wanted, I was very pleased. Adult attitudes towards these photographs did not change much, despite my care in bringing back each photograph I took and discussing it with the person involved. But adult attitudes towards my taking the photographs did change as I was accepted more fully as a participant. Among my fondest memories is the time that one of my very best informants looked for a long time at a picture of himself, then folded it carefully in quarters and put it into his wallet.

In converting my role from that of overfed guest to that of participant, I also had to learn that I could not hang onto my self-presentation
as an "innocent bystander." The Irish, having no such concept, actively
involved me in whatever was going on, with or without my consent. In
small-scale societies the number of roles available are often limited.
And in Ireland there are three categories: neighbors, kin (called
"friends"), and others. Others could be guests for a while, especially
if they were chicken inspectors and likely to pass on quickly to the next
set of fierce birds; or they could be officials intent on ferreting out
damaging information, or livestock buyers determined to cheat the
farmers of their profits.

When it was clear that I was determined to be more than a casual
"other," and that I had no Irish relatives, so could not be relegated to
the category of "friend," I was assimilated into the group as a "neighbor"
and lost my status as an innocent bystander. Because I was determined
not to go away but to remain on whatever spot seemed to me of most
interest, the Irish dealt with me by making me part of the local group.
It was only after many cream cakes that I became their neighbor.

CAMERA WORK AND MEMBERSHIP

In going from invisible tourist to guest, to neighbor, and participant,
I encountered most of the problems that researcher-photographers
face: the suspicion of outsiders, the feigned indifference, the mistaken
apprehensions about the uses to which the photographs will be put,
and the never fully resolved question of "observer effect." In the Irish
case I decided that photographs were worthwhile only if people were
conversing freely while they were being taken. The tourist who had
leaped from his car to photograph the fair was met with silence and
stilted attitudes; my photographs were of people engaging in some
activity and discussing it at the same time—not necessarily for my
benefit, but because the occasions were both social and task oriented.

Good photographs, within this context, were those taken while the
person was talking, and the most useful ones were those that I took
back to informants and discussed at length with them. Sometimes
comparison helped—a photo of the informant shearing a sheep and
another photograph, say of an Australian shearing a sheep—and
brought out information that I would never have known enough to
ask about. Photographs were useful, too, for eliciting information
about what informants see as important and outstanding features of
the landscape. What a tourist sees as a beautiful landscape, with pictur-

esque rushes and stone fences, the informant may see as barren ground with poor drainage and many rocks.

Having gone through the stages of invisibility, of guest, and of participant, I came to share many of the feelings that the local people had about being the objects of a tourist's idle curiosity. Technically, the tourist's photographs may have been better than mine, but the artificiality of the circumstances rendered his worthless and even misleading. Mine, on the other hand, were hard-won and animated records of people at work, and they represent a reasonably accurate record of the way things actually get done. Analytically, they are a useful set of visual "field notes," and they represented to my informants variations on some of the photographic themes with which they were already familiar. Both analytically and sentimentally they are worth more than several million words to me. They recall my experience as a member of the culture I studied. As reminders of my participation in the social role of neighbor, they reflect both my minor and major triumphs in the field.

AVOIDING ERROR 10

Jon Wagner

Several years ago (1972) the British government sponsored a project and exhibition in which six different towns were photographed by two photographers each. Six photographers were selected to participate, each of them taking pictures of two towns, and all together they generated twelve sets of photographs. Each town looked dramatically different as seen by its two photographers, but the work of each photographer was so distinctive as to make two different towns look alike.

The exhibition was a remarkable illustration of what might be called the "subjective" nature of photography. On closer examination, however, the towns could be seen to play an important part in the creation of the images, and a person familiar with them could find, here and there, a few distinguishing features. A skilled observer, for example, could tease apart their identities through careful reading of the kinds of clothes worn by residents, construction details, and the signs in shop windows. The photographers' visual strategies might have dominated how the images appeared at first glance, but the towns' identities were preserved in the details of social life and physical structure out of which the images were made. For the skilled observer, the photographs thus had an "objective" as well as subjective value.

What was true of these images of British towns is true as well for other photographs. In every case, a photograph is something created by the photographer, an image selected from all there is to see, framed in a distinctive and at times peculiar manner, and processed—through exposure, development and printing—according to a set of highly manipulable techniques. In every case as well, a photograph is *of* something, a record of light passing through, around, within, or bouncing off what we know as the material world. As with other forms of observation and record keeping, the question this poses for social scientific work is both technical and conceptual: In looking at a photograph, how can we distinguish that which is contributed by the setting or subject of the image, and that which is contributed by the photographer?

There are a number of ways we can answer such a question, and the exhibition of British towns suggests at least one approach. By comparing the work of two photographers—especially when they have photographed the same "subject matter"—we can begin to identify their distinctive "visual style." With a sense of this "style" we can make better judgments about the informational nature of the images they produce. We can question their strategies and suggest our own. In a small country town, for example, what kinds of information will be left out of the work of the local portrait photographer? What will the images made by this local photographer include that will not be found in the work of a traveling fashion photographer who uses the town as a backdrop for posed models and the latest clothes? What kind of information will be passed up by a photographer who works in close to the subject, and what kind will be missed by one who works at a greater distance? What choices of camera format, lens, image contrast and size, clarity, and composition will leave out or include which kinds of information? Questions such as these, when used to sort out the distinctive "pattern of seeing" taken on by each photographer, can provide us with a useful framework for assessing the photographs themselves and making judgment about their adequacy as an account of the phenomena they portray.

Error, bias, and validity in photographic work have been discussed by a number of other researchers. Howard Becker has identified some of the issues involved (1975) and provided a framework for the fine-grained analysis of photographic validity and reliability (1978a). Bruce Jackson (1978) has commented on similar issues in terms of his own photographic work in prisons; Margaret Mead and Gregory Bateson (1976) have debated the merits of "systematically removed" versus "artistically informed" photographic strategies in a recently published interview, and Paul Byers (1964, 1966) has discussed these matters as well.

In addition to these more general orientations towards photographic work, there are a number of techniques which can be used to increase our confidence in photographs as coarse-grained social science statements. These can effectively identify and reduce the amount of sampling error, increase intersubjective reliability of interpretation, and in some cases provide an important test of the validity of visual statements about human subjects. None of the techniques are particularly complicated, and it is remarkable that they are so seldom used.

TO AVOID ERROR IN PICTURE TAKING

USE SEVERAL PHOTOGRAPHERS

The British photo show mentioned above suggests that if we want to record visual information about a town, we will do well to use more than one photographer. In a community study of Twin Rivers (reported elsewhere in this volume—see Chapter 5) we took this suggestion seriously. After more than a year of recording by one photographer, we brought in a second. In this case, the second photographer's images confirmed the reliability of those of the first, rather than contradicted it. As an additional check on our potential "visual bias" during the remaining two years of our study, we asked a number of other individuals to take twenty or so photographs of the community. By comparing their photographs with the images we had already accumulated we accomplished two tasks. First, we were able to sort out personal visual styles of composition, lighting, and so on from the visual dimensions of the community itself. Second, we were able to identify community themes and content areas which we had underrepresented or overrepresented relative to others in our own work.

PHOTOGRAPH FROM SCRIPTS

One of the first decisions we made about studying Twin Rivers was to allow room for the expression of a photographer's personal vision while also insuring that certain general and essential features of the community would be systematically recorded. Photographers were thus instructed to follow specific "shooting scripts" as well as to take pictures of whatever struck them as interesting or exciting. In some cases the scripts were direct and inclusive: e.g., "Take pictures of all public facilities." In other cases they were geared to a particular time span, e.g., "Take a panorama of photographs from this particular spot every month." The camera was used to document—"Take photographs of the apartment fire in Quad III," and to replicate—"Re-photograph the houses near the pool." The scripts were not intended to restrict photographs to be taken of the community but to provide a basis for inclusion and selection.

The number of scripts used are listed below:
Scripts involving photographs of:

public facilities
social activities
signage
commercial facilities
children at play
embellishments and defacements
residences
visual change
people "using" the community

Other scripts, contemplated but not realized, included:

interiors of residences

aerial photographs of land use

basements of the townhouses

a day in the life of a Twin Rivers housewife

a day in the life of a Twin Rivers commuting businessman

particular events (e.g., new family moving in, holidays, community meets, and the like)

The scripts introduced some order into the photographic recording and helped us develop a set of working hypotheses with concrete visual referents. They were thus valuable not only in ensuring that certain features would be covered on a regular and systematic basis, but also in refining our conceptual scheme for the photo-analysis.

As an additional contribution, the scripts made our photographic work understandable to others. As a check list of what it was we were looking at, they were absolutely essential to our solicitation of advice and critical input from other social scientists, most of whom were unfamiliar with visual research methods and many of whom were unfamiliar with the particular community we had chosen to study.

ASSESS PHOTOGRAPHS IN LIGHT OF OTHER DATA

A third corrective for our photographic work in Twin Rivers was the continuing assessment of visual and verbal portraits of the community. The verbal descriptions came from two major sources: our own field notes as participant observers, and the comments of residents as reported on a series of in-depth interviews. By moving back and forth between examination of the photographic contact sheets and a review of the verbal data, we were able to refine the meaning of each. The verbal data was no more valid than the visual, but taken together they gave us a useful triangulation for studying the community.

At times, we revised work in one media to take into account insights gained through the other. Photographs of the "open green space" in the community seemed so barren to us that we designed questions about it for interviewing the residents; the interviews revealed that many residents saw the community as a good place to raise their children, and so we revised our photographic shooting scripts to specifically include "children at play."

MAKE RANDOMIZED EXPOSURES

In order to further overcome the limitations of our routine "visual sampling," we developed a simple coordinate model for making randomized photographs, thereby supplementing "personal" and subjective procedures for taking pictures.

We first marked off a grid on a map of Twin Rivers, and via a table of random numbers, selected sixteen sets of coordinates from which to take our photographs. For each coordinate point we then selected an angle of orientation. We accomplished this by using random number tables to generate sixteen three-digit numbers, each of which represented degrees clockwise from direction North as indicated by a compass. With the use of a protractor and our grid map of the community, we marked off sixteen "views" in this fashion, and then went to the community and, with our map as a guide, made photographs of each. We used a 35mm camera with a 35mm lens (slightly wide angle) and a tripod with a pan (rotating) head. In every case we aimed the camera so that its lens projected in a line parallel to the ground.

The photographs generated in this random manner were an important complement to those generated more "subjectively." While they did not show us a community dramatically different from that presented in our other photographs, they did direct our attention to a number of features which we had overlooked, neglected, or recorded poorly, such as the view "outward" from Twin Rivers to the surrounding countryside and the presence of an industrial-commercial complex at one point on its perimeter.

As we were interested in activity *and* environmental settings, random sampling at Twin Rivers was somewhat straightforward, and we used it as well to select times of the day, week, and year in which to pursue our thematic scripts. In less "environmental" contexts, of course, social researchers may find this technique more difficult. To randomly sample views of a gathering, for example, we would need to know ahead of time how long it would last and the area it would occupy. For family interactions, we would need to know something about the pattern of family encounters and the settings in which they occur. In every case, to design an appropriate sample requires prior familiarity with the structure of the subject we are investigating. This is true as well, of course, for nonvisual research methods. In visually recording "events" and other dynamic processes, however, we are dealing with complex phenomena, and the "universe" from which we would like to sample includes far more than individual people. As a random sample of views of a religious ceremony, baseball game, or community meeting we would like something more than a picture of every fifth person, however interesting such a set of portraits might be.

Looking at photographs can be just as creative an activity as taking them. As a result, there is potential not only for insight and conceptualization, but also for bias and error. As in the case of making photographs, however, confidence in our interpretations can be enhanced through a number of simple but important techniques. Once again, it is remarkable that these are not used more often. Not only can such strategies serve as important correctives to more casual examination of a set of images, but they can generate rich and varied data in and of themselves.

TO AVOID ERROR IN ANALYZING PHOTOGRAPHS

USE SEVERAL ANALYSTS

It should go without saying that intersubjective reliability of an interpretation increases as more observers examine and agree about the meaning of a set of photographs. What may be less clear, however, is that bringing together a number of people to assess a set of photographs can expand the process of conceptualizing far beyond what it would be for an individual alone. In their disagreements about the meaning of an image or a set of images, individuals can begin to articulate and refine relevant dimensions of social theory. The consensus in which some images are interpreted can suggest an important area of conceptual clarity. Controversial images similarly suggest areas in which theory is ungrounded or confused. Collective analysis of a set of photographs thus provides both a strong corrective to the idiosyncracies of individual interpretation as well as an exciting arena in which to analyze the subject of the photographs themselves.

As an added dimension, photographs can in some cases be shown to the subjects of the study. In Twin Rivers, for example, we were able through the photointerviews to compare our understanding of an image of the community with that of a number of residents. This corroborative mechanism has a wide applicability to social research. While informants may have neither the inclination nor the aptitude to read technical research reports, they are in many cases willing and able to discuss photographs of themselves and their surroundings. A series of photointerviews (such as those described in chapter 5) can give researchers some idea about whether or not their understanding in any way corresponds to that of their informants.

EDIT ANALYTICALLY

If we are willing to move from casual readings to careful study—and we ought to be as willing for images as for words—there is something to be learned from organizing a set of photographs in different ways. Confidence in our interpretations can be enhanced by trying to say different things with the same set of images. Engaged in a process of what might be called "analytic editing," we can assess the contribution of each photograph to statements about the whole set. Are there certain images which in and of themselves are sufficient to make such statements? What is lost or gained by dropping or adding images from those before us? What statements could be made if we had additional images, and what might these other images be?

Based on questions such as these we can delimit the kinds of statements reasonably made with a given set of photographs, and we can exclude interpretations which the set cannot support, even if an individual photograph or two within it offers some confirmation.

In the Twin Rivers study, for example, we wanted to use photographs to make statements about how people used open space. We found, however, that we could not make such statements based on the photographs alone, simply because we could neither make nor find images in which people were using the space. This observation led us to question the residents about the open space, and we found—through a process begun by our analytic editing—that, in fact, the space was rarely used. In this case, the photographs could not support the kinds of statements we first wanted to make, but they could support our subsequent conclusion about the underutilization of the open space in the community.

EXAMINE RANDOM SAMPLES

Images receive our attention for their formal features as well as for their content. If we were to select the most interesting from a large set of photographs, we might well overlook those whose aesthetic possibilities were poorly realized. In analyzing a set of photographs, however, it is important that we become aware of such oversight and its potential to skew our understanding. One simple corrective to such error is to study quite closely a subset of the images before us. If this subset is randomly selected, we can be somewhat assured that our choice of images for analysis will not be prejudiced by aesthetic concerns alone.

In the study of Twin Rivers we occasionally performed the following exercise: We first selected a set of fifteen images which we felt gave the most vivid *and* accurate portrayal of the community features we had investigated. In this selection, of course, we were guided by aesthetic impact as well as by information. After putting this set together— through the process of analytic editing described above—we then made a random selection of fifteen images from all the photographs we had taken. Putting the two sets side by side, we could get a clearer sense of how well the "impact" photographs corresponded to the set of images as a whole. We might find, for example, that in making the first selection, we had unconsciously left out photographs in which there were "obtrusive automobiles." If we saw these in great abundance in the second set, it would indicate one respect in which we were misreading and misrepresenting our visual data about the community. The random selection of a sample of images can provide, in this way, a useful reminder about important features of the community for which no visually interesting photographs may have been made.

PERFORM CONTENT ANALYSIS

The example of obtrusive automobiles suggests "content analysis," a process in which a set of materials—which can be visual or verbal—is systematically surveyed with respect to predetermined variables. Such analysis can be performed during at least three stages of photographic research: before pictures are being taken (in which case the situated activity itself is surveyed); after photographs have been taken (in which case contact or proof sheets can be surveyed); and after photographs have been selected for presentation of research findings.

In the study of Twin Rivers, we performed content analysis at each of the three phases. Before we began making photographs, for example, we made a survey of the community and identified those features we thought most important to record. The variables we noted in this survey became the content of our various shooting scripts. At the other end of the line, we reviewed our set of "presentation images" to see if it represented all the variables on which we intended to comment, and as this suggests, content analysis of photographs is closely connected to what I have called analytic editing. By far the most interesting application of this method to our work, however, was in between these preliminary and final stages. A content analysis of all the images we had taken was not only useful in checking the reliability of what we intended to say with our images, but also in generating information which we had not previously considered.

In order to survey our proof sheets we developed a simple set of categories. First, we coded for the *presence* in each image of each of the following: automobiles, automobile pavement, pedestrian pavement, residences, commercial facilities, public facilities, open space, vegetation, signs, humans, and sky. Then we coded for the *amount* present in each image for some of these elements. For cars, people, and signs, the amount equalled their actual number. For pavement, vegetation, and sky we used the following categories:

1 = 10% or less
2 = 10-25%
3 = 25-50%
4 = 50-75%
5 = 75% or more
6 = N.A.

Each value represents the area of the total image taken up by vegetation, sky, pavement, and the like.

Finally, we coded for the copresence of two, three, or four of the central features of Twin Rivers: residence, open space, commercial facilities, and public facilities. A summary of some of the data generated by this content analysis is presented in the following tables:

TABLE 1: Presence of selected elements visible in photographs of Twin Rivers

	# of frames in which element is visible	% of total frames in which element is visible
Automobiles	704	43.8
Automobile pavement	808	50.2
Pedestrian pavement	782	48.6
Residences	1174	73.0
Commercial facilities	373	23.1
Public facilities	415	25.8
Open space	272	16.9
Vegetation	955	59.4
Signage	467	29.0
Humans	339	21.1
Open sky	1403	87.2

TABLE 2: Amount of selected elements visible in photographs of Twin Rivers

	Total # appearing in all frames	Average per frame
Automobiles	4346	2.7
Humans	1298	.81
Signs	1355	.84

Total Frames = 1608

TABLE 3: Amount of selected elements visible in photographs
of Twin Rivers

	Total # frames in which element accounts for 25% or more of image area	% of frames in which element accounts for 25% or more of image area
Automobile pavement	400	25
Pedestrian pavement	38	2
Vegetation	18	1
Open sky	858	53

Total Frames = 1608

TABLE 4: Frequency of occurrence of selected elements in
photographs of Twin Rivers

	# of frames in which element(s) is (are) visible	% of total frames in which element(s) is (are) visible
Residences	1174	73.0
Commercial facilities	373	23.1
Public facilities	415	25.8
Open space	272	16.9
2 of above in same frame	325	20.2
3 of above in same frame	162	10.1
4 of above in same frame	13	0.8

Photographs—except for those taken in studios—usually contain information not intended by the photographer. In making up our code, we were trying to develop a mechanism which would not only summarize the visual data we *knew* we had collected, but also identify some of the information we had unintentionally recorded while photographing from personal interest and shooting scripts.

The survey itself generated new insight in three major areas, the first of which was the segregation of physical facilities. Twin Rivers was designed to be a complete community, providing all the facilities characteristic of a small town. In only 13 of the 1,608 photographs, however, could we find all four of the central features of the community, and in only 162 photographs could we find as many as three (Table 4). Thus, while the planner may have included a number of facilities in Twin Rivers which are typically lacking in unplanned developments, they are not apparent from the way Twin Rivers "looks." The facilities may be there, but they are not to be seen together within the same frame, a condition which makes the community look more unplanned and less self-sufficient than was originally intended.

Our second insight involved the dominance of the automobile over the Twin Rivers landscape. One of the planning priorities for Twin Rivers was that there was to be a separation between pedestrian and vehicular traffic; another was that this be a "walking distance" community, one in which residents would get around from stores to schools, to playgrounds, and to neighbors' houses on their own two feet. In terms of the site plan these objectives are somewhat realized. There has been an effort to separate pedestrians and cars and to provide centrally located facilities within walking distance of the community's residences. As with the previous example, however, this overall design is contradicted or undermined by how Twin Rivers looks.

For example, 43.8% of all the photographs we made of Twin Rivers contain automobiles (see Table 1), so many, in fact, that we find an average of 2.7 cars per photo (see Table 2). These figures are particularly striking because none of our explicit photographic scripts called attention to cars. The automobiles which appear in our photographs, then, are those which could not be kept out. They appear in the background and the foreground, at the center and at the periphery of photos focusing on other aspects.

In contrast, there is a paucity of people in the photographs. Despite our explicit attempt to show as much as possible about how people "used" Twin Rivers, our efforts yielded people in only 21.1% of all photographs taken. This is less than half the frequency with which unsought-for autos appeared. In fact, out of 1,608 photographs of Twin Rivers, we find a total of 1,316 people and 4,346 cars. Had we photographed cars with the same tenacity we used in photographing people, our contact sheets would have appeared to be a record of a huge parking lot. The visual predominance of the car in this landscape thus challenges the notion of the walking distance community and the effective separation of pedestrian and vehicular traffic.

A third insight emerged from surveying the presence of sky in our photographs. The sky is present in 1,403 or 87.2% of all photographs made (Table 1). This means that when we are taking a picture of something in Twin Rivers, the most common background against which it appears is the sky. We know that the community has a rather uniform and even elevation; nothing in Twin Rivers is over two stories tall. Translating this design feature into the appearance of the community, we notice a lack of what Kevin Lynch (1960) has called "legibility"; absent are orienting landmarks by which individuals can tell where they are.

This is demonstrated by the fact that in 828 (53%) of the photos, the sky takes up more than 25% of the image. This is no doubt a reflection of certain photographic conventions: when we take a picture, holding the camera at eye level, we are inclined to aim the camera along a line parallel to the ground, providing us with an image about half of which is above and half below the horizon line. This convention is abandoned, of course, when there is something of interest above us or below us. In Twin Rivers, however, there are no hills, depressions, tall buildings or other vertical elements which draw one's attention up or down. The dominance of the horizontal line appears everywhere: in the rows of townhouses, the elevation of the shopping center, the parking lots, streets, walks, and fields; and this line is recorded in the horizon line of the photographs. By surveying our contact sheets, we found a way to articulate what we sensed was a monotonous landscape, a point on which both residents and researchers tended to agree.

This content analysis of Twin Rivers photographs calls attention to both social and physical variables. In some respects the social variables are less directly examined—knowing how many people are present does not tell us what they are doing, and views of the community are only suggestions of the phenomenal world of its residents—but they need not be. Had we the appropriate images, we could have analyzed photographs for the social relationships they portray between different members or groups in the community. Photographs of individuals can be surveyed for the record they provide of gesture, posture, orientation, movement, and spatial positioning. While physical relationships should not be taken to be social relationships, the two frequently participate in a sophisticated congruency.

IMPACT, VALIDITY, AND RELIABILITY

These strategies described above can increase our confidence in both making and analyzing photographs. With them we can answer a range of questions which might otherwise be taken to imply severe limits to visual social research: Are these images representative of the phenomena studied, or just a personal vision of it? How were these photographs selected from all those taken? With what frequency do certain variables occur in the photographs? Would someone else photographing the same phenomena come up with the same kinds of images?

These questions are asked in other ways of all social research. Conventions for assessing photographic work, however, are less agreed upon by social scientists than are those for evaluating written presentations, and as a result, questions of "proper method" may carry a high charge. The techniques for reducing error described here, however, can be valuable even if the questions are never asked. In addition to providing the grounds for a good defense of visual statements, they can generate interesting information in their own right.

They do take time, effort and, at times, money, however, and we ought to determine when it makes sense to use them. In a discussion of parallel questions in "field studies," Morris Zelditch (1962) suggests that research techniques ought to be chosen on the basis of the kinds of questions being asked. His model for choosing between interviewing informants, participant observation, and enumerations and samples is an excellent framework for choosing as well between analogous methods of photographic research.

To make a visual statement about the life of a community or sub-culture, for example, we might want to pursue our own informed "participant" vision, much as Robert Frank did in *The Americans*. To generate an exhaustive visual statement about the "themes" of this setting, we might want to use several photographers working within carefully structured "scripts." To make statements abut the frequency with which these themes emerge in different physical or social settings, we would have to code, count, and tabulate such images and the information which they contain.

By looking at this variety of strategies for avoiding error, it should become clear that there is nothing about photography per se which makes it a "hard" or "soft" in applications to research. In fact, it can be both, and as a result of this dual potential, it provides an interesting vehicle through which to explore these matters. In popular and commercial contexts, for example, we encounter images of great power, which affect us deeply and at times contradict what we thought to be true. In applications of this media to the social sciences, we will lose something of great value if we dismiss or reject this potential power of the image. Our personal experience in viewing such photographs, however, leaves us suspicious of those who make them, and when confidence is at issue, it should be asked for and supplied as well as possible. Photography can contribute to both the science of understanding the world as well as the art of communicating what we have come to understand. We certainly cannot ask for more than that, but it seems to me we should not settle for anything less.

EVALUATING VISUAL DATA

John Collier

The productive assessment of photographic evidence rests on the style and methodology by which these camera records are made. Therefore, a discussion of the problems of evaluating photographic data must first review how creditable visual evidence can be gathered.

The production of photographs for purposes of research requires at least two elements. The first is an overview of the culture or setting which allows all details to be seen within a *context*. In the study of community, context is found in the total of proximal relationships of earth space and floor space. In archeological excavation, context is found in *time space* as well as *earth space*. In both cases, analysis can become impossible without records of these larger relationships; without context there can be no correlative insights.

The career of the anthropologist Robert Redfield has been devoted to the study of the function of communities. In his text *The Little Community*, Redfield describes a variety of ways in which this whole view of community can be achieved. I restate two of these approaches that can yield cohesive analyses. Follow a man, woman, or child as he or she passes through the community over a period of time fulfilling the material and social welfare needs of that community, and you will observe the culture in functional association, "ordered like the beads of a necklace." Or, describe ethnographically the typical roles of the men, women, and children of a community and you will have observed the functional relationships of social structure.

The second necessity is that photographs contain creditable research tangibles, such as those provided by photographic redocumentation and sequential recording of visible change, social interaction and process; photographs should offer a way in which we can do accurate measuring, counting, and tracking. Photographic observations should thus be consistent samples or records of phenomena holistically documented, and offer evidence of distinctive cultural patterns that can be responsibly researched.

MAKING VALUABLE PHOTOGRAPHS

In a tantalizing way, the camera record *is* an infallible account of all the elements within the focus of the lens. In terms of recording both the overview and tangible detail, photography has been responsibly used by science as a tool for obtaining the central evidence of research. Archeology uses the camera as a mapping tool and a recorder of all spatial relationships. Medicine, physiology, zoology, and botany, as further examples, consistently use photographs to measure growth and change and as accurate evidence for comparative studies.

Throughout sociology and anthropology, however, there is anxiety over the credibility of the camera image. I see this distrust as resting not on the camera record itself, but in the fallibility of the process of human selectivity. As working photographers know, cameras by themselves do not take pictures (Byers, 1966). It is not the camera image that creates the inaccuracy, but where, when, and how the records are made. It is in these decisions that we may be mistaken and lose the validity of photographs.

There is a dual meaning to "subjectivity" in social science, however, that is often overlooked. In anthropology, for example, field workers try to keep the data clean and avoid projecting subjective feelings into the objective record. On the other hand, any and every response of the native informant, no matter how subjective, must be recorded word for word for inclusion in the raw data files, for any reaction of the native is valid and creditable data. For this reason one of the most valuable applications of community photographs is their use in projective interviewing to gain the emotional nuances and values the informants have about their community world.

In addition to helping us understand the subjective nature of the informant's experience, there is one kind of photographic recording which will always be affected by the personality of the observer. These are records that are made within a human relationship, or more precisely, photographs made over the human bridge between the native subject and the photographer. Photographs made within private air space, interiors of homes, portraits taken on village streets—all these invariably reflect the sympathy and transfer of human feeling on the part of the field worker-photographer. This is equally true of verbally recorded information, and in the interview, as in photography, communication must move over a two-way bridge of human relations.

This subjectivity is an asset, however, as well as a liability. Wagner (see Chapter 6) asked his Twin Rivers photographers not only to gather information but also to record this town with all their artistic (subjective) feelings, and I have found this free approach valuable in recording the whole view of cultural circumstances. Edward T. Hall has pointed out the particular value of open reception as the first step in creating research procedures. Robert Redfield (1960) also suggests that the first open response to a strange environment often reveals character that is never clearly seen again after the research descends to the micro details of the culture. Charles Hughes, principal author, prefaced each chapter of the Stirling County ethnographic study, *People of Cove and Woodlot*, with an introduction by an artist-writer. He felt the artist's perspective was likely to contain more of the character of the *whole view* than the disciplined scrutiny of his anthropological field workers.

This does not mean that we should abandon efforts to increase the reliability of photographic evidence. We can make use of several photographers, for example, in obtaining the visual record, for the social intelligence of each offers a distinctive organization of information. In the Stirling County study, in the Maritime of Canada, directed by Alexander Leighton (see C. Hughes, 1960), field investigation was made by a team highly versed in the ethnographic phase of this social psychiatric study. Field workers included a Franciscan priest, a medical doctor (Leighton), a specialist in labor relations, a British sea captain, a sociologist, an agricultural economist, two anthropologists, and a photographic visualist. Each of these specialists contributed unique insights to the ethnographic portrait of Stirling County.

Or, we can make random samples when that is appropriate. If you want to survey housing in a social territory with living units of many thousands, a random sampling becomes a method of practical value. In the Andes of Peru, I photographed a cultural inventory of two thousand Indians (1957) by sampling every eighth house on a government housing census. The return of this sampling was excellent and gave us a reliable visual baseline for the measurement of social and technological change (The Cornell Peru Project, 1956).

Regimented and systematic research designs, however, do not guarantee that the photographic record will be valuable. Research questions may evolve so that they eventually focus on information which exists between the random or scheduled points which are known. In doing a anthropological study of a community I recommend a process of photographic tracking and selective response to "peaks of information," where and when they happen. This is a flexible approach, one that can be responsive to unpredictable and uncontrolled behavior in social and cultural field settings. It is a process in which selectivity is not an immaculate and mechanical exercise, but a manifestation of human sensitivity, one that rightfully portrays significant research as an accomplishment of human judgment.

In recording social behavior I believe the most rewarding control in the gathering of scientifically valid information lies in the disciplined responsiveness of the photographers. They must recognize what a researchable record is and be involved themselves in the visual analysis. The process of extracting tangible information from photographs is the best preparation for insuring that optimum researchable content will be present in subsequent photographic records.

MACRO ANALYSIS AND OPEN INQUIRY

The camera record is the least abstract of all recorded information. Because photographs are a close replica of reality they offer insights difficult to find in other field evidence. Technologically, photographs are the result of an imprint similar to a shadow graph or an x-ray, and this nature of the medium deeply affects both research methods and the conclusions it is possible to draw from the camera image. Photographs can be both baffingly complex and at the same time fluently understandable to our sensual and intuitive intelligence. (I see intuitional response as a part of the total response in which decisive information is registered in the cortex faster than the relay of intellectual judgment.)

We should first approach photographs *openly* (Hall, 1974) in order to respond to their holistic content. We could call this initial experience "listening to the visual voice of imagery"; the researchers respond with all their senses open so that they may be deeply affected by this documentary realism. If we first approach photographs with more structured inquiry we encourage a *closed process* which may itself impose meanings that could obscure the authenticity and value of the visual record.

Photographs can send out vivid impressions which invite both judgmental recognition (response with the whole intelligence) and analytical deduction (a summation of the details of micro evidence). When Dr. Paul Ekman et al. (1972) made their preliminary visual index of the emotional signals of the face (analyzed from slide images), they stabilized interpretation by drawing judgments from a psychologically trained team of observers. The question could be raised: "Could we not carry out judgmental research on verbal evidence as well?" We could, but with considerable loss of definition—for verbal statements are already in a shorthand code and hence contain limited opportunities for further refinements in value and behavior.

In my own film research of the culture of multiethnic classrooms we first respond to the film projectively. (Responding to the projections of the film with intuitive insight.) We screen the classroom records at normal speed and then in slow motion, turn on the light and interview each other about the *feelings* evoked in us by the classroom environment. These communications are not consciously analytical but a direct reaction to the voice of the film, and tape recorded, they prove invaluable in writing up our conclusions. This projective examination can also be made from color slides of a community.

The second step is to assemble photographs in structured units of documentation which offer a narrative understanding of the record. Imagery can be arranged, for example, as *chronological experience*, a record of the way the photographer moved through circumstance. Photographs can also be organized as an illuminated *map* of a community with every house placed in its spatial position. If the records are of a habitation, photographs can be assembled as a *model*, creatively, like a projected doll house, with every item related to its floor and wall space. Pictures observed in this structured way allow us to absorb the vivid details of the environmental context, the background for all micro analysis.

The visual narrative of photographic evidence can be pinned on a wall in filmic order; community photographs can be mounted on real site maps. These approaches are especially rewarding in group analysis for the assembled materials will forcefully establish the relationships within which individual research questions can be oriented. I suggest that these narrative maps and model assemblies remain on the laboratory wall throughout the period of community research. As photographs are dissected by statistical and micro insights, the whole views of community process which they provide will become increasingly valuable. A second set of photographs should be made for the specialized and structured analysis.

STRUCTURED AND MICROANALYTIC STUDY

The function of all analysis is to find patterns. Based on the evidence of patterns we attempt to deduce significance. The shape of significance can allow us to make conclusions. Patterns are the compounding effect of photographic details, hence, an initial step in analysis is to qualify and count what each set of photographs contains.

The second step in summarizing is to make a systematic inventory of the content of the photographs. There appear to be three possible schemes for inventorying: an *item listing*, an enumeration, for example, of all the possessions of a home, or every image, human or technological, seen in photographs of a street; a *categorical listing* such as that of all kinds of a dwelling's possessions; and finally, an *inventory of cultural significance*.

What is the research value of an *item for item inventory* which lists all the possessions of a room or visual elements seen on a street? This is just a direct transfer of information from the photographic document to the verbal document, and no matter how thoroughly this inventory is compiled it offers little insight. Such listing would have to be classified in categories before any research refinement could take place.

The *categorical inventory* creates a statistical design for summarizing repetitious artifacts: how many chairs in the room, beds in the house, varieties of pictures on the walls? The significance of these statistics is limited, and they offer by themselves little cultural understanding. What is needed is an inventory that reveals function, values, beliefs, and identity: an inventory of significance.

When artifacts are placed together with their intrinsic meanings in *categories of significance* the inventory contains reference to both cultural process and structure, not just an index of visible content. Statistical accounts can emerge from this inventory and they can describe meaningful patterns. Categories selected for this *inventory of significance* should be chosen to reflect the inquiry in which the documentary content of the photographs can be distilled into refined insights.

Step three involves abstracting insights from photographs through detailed study, an advanced step in the refinement of research. As with film, still photographs are overwhelming in their volume of detail, and the sheer mass of material makes it urgent for the analyst to seek ways to capsulize and codify content so that it can be mobile and flexible in the analytical processes to which it is being subjected. One of these efforts is to place the content and significance of photographs on *code sheets*. This certainly makes the photographic information mobile for it moves details wholly from the visual and makes them a part of the cognitive verbal process.

Code sheets can be duplicated and cross-filed for rapid correlative analysis, a sophisticated abstraction that also prepares content for later computerized analysis. Code sheets are attractive for specialized research, and they make it possible to short-cut some of the difficulties of analysis by moving photographic complexity towards condensation and abstraction of information.

But the transfer of visual content to verbalized code sheets can also frustrate understanding. We have experimented with this methodology in complex film analysis and were defeated by the very abstract nature of this information. Writing a summation from the verbally codified information proved very difficult, for the extraction process had destroyed the context of the film imagery. We were unable to reassemble the whole artistically and write a satisfactory anthropological conclusion. Edward Hall, after critiquing our final writings, observed: "You have destroyed your most important asset, the vitality and organization of film." Our experience illustrates how important it can be to have the undisturbed narrative image before you on the wall when you write conclusions.

I now recommend a modified process in which a contact print of each research photograph is mounted on a five by seven punchcard, which also contains an abstract of the significance of each image. These are filed in cross index so that a variety of relationships can be drawn from each card by lifting out any correlative set of images desired.

MICRO IMAGE ANALYSIS OF BEHAVIOR

In dealing with visual records of social interaction and communication the problems of categorizing behavior are too complex for a simple inventory of content. With a magnifying glass you can count and identify (with the help of an informant) personality and artifact. But to go beyond such identification requires more detailed and complex work with the image. In motion picture analysis this means frame-by-frame study, and this is exactly what is required for interpreting the subtleties of behavior in still photographs as well. To do this, we must again go back to the field recording circumstance, for without a *sequential* record of the phenomena, our reading of the images will be only suggestive of the action. Photographers in the field must understand these research needs and be able to synchronize their exposures with the peaks of communication imagery, for it is the sequential flow of film that makes comprehensive understanding possible. Exposure for exposure, whether in moving or still imagery, the micro signals of behavior are the same.

Still photographic records of communication thus attempt to track the action through time in a way that is characteristic of motion pictures. If the photographer can produce a reliable sequential record, this body of images can be pinned on the wall in precise chronology. The edge numbers of 35mm film lock together the authentic image-sequence.

We can study the action captured by such photographs holistically, as if it were the subject of a movie, and track the communication through time. Below the sequence of images we can represent the action-message as a series of unbroken graph lines tracking the behavior flow of all participants. This is critical, for the interaction strategies

can only be reliably evaluated when seen choreometrically (the choreography of behavior) moving through time. The flow of the sequence
allows us to track and interpret all activities involved with sending and
receiving communication. The study of spatial relationships (proxemics) is important for what it can reveal about social structure as
well as for the psychological insights it makes possible into communication, and it is the full volume of nonverbal behavior that reveals the
nature and current of interaction. In most Western cultures eye behavior is locked into the communication process, along with body
sensing and listening. The study of the extremities of both hands and
feet also reveal something about response and message focus within
communication. There are thus three behavior patterns that constitute
the evidence for micro analysis: *proxemics* (measurements of space);
kinesics (messages of body behavior); and *choreometrics* (patterns
of behavior through time). The significance of the most involved and
detailed evaluation of still imagery or film rests on these three components.

DRAWING CONCLUSIONS
FROM PHOTOGRAPHIC RECORDS

The still photographic image offers accurate information about
all static elements: geography, topography, ethnographic detail, the
proximal relationships of social order, and reliably identifies places,
objects, processes, and personality. Photographs can state what has
happened, what is happening, and imply what will happen in the future.
The still camera's ability is to establish fixed points of visual information over a broad environment. Even in saturated sequential records
interpretation *still* moves between fixed tangible points of insight.

With moving images, visual information can flow through time, and
the scope of observation and intelligence is therefore far more complete than it is in still imagery. But a variety of phenomena can be
reliably studied through use of the still image alone. At a particular
point in time and space we can recover a cosmology of relationships—
ecological, technological and social structural. The still camera is
superior to the film camera as a tool in most surveys of cultural territory
and the welfare of people as reflected in housing, body structure, and
clothing. The research challenge is that when we track behavior through
space and time we must move from one static fixed point to another,
from one informational tangible to another; we must project both
action, qualification, and significance across previously unrecorded
space.

When we study community life with still photography and use the keen eyes of informants as image readers we can tangibly anchor our insights into ecology and community structure. We can assemble embracing indices of life process, identify community boundaries, both urban and rural, and build a personality identity file of enormous proportions. As an example, photograph any small trading center on Saturday afternoon, sweeping the streets to make wide angle image-records. One interview with a native will identify *all* the people present in the photographs, in most cases even when their backs are turned. People at home in this place can be distinguished from out-of-town shoppers. Finally, with the help of a regional map, the dissemination pattern of the trading center can be reliably established. By establishing fixed points of visual reference throughout regions and communities, we can use a scientific imagination to understand social and cultural processes and arrive at responsible conclusions about their significance and shape.

PART III

ISSUES IN TEACHING

Introduction

Many of the issues discussed in connection with research activities can be productively examined in social science teaching. The complex relationship between verbal and visual information, for example, can be better understood through experience with both in the "field setting" of college classrooms. Processes by which photographs are interpreted—and meanings assigned to them—can be explored as well through teaching. And, the ambiguity of the medium, as both a matter-of-fact record and a complex symbolic language, becomes apparent to anyone who attempts to use it in communicating with students.

In addition, however, photography can enhance a variety of teaching strategies and serve as a powerful resource for social science teachers. In the first chapter in this section Curry and Clarke describe a wide range of teaching exercises in which photographic images can play a central role. In the chapter following I discuss issues which emerge through use of the most conventional of visual presentations, the classroom slide show. The section concludes with a description by Cheatwood of the techniques, problems, and procedures of encouraging and evaluating student photographic projects in the social sciences.

Taken together, these three chapters move from a discussion of photographic "experiments" to the articulation of guidelines for photographic projects. As these matters are central to issues of inquiry—whether performed by students as "course work" or by their seniors as "research"—they should be as useful to those working within visual research designs as they are for those involved primarily with teaching.

—*J.W.*

PHOTOGRAPHIC EXERCISES 12

Timothy J. Curry
and Alfred C. Clarke

In recent years a number of projects and exercises in still photography have been developed as aids to the teaching of social science. In this chapter we will attempt to describe some of these and to suggest as well some of the issues they raise. Our hope in doing so is to demonstrate to students and teachers that photographic course work is not such a mystical or unusual activity after all, but an extension of social science methods and principles into an exciting new arena of experimental teaching and learning.

Photography is a very flexible symbol system, and our account of present efforts by no means suggests all the ways that it could be used in years to come. As social scientists, we are only just beginning to grasp the potential of the photographic process and the images it produces, but as teachers and students we have developed an appreciation for the manner in which it can enhance the teaching of social science.

PHOTOGRAPHY AND EDUCATION

It would be unthinkable for art historians to teach art history without using visual images to refer to the works of important artists. It is, at the least, unusual for the physical and natural sciences to be taught without the tactile and visual aids of laboratory sessions and demonstrations. We in the social sciences, however, are often expected to teach with no more than a piece of chalk, a blackboard, a strong voice, and a text which may or may not contain appropriate visual illustrations. It is our contention that instruction in the social sciences can dramatically benefit from exercises and presentations analagous to those which appear as a matter of course for art history and the natural sciences.

Photography and education are hardly unacquainted. Four decades ago the *Leica Manual*—then one of the foremost authorities on the application of still photography to a variety of fields—included a chapter entitled, "The Leica in Visual Education" by Ellsworth Dent. There is, however, a crucial difference between these early accounts of photography in education and today's efforts. While photography's earlier role was primarily that of illustration—making images of far-away places, subminiature processes, or even local events of some special value—photography's current use goes much further. While respecting the power of photographs to illustrate, contemporary use of the media in education has begun to capitalize on the photographic process itself as a model for revealing much about social life.

The best way to indicate some of the new uses of photography in the classroom is to outline the developments which have occurred in the concept of the "documentary image." Before examining this in greater detail, however, it is important to raise a more fundamental concern, that of "visual literacy." Photography is at least a technology for recording observations of the world. To make good use of its capacity to do so, both instructors and students must develop their ability to "read" photographic observations. In this context, it seems appropriate for students and teachers of social science to take seriously the task of improving their visual literacy as a means of enhancing their skills in observing the social order.

VISUAL LITERACY

A number of scholars have asserted that we are reentering a period in which the image will be dominant over the written word. As Platt (1975: 6-7) has noted, much communication took place before the invention of movable type; and the hieroglyphics of ancient Egypt, the pictographs of early China and America, even the cave paintings of prehistoric times, were all attempts at visual forms of communication. So, too, were the glass and stone textbooks, the great cathedrals of medieval Europe. We may now be entering once again an historical epoch in which the image will take precedence over the written word. Does our photoelectronic technology have the capacity to bring us all into the "global village," where the primary form of communication is visual? A stimulating question, but at this point the answer to it must remain conjectural. While a new age of imagery may be dawning, no one would seriously consider holding a requiem for the written word, and what is important to note in today's world is the mutual expression and interdependence of visual and verbal forms of communication.

Many of us, however, are generally unaware of our participation in visual forms of communication, and some of us are noticeably unperceptive of the visual messages which surround us. Some people are highly skilled at both producing imagery and discussing it, but others find it difficult to do either, for even the simplest of images. In the classroom these different levels of skills and abilities present a real challenge for the instructor seeking to use photographic exercises in teaching social science.

Our experience suggests, however, that early diagnosis of relevant visual-verbal skills can help both the student and instructor design appropriate course objectives. Table 1, which appears below, suggests one way of classifying such abilities, and indicates that student skills may vary along two dimensions: (1) their ability to discuss imagery (in this case from a social-scientific point of view); and (2) their ability to produce images. As this cross-classification reminds us, these abilities are not necessarily directly correlated. A student skilled in making photographs may not be able to discuss them; a student able to discuss photographs may not be able to make them.

When both students and instructor are aware of the different clusterings of skills among members of the class, a number of approaches can be undertaken to maximize learning for all students. One strategy is to divide the class into smaller groups on the basis of homogeneous or heterogeneous abilities. For homogeneous groups, projects need to be designed in careful correspondence to the skill level of each group. With heterogeneous divisions, each group will have a mix of more and less able students, and the group as a whole can work on a wider variety of tasks.

A second strategy is to design a number of different projects and activities for each individual to complete. If these projects range in the level of activities and abilities required to complete them, each student can work as hers or his individual abilities and temperament warrant. In any case an instructor for a social science course which calls on visual literacy should not expect all students to perform equally well, *even if* those students have equal ability in the social science itself.

A number of exercises have been devised to help diagnose an individual's visual literacy (here defined as the ability to both produce and discuss imagery), and the most elaborate of these have emerged from the field of education. Picture analysis, for example, can proceed from the statement of tentative hypotheses through phases in which people, objects, physical features, and functions are identified and described (Hawkins, 1971). Discussion of these phases, of course, can underline their interdependence, and students can be instructed to move from identification and description into more general inferences. Tentative hypotheses can be restated and verified; descriptions can be clarified. The point of providing students with such a model is not to teach them the *one* correct way to analyze a photograph, but to give them at least

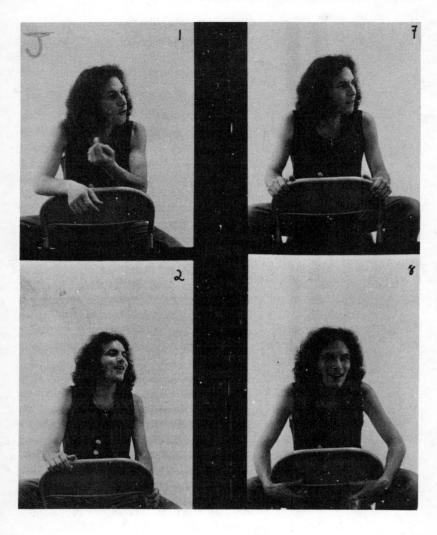

Diagnostic projects and exercises designed to develop visual literacy are
the means by which students can be prepared for a greater involvement
in visual methods and materials. The above images are part of an exercise
designed by Byers (1964). These images are produced in controlled
settings and may be used to reveal different abilities, preferences, and
styles students have in photographic observation and interaction. For
example, how many times did ths photographer record eye contact with

Table 1: Conceptual Cross Classification of Verbal and
Visual Skills in a College Classroom

		Verbal skills	
		High	Low
Visual skills	High	Student is able to produce and discuss imagery	Student is able to produce imagery
	Low	Student is able to discuss imagery	Student is unable to produce or discuss imagery

some idea of how imagery can be viewed from the perspective of social science.

Byers (1964) also provides some excellent exercises for teaching students about photography as a means of observation and social interaction. Some of the projects he describes lend themselves well to the development of visual skills; others provide sophisticated approaches to the analysis of information available from still photographs. Byers suggests, for example, that much can be gained by simply having students photograph each other in carefully controlled situations. Besides creating solidarity among class members, such exercises indicate who is comfortable in the role of photographer and who is not; who can discuss the interaction that occurred during the photographic session and who cannot. Of course, these projects are only suggestive of the variety of activities that could be used to diagnose and develop a student's visual literacy and awareness. The best projects are those that evolve from a specific substantive interest on the part of the student and instructor, and consequently manage to combine a deepening awareness of visual imagery with examination of a course topic.

Diagnostic projects and exercises designed to develop visual literacy are, in themselves, only the means by which an instructor can prepare his or her students for more sophisticated work with visual materials and methods. The exercises by which this work can be encouraged represent

---

the subject? Was a particular body arrangement and set of gestures photographed repeatedly? When a number of students photograph the same person, additional questions that may be asked are: Which photographer seemed to capture the greatest range of expressions, which the least? Which photographer seemed to make the subject most tense, which the least tense? Finally, which photograph produced the "most accurate portrait of the subject" (according to the subject's own choice). Why?

some of the new uses of still photography in the classroom, and many of these stem from the central tradition of photography in education, the documentary image.

THE DOCUMENTARY IMAGE

To see life; to see the world; to eyewitness great events; to watch the faces of the poor and the gestures of the proud; to see strange things—machines, armies, multitudes, shadows in the jungle and on the moon; to see man's work—his paintings, towers and discoveries; to see things hidden behind walls and within rooms, things dangerous to come to; the women that men love and many children; to see and take pleasure in seeing; to see and be amazed; to see and be instructed [Declaration of intent for *Life* magazine, 1936].

The documentary approach has a long history in sociology and anthropology, and it is probably the conception most frequently held by social scientists when they think of the way in which visual data provide insight into understanding specific segments of society. Documentary photography is sometimes associated with images that portray the lives of unusual people in distant parts of the world. While many documentaries are of the travelogue variety, the realization that photographs could become social documents led photographers and social scientists to explore not so laudable as well as more favorable elements of society. As Stasz has reported elsewhere in this volume, documentary photographic images were used in the early years of the *American Journal of Sociology* to illustrate several articles. Anthropologists in particular have been interested in documenting various aspects of cultures throughout the world, and many of their efforts are discussed in a recent book, *Principles of Visual Anthropology,* edited by Paul Hockings. Photojournalism, "the handmaiden of history," has become a well-established tradition of modern society. Nowadays, we routinely expect any newsworthy event to be photographed, perhaps forgetting that before the advent of *Life* and other such picture magazines, photographs of news events were the exception rather than the rule.

Doucmentary images, whether produced by social scientists or by professional photographers, can be used in a number of ways in the classroom. One of the most popular methods is to use the documentary image as a "straightforward" portrayal of an exotic subculture or unusual event, allowing the images to present in graphic terms a visual description of a previously unknown people, place, or process. The teacher or student can link relevant concepts and perspectives to the images presented, even if the producer of the images was unaware of such possibilities. In our own lectures, for example, we draw upon the work of such contemporary photographers as Owens (1973) and Slavin (1976) to make sociological observations about social class differences and apparent social structural characteristics of groups, observations that may not have been apparent to the photographers themselves. Even for today's students, reared in a photoelectric society, the impact of a realistic documentary image is considerable, and often exceeds the possibilities of the written word.

A more advanced series of exercises, however, lies beyond this traditional use of the documentary photograph. As Ohrin (1977) has noted about the genre, "What You See is What You Get," an observation based in part on her analysis of the documentary work of Dorothea Lange and Ansel Adams at the Manzanar "relocation" camps for Japanese-Americans during World War II. Ohrin argues that the documentary photographs produced by Lange, while originally viewed as inaccurate portrayals of life in such camps—and suppressed by governmental authorities—are now viewed as more acceptable documents of this unhappy era in American life. Adams' work at Manzanar shows the opposite trend. Originally viewed as accurate, acceptable to the government, and understandable to the majority of citizens then angry at and suspicious of Japanese-Americans, more of his work now seems contrived and nonauthentic. Ohrin thus concludes that the documentary image may reflect, not the event itself, but an interpretation of an event made by "the person behind the camera and the people in front of the photograph."

Becker (1975, 1978a) has raised a number of other issues concerning methods by which one can assess the validity of information presented in documentary images. He provides a number of interesting questions for discussion. Some of these concern the nature of imagery itself, and what is or is not appropriate to expect from photographs as data; other questions focus on sampling procedures used in producing imagery, and criteria for determining when to terminate a photographic research project. An imaginative course in visual social science can be constructed around topics such as these, for they are basic to verbal as well as visual forms of presentation. It is important to remember that discussion of such issues can be based on the analysis of images produced by others, including contemporary and historically significant photographers. A course designed around discussion of existing imagery can thus be used both to acquaint social science students with the extensive visual literature of photography, as well as to acquaint students familiar with photography with some of the research traditions of social science.

Sequencing ambiguous imagery can be an interesting exercise for developing a student's ability to both theorize about and find evidence for social processes and events. Here, for example, are three photographs taken within seconds of each other at a wrestling match. Can you correctly sequence these pictures? What evidence, particularly of an anthropological, sociological, or psychological nature, can you use to support your sequence?

A second approach to teaching this material draws upon the production of images themselves by students in the class, and a number of sociologists and anthropologists have developed curriculum around the issues this image-making generates. The decision to involve students in producing images, of course, immediately brings up a number of technological concerns (some of which are discussed by Cheatwood in this volume). These matters can become exceedingly complex, as McPhail and Wohlstein (1978) and their associates have discovered in their efforts to accurately record crowd movement. Francis (1971) has suggested, on the other hand, that modern film and camera technology has greatly simplified many of the demands placed upon photographers. Even so, a social scientist unfamiliar with photography may need technical assistance in designing a course in which students are to make photographs as well as discuss them. For these reasons, those interested in developing such courses would do well to befriend a professional photographer or develop institutional ties with an existing photographic facility.

When we begin to ask certain theoretical questions about documentary images, particularly in conjunction with an effort to produce photographs, a number of interesting issues emerge that go far beyond purely technical concerns. One of the conceptual problems we encounter is that there are many more unknowns than knowns in the social process of making and interpreting photographs. In going beyond the notion of "the image as evidence" and questioning the separate roles of viewer, subject, and photographer—as well as questioning the influence of the nature of the event being recorded and the demands of the setting in which the event takes place—we find that an unsettling number of issues have been raised, none of which are easy to resolve. As we try to develop an understanding of these concerns, the central role of social theory becomes increasingly clear, and the production of a straightforward documentary image becomes increasingly difficult. We have then the opportunity to work with a different type of photographic exercise, one which we can use to derive visual images more self-consciously from explicit theoretical bases.

PHOTOGRAPHING THEORY

A number of classroom projects have been developed in an effort to derive images from theory. A popular attempt was made in *Conceptual Sociology*, a text-workbook written by Larsen and Catton in 1962. The exercises in this work call upon students to find "specimens"—cartoons, written passages, or photographs—of sociological concepts. The idea behind the exercise is to assist students in apprehending a theoretical concept by developing a visual or verbal extension of it. Because existing theoretical concepts are a given condition of the search activity, deductive thinking is implicitly stressed throughout the exercises.

Another form of logic, "retro-duction," can be used with success in a somewhat different kind of exercise. Here images are used to test out the concept as well as to illustrate its meaning, and students find themselves working back and forth between theory and image to develop a richer understanding of each. Becker (1975) has outlined the possibilities of this practice in his discussion of concepts and visual indicators. As he has written, "If we cannot imagine or discover a visual image that embodies our understanding of a concept, we might take that as a warning that the concept is not explicitly related to its underlying imagery. Looking for an appropriate visual image might help clarify the relationship." This connection between social theory and visual image has also been discussed by Blumer. Writing in 1969, he observed, "When the image underlying a concept is explicit, it can more easily be criticized and revised. . . . When the underlying imagery is lift implicit, the reader invents his own, and the critical assessment of that relationship tends not to occur." Observations by both social scientists point to the fruitfulness of an effort to connect imagery and concept, a process to which photographs can contribute greatly in the classroom setting.

Imagery derived from theory can be an especially useful photographic exercise. This image was produced in connection with a study that explored some of the visual dimensions of interpersonal attraction and similarity. How many aspects of similarity do you see between the two persons in this photograph?

If we move beyond the use of imagery to "flesh out" or clarify concepts into the more demanding task of producing imagery out of an explicit theoretical perspective, we are presented with some interesting challenges for both students and teacher. As Ruby (1975) has warned in his discussion of social scientific film statements (specifically, ethnographies), no definitive social science tradition currently exists for carrying out and presenting a theoretical argument on film. Although there have been some noteworthy attempts—early work done by Bateson and Mead (1942); more recent work by Worth and Adair (1972); and some of the work presented in this volume—there is still a great deal of ambiguity and confusion surrounding the communication of social science ideas through visual media.

For all these reasons, we recommend that students, particularly those just becoming familiar with visual social science, work on topics that have both a relatively strong visual dimension and an existing social science literature associated with them. It is often wise as well to encourage beginning students to use visual methods as a supplement to, rather than a replacement for existing research strategies. In such a context, visual imagery can become an important part of the research process itself, facilitating and generating new ideas and methods. To be too ambitious, to expect students to both devise new formats for the presentation of research findings and ask original research questions, is to court dramatic failure rather than build gradually towards success.

In working out the relationship between theoretical content and visual methods of research, it is good to keep in mind an observation made by Barndt (1974: 38): "We do not pick up our cameras and aim them at any research problem . . . we begin with a problem, an interest, a hypothesis. Then in building a research design, we ask if there are visual manifestations relevant to this problem, and if visual methods can be used to facilitate any part of the research process." In other words, our goal is the examination of the social order within the discipline of social science, and our photographs are but the means to that larger purpose of our teaching.

THEORIZING ABOUT PHOTOGRAPHS

Much of the recent research and related teaching exercises in sociology and anthropology have focused on the derivation of images from theory. Much of the work recently conducted by social scientists from other disciplines (particularly psychology, geography, and communica-

Another approach to using photographic imagery in the social sciences is to derive theory from the images themselves. This hundred-year-old picture of two sisters—one dead, one alive—usually is viewed with some dismay by contemporary students. Our conventions regarding what is appropriate for the family album have changed, apparently. What are those conventions? Can an existing snapshot of a modern family be used to provide information about that family's emotional health, rituals, social class standing, and sociological organization? Photograph is courtesy of the Walter C. Johnson collection. All other photographs were by Timothy J. Curry.

tions study) has been directed towards constructing theories from sets of images produced by either individuals, groups, or societies. Not all images in this latter context have been photographs. Indeed, we can trace many of the current interests in social science photographic exercises to research on nonphotographic imagery, particularly through the work of Arnheim (1969). Studies of this genre are relatively new, and only a few exercises have been developed and classroom-tested. As a result, those interested in training their students in this form of analysis may have to consult actual research reports in developing teaching materials and designing effective course projects.

Milgram (1976), for example, describes a number of activities he has developed for his students. While some of these flow from his own research activities, others are extensions of the work of researchers in related fields, particularly other psychologists and geographers who have articulated the notion of "cognitive mapping." Milgram's adaptation of this related work has increased his resources for teaching psychology, for which he feels photography is particularly suited: "Photography is a technology used to extend specifically psychological functions: perception and memory. It can thus teach us a good deal about how we see and how we remember. The challenge is to identify psychologically interesting components of photography and to deepen our understanding through analysis and experimentation."

Those interested in communication processes also find the analysis of still photography fruitful as well as fascinating. Goffman (1976) for example, has analyzed over 500 advertisements in terms of the ritualistic displays of gender-related behavior they communicate. Students, when presented with guidelines for conducting such an analysis, often are surprised to find that advertisements contain a remarkable amount of information about cultural stereotypes and the assumptions of advertisers, much of which previously went unnoticed. In a similar vein, family photographs can be analyzed according to the cues discussed by Akeret (1973), a psychoanalyst, or within the sociovidistic framework of Chalfen (1974a, 1975), a communications theorist. In both cases, the perspective of social science can heighten the meaning of the most commonplace of family snapshots. And finally, newspapers and magazines are full of interesting images ready to be mined by the creative teacher who can provide students with guidelines for looking and interpreting. While this is not a simple task, time, attention, and experimentation can frequently generate a framework that makes analysis of existing images both fruitful and interesting.

GUIDANCE AND PREPARATION

Our own experience in designing the projects used in *Introducing Visual Sociology* suggests that it is unrealistic to expect students on their own to ask sophisticated questions about imagery. There are exceptional students for whom such questions come naturally, but they are truly exceptional and do not reflect the great majority of students enrolled in college classes. This is the case even for such simple tasks as comparing and contrasting sets of images, or arranging a set of ambiguous photographs in a meaningful sequence. Unless considerable care has been exercised in selecting such images, these elementary exercises in analysis can generate more confusion than insight. As always, the teacher should try to anticipate what might go wrong, as well as plan for what ought to go right. With this kind of thoughtfulness and preparation as background, however, even a student's failure to "get the sequence right" can be used by the attentive teacher to illustrate or reveal an important concept.

CONCLUDING COMMENTS

Images begin and end with words [Robert W. Wagner].

The Ninth International Congress of Anthropological and Ethnological Sciences met in Chicago, September 1973, and passed a "Resolution on Visual Anthropology." According to Hockings (1975: 483-484), that resolution called for six far-reaching goals, several of which concerned the development of a worldwide filming program to collect and preserve visual records of traditional cultures whose ways of life are threatened with extinction.

Perhaps the time has come for other social scientists to come forth with their own resolutions about the visual orientation of their discipline. It may be important to keep in mind, however, that the disciplines each have their own distinctive ways of formulating problems, posing questions, and pursuing research. As a result, a resolution passed by sociologists might reflect a different set of concerns than one passed by anthropologists, psychologists, economists, geographers, or others. While each social science may eventually become more familiar with the use of visual equipment and the analysis of visual data, each may also be expected to pursue different lines of investigation. Thus, while a visual orientation holds out some promise for an integrated social science, it is by no means dependent on such integration for its value within each discipline.

In general, however, the future of the social sciences lies within the kinds of questions and inquiries they choose to raise about their subject matter, and based upon current trends, societies of the future will continue to use increasingly visual means of communication. Perhaps coming generations of social scientists, conditioned by these influences, will be more visually literate than their predecessors. There may indeed come a day when research and teaching which ignores visual methods and visual data will be seen to be lacking, a manifestation of truncated and incomplete approaches to the understanding of the social world. That day will not be tomorrow, nor the day after, but it may arrive sooner than any of us can presently anticipate. In preparing our students to think critically within these visual and societal terms, we may be preparing ourselves as well for participation in the future.

PHOTOGRAPHS AS BACKGROUND, ILLUSTRATION, AND DATA

13

Jon Wagner

For the past ten years or so I have had parallel interests in photography and social science, and at a number of points along the way, the logic, concepts, or techniques of one have worked their way into my practice of the other. This began quite early, during my years in a graduate school of sociology, when I cotaught with a photographer a course entitled "social documentary photography." It continued as I used the camera to systematically record pedestrian movement on city streets, and a second kind of "interbreeding" led me to examine the social structure of photography within contemporary American culture. My parallel interests were further integrated in the study of Twin Rivers reported elsewhere in this volume (Chapter 6 and 10).

By the time I completed my graduate study, this cross-fertilization characterized my participation in both photography and social science, with the singular exception of teaching sociology. For some reason, it was easier to apply social science to the teaching of photography than vice versa.

In retrospect, I find that an important conceptual dilemma had kept me blocked from using photographs in teaching social science, one that stood as an overwhelming complication of the relationship between theory, method, and data. In simple terms, I was confused about the meaning of whatever photographs I might show to students, and I was afraid of passing my confusion on to them. In presenting a set of slides, for example, would I be giving them "illustrations" of the concepts in my lectures? Or would such images be less visual aids than data about the topics we were to examine in class? While I had the intuitive feeling that there was a great deal which they could learn from looking at photographs, I was reluctant to show them "just anything" and unclear about how to show them something more than that.

I have since moved beyond this impasse, not by achieving complete clarity about the meaning of photographs, but by becoming more comfortable with my confusion. The dilemmas which held me in check have not been resolved, but I now see them as an essential characteristic of the practice of social science. As such, they have become something to share with my students rather than hide from them.

The rewards of presenting photographs to students in regular social science lecture classes have far outweighed the problems associated with doing so, but it remains a business far more complex than that suggested by the term "visual aids." In order to outline some of the assets and liabilities of this practice, I will describe in some detail the kinds of photographic presentations I have made.

TEACHING "DEVIANCE"

While photographs have become an essential feature of all my classroom teaching, they have been most fully developed for courses I have taught on deviance, social control, and contemporary social institutions. My courses in this area have focused on three kinds of questions: "What is life like for those individuals popularly characterized as 'deviants' (e.g., criminals, mental patients, nudists, sexual innovators, the disabled, and the like)?" "How are such people treated and processed by institutions of social control?" and "What part is played by social convention, economics, and political ideologies in classifying individuals as 'deviant' and designing institutions for them?"

In teaching a course on a topic such as deviance—one with a high emotional charge—it is important to recognize that students already have rather clearly formed feelings and ideas about the subject matter. These may be grossly misinformed and highly particularistic, but they serve as the lens through which new information will be processed. In working through the three kinds of questions identified above, I found it was not enough to provide "verbal" answers, for these rarely had the power to contradict or transcend the students' performed images. On the other hand, by presenting them with more complete and accurate imagery, it was possible to suspend and contradict their predispositions—change the configuration of their perceiving lens— and make available to them written material which they otherwise would simply dismiss.

The slides I showed to students were organized into sets around particular topics, and I presented them in conjunction with appropriate readings. I was not interested in finding photographs to go with every reading, but I did want the images to make sense to the students within the context of the course.

For the course on deviance, I presented slides arranged into the following sets: "Inmates," "Prostitutes," "Freaks," "Nudism," "Rule Enforcers," and "Total Institutions." The slides, made from photographs, might be drawn exclusively from the work of a single photo-grapher. The images in "Prostitutes," for example, came from E. J. Bellocq's *Storyville Portraits*, those in "Freaks" came from the work of Diane Arbus (1972). Other sets were composed of photographs taken from a wide variety of publications. The set on "Nudism," for example, included photographs from *Playboy* and *Playgirl*, the Sears catalogue, Time-Life's history of the 1920s, *National Geographic*, and the work of several serious "art" photographers.

In many cases these photographs were powerful contradictions of stereotypical images of "deviants" and the institutions designed to process or control them. As a result, looking at the photographs was not necessarily a pleasurable or comfortable experience for the students. To help students better understand this difficult visual material, I explained my reasons for showing the photographs in the course, and described as best I could the context in which they were originally made. In whatever ways that I could, I prepared the students to look at the photographs as "examples" and "images" of the phenomena they portrayed, and through such efforts, I worked to create a meaningful context in which they could be viewed.

After several small disasters I learned to leave as well a reasonable amount of time for discussion after the photographs had been shown. To the extent that the images were powerful and new, students were disturbed, provoked, or excited about having seen them. As a rule, I quickly divided the class into small groups for five to ten minutes worth of discussion, and insisted that everyone in each group be given the chance to say *anything* he or she wanted to about the photographs. Having made a place in this fashion for the most personal of responses, we were then able to undertake a more collective discussion of the images and their relationship to the topics we were investigating in the course.

CONTEXTS FOR VIEWING PHOTOGRAPHS

As indicated earlier I brought photographs into the classroom without being perfectly clear about their meaning, but only after I had become comfortable with and clear about my purposes for doing so. Through both teaching and research I found that photographs can provide a wealth of visual detail and physical context in which to "place" a particular social phenomenon. The *Storyville Portraits* of E. J.

Bellocq, for example, are not only pictures of prostitutes in New Orleans, but pictures of the physical settings in which they lived and worked at a time when such activities were momentarily legalized. As a *background* to discussing prostitution, the photographs provided an image in marked contrast to the one with which my students had become accustomed.

Visual background information is of great importance to teaching in the social sciences as the following example illustrates. Students had brought to the class an image of prostitutes as hard, harsh, ugly women who were obviously immoral and engaged in illicit and illegal activities. For these students prostitutes were a special kind of human being, more than participants in a special kind of activity. This image had been formed, no doubt, by the fact that the only prostitutes they had seen were at work, harassed, tough, and "dressed up" on city streets. In contrast, the women in *Storyville Portraits* are seen relaxed in the settings in which they lived as well as worked. They seem less a special "kind of person" than normal people engaged in distinctive activity. In many cases the activity in itself seems normal—and seems so to the women themselves—and to cover this new "information-image" the students had to increase their understanding of social deviance. As a number of students remarked on this change in their perceptions: "I thought all prostitutes were really sick, but some of these women look like they could have been by grandmother. That's just how she looked back then."

Photographs were also useful as *illustrations* of concepts we discussed in the course. The pictures of inmates, for example, showed them engaged in behavior which Goffman has described in *Asylums* as "removal activities," "secondary adjustments," and "institutional displays."

In addition, photographs were useful as *data*, and in many cases we were able to discuss the quality of the information before us and suggest appropriate questions to ask of it. With the slides concerning nudism, for example, we found images in the Sears catalogue which were at least as "suggestive" as those in *Playboy* magazine. Another image showed women being arrested for indecent exposure in the early part of this century, women more fully clothed than cheerleaders at football games which are now nationally televised. Our attention was also called to the manner in which "natives" in *National Geographic* magazines did not seem nude in the same way as did contemporary pin-ups. The question of whether these observations were ours alone, or accurately reflected the social structure of nudism in this century, was one which we could explore through analysis of additional images. As suggestions of the range of contexts in which people are seen to be nude, the photographs were raw but useful data.

The more I used such photographs in my classes, the clearer it became that the difference between *background, illustration,* and *data* lay not in the images themselves but in the manner in which they were used. Thus, the context which I had created for viewing them—albeit one which I created with the students—determined to a large extent how the images would be examined. Any photograph could serve as background, illustration, or data, if we could agree to look at it as such. By making this lesson explicit to my students it was possible to introduce them to a complex and subtle feature of social research.

What students learned from and about the photographs, they were able to apply to other work as well. The course readings, for example, became more understandable and slightly less inviolate to the students as books and articles were seen to participate in the same ambiguities of meaning which characterized the photographs. Was Goffman's (1961) book an illustration of concepts, a source of background information, or a set of data about total institutions? After their work with the photographs, students had no trouble in seeing that it might well be all three, and more successful in one respect than in another.

THE DISSOLUTION OF VERBAL AUTHORITY

A second feature of showing photographs to students in the classroom was that it undercut my authority as a teacher, at least in the conventional sense. This occurred in part because of the student's willingness to look at the images more carefully than they might listen to my words. It also occurred, however, because communication within the classroom was expanded from one "channel" to two; with both verbal and visual messages in play, one medium could be used to comment on the other.

In simpler terms, the photographs gave students access to at least part of the original "data" from which I was drawing inferences. While I called on much more than photographs in preparing lectures and organizing the course, I chose images which I thought were congruent with my analysis of a subject area. Once the photographs were before the students, however, they were subject to interpretations other than my own, and at times, I heard that the images contradicted rather than confirmed my analysis. For example, I had presented Diane Arbus' photographs as images of freaks, as she herself had described their subject matter. Several students argued, however, that she was the "freak" for having taken them. This ran strongly counter to the kinds of arguments I was trying to make in class, and I strongly disagreed, referring as I did to Arbus' verbal and written comments on the kind of "attention" she paid to her subjects (1972). What I reported of what Arbus had said, however, cut little ice with these students who remained convinced—as they put it, "by the kinds of photographs she made"— that Arbus was an out-and-out degenerate. Comments such as these represented a dramatic change of climate in the classroom, one which I found at first disconcerting but later grew to appreciate profoundly.

SHARED STIMULUS

Classroom discussion typically calls upon some domain of shared experience and familiarity. The teacher can help identify and enlarge this domain through assigned readings, written exercises, illustrative examples, personal disclosure, and formal lectures. There are certain problems associated with these other vehicles for which photographs can provide a partial solution. Notable among them is the difficulty of beginning a discussion when some students have not completed and may have not understood the assigned readings.

Presenting a set of photographs may have the distinct advantage of ensuring that all students have "seen" what it is that will be discussed, and done so immediately prior to the discussion itself. This feature of classroom visual presentation contributes both mutuality and specificity to such discussions. The images provide a common stimulus for all members of the class—although differences in individual perception of them can be important to explore—as well as a common and concrete reference point for subsequent comments and analysis.

This is not to say that similar classroom processes cannot be based on other forms of presentation. The careful reading in class of selected sections of a written work—as is the case with *explication de texte*— can achieve many of the same results as a presentation of photographs. In the social sciences, however, photograpahs offer a direct opportunity for connecting "observation" with "analysis," and to do so in a way that texts themselves can only suggest. In my own teaching I have found such photograph-inspired discussions to lead students back into the assigned readings, and establish a context in which scholarship and research take on increased significance.

For example, in reviewing the photographs of inmates, we usually noted not only characteristics they shared in common, but also the manner in which individuals differed in their posture, expression, and demeanor. This led some of the students to reread sections of Goffman's *Asylums* to see if he had adequately accounted for variation in individual experience, and several decided that he had not.

ENCOURAGING CRITICAL THOUGHT

As a result of these factors operating together—the variable meaning of photographs, dissolution of verbal authority, and the use of images as common stimulus for classroom discussion—I have found that photographs can be very useful in encouraging students to engage in critical, analytical, and dialectical thought. In part this is because students are less intimidated by images than they are by words; it is as if they know that all pictures were made by a photographer but are less sure that all words were written by a writer. It is also a consequence, however, of expanded opportunities for comment which are provided by bringing *both* visual and verbal information into the classroom (I suspect that a course which relied on visual materials alone would suffer greatly as an exercise in social science). By combining the two media, structural conditions are established for critical comment on images through words, and on words through images.

In order to realize this potential for encouraging critical, analytical, and dialectical thought, however, normal conventions for visual presentations have to be somewhat modified. In popular and professional contexts, for example, visual materials are frequently analyzed first in terms of their aesthetic or formal characteristics. Thoughtful use of photographs in the social science classroom does not rest on a repudiation of these criteria, but it does require that another logic of inquiry take precedence over them. In showing photographs to students, for example, I tried to answer questions about the "art of photography," but I also limited the amount of time we would spend on such matters before moving on to discuss the relationship of the images to the phenomena they portrayed. Students would at times resist this strategy, calling on a number of folkloric simplifications in doing so: "You can't tell anything from a photograph anyway," they might say, "so why even try?" Or, "All photographs are lies." While it is important to respect the grains of truth which are contained in such dismissals, I found it important to move beyond the limited analytical frame which they imply.

In my own teaching I found such dismissals of the "truth" value of photographs to be used by students frequently as a mechanism for rejecting information at odds with their own preconceptions. Those photographs which were most quickly categorized as "lies," for example, were not those which were the most heavily manipulated through photographic processing. Rather, these "photographs which can't tell you anything" were images which students found disturbing, unsettling, or infuriating. Students would insist, for example, that I must have "doctored" the photographs of women in the Sears catalogue in order to make them more like those which appeared in *Playboy*—I had not. In their minds, the Sears catalogue was a clean, asexual, and safe component of adult domestic life; *Playboy* was just the opposite. In suggesting that women are portrayed in much the same way in each context, some aspect of the students' world view was seriously threatened.

The complications introduced by the partial truth that photographs are lies and the threat posed by images contradictory to personal values becomes part of a more general process in which the images seem to have a life of their own. Both students and teachers can be profoundly moved within the classroom—an environment which is usually defined by low affect and minimal dramatic content—and personally affected in ways which are both surprising to individuals but predictable for the group. In selecting a set of slides about total institutions, for example, I included several cartoons and photographs of Japanese-Americans in "relocation centers." I had also included in the set other images of Vietnamese refugee camps, Nazi concentration camps, medical hospitals, a luxury ocean liner and a Zen monastery in Japan. While I had viewed these images myself many times, on several occasions I became quite disturbed by seeing them in the classroom setting. The images gave a dramatic illustration of some of the concepts we had been discussing. The power of the photographs themselves, however, took my attention away from such concepts to the lives of people who were actually affected by these particular institutions. After the whole set had been shown, I would find myself quickly joining one of the small discussion groups in order to express my personal feelings about the photographs. The services I had provided for students became, at these times, an important resource for me as well.

This same set of slides, however, was useful in refining concepts as well as particularizing the phenomena we investigated. Commenting on the photographs in small groups may have taken all of us outside the boundaries of our normal institutional roles, but discussing them as a class brought us back to the business of teaching and learning social science. After the space for personal expression, for example, we could build on our "viewing" and identify a number of distinctions between the total institutions illustrated by the photographs. In what ways were they the same, I asked, and in what ways did they differ? Do Buddhist monks feel the same way about their total institution as do their relatives in American "relocation centers"? In what ways are refugee camps for Vietnamese different from luxury liners? Working from the images through the concepts discussed in course readings, we were able to identify variables which distinguished between kinds of total institutions and have important consequences for the experience of those who spend time in them. In this way the photographs were an important resource to students to resisting the temptation to see course readings as the last word, or—if that locution is appropriate—in suggesting that there are images to come beyond even the most final of words.

TAKING RISKS

A classroom in which visual images are presented is different from one in which they are not. The distinctions between the two can vary from small to large, depending on how the images are used, but they remain a complicating factor to conventional classroom teaching. I would argue, based on my own experience, that the complications are neither unproductive nor overwhelming. It is true, however, that a different set of risks are encountered by the teacher who seeks to teach social science through the use of photographs.

Some of the risks involved are practical and technical; and the use of slide projectors, opaque projectors, and related equipment certainly increases the number of things which can go wrong in a class. Technical questions and uncertainties, however, can be answered and resolved rather easily, and trained audiovisual personnel are available on most campuses to help teachers with such presentations. In order to make their own jobs somewhat less demanding, these personnel are also usually quite willing to train teachers in the use of audiovisual equipment; a sense of familiarity with slide projectors and photocopying set-ups is not at all difficult to achieve within the space of a few half-hour sessions.

Not all the risks are so mechanical, however, and the teacher who is interested in working in this format should be prepared for some of the other outcomes described above, the most unsettling of which may be the deterioration of her or his "absolute" authority in the classroom. To the extent that the teacher has taken on the role of presenting the truth about a matter to the students, that teacher's in-class presence may be made more vulnerable through the use of visual materials. This condition applies because of the great difficulty encountered with photographs in avoiding questions of epistemology and method. To work comfortably within such a format, teachers should probably be willing to discuss the processes by which statements are made about the social world as well as interested in cataloguing and commenting upon those already made by other social scientists.

For some, these risks are what give teaching its peculiar fascination. In their commitment to the use of the classroom to create knowledge—as well as pass it on—they take chances with what they have always thought to be true and try out new versions of their understanding. For teachers whose primary commitment is to processes such as these, photographs may serve as an extraordinary and valuable resource.

SUGGESTING AN ORDER OF INQUIRY

In a number of ways, the best use of photographs in social science presentation—whether from teacher to students or from one colleague to another—will require the creation of a distinctive order of visual and analytical inquiry. In its simplest terms, such a framework must address at least three questions: "What is *out there*, beyond the boundaries of our personal and social selves?" "What of that which is out there do you and I *notice and remark upon*?" and "What do you and I *invent* in our processes of investigating the world?" These questions apply as well to verbal material as they do to visual, but the power of images to both transmit and transmute gives them an added salience in the use of photographs.

The order of inquiry which these few questions suggest, however, is not one for which answers will come easily. Answers themselves will participate in the order and be continually subject to the questions that inspired them in the first place. Those which stand up to such trials will probably lie somewhere in between absolute truths and absolute invention, and this should come as no great surprise; our most useful theories about the social order may be found there as well.

In all of this, I suspect we will find both poetry and axiomatic formulations to have great heuristic value, but little of the essential substance of social science. Each of these more extreme versions of the truth can illuminate contradictions in our routine understandings of the social world. They cannot, however, transcend the process itself of "framing" and "inventing" that world, and they offer no great promise for the future of social science. Such promise, where it is to be found, will be substantive to the extent that ideas are tied to the worlds in which we live, and photographs are one way of pursuing that reflective and elusive goal. Within the contexts of background, illustration, and data, they call our attention to intricacies of the process by which we create our knowledge of the world.

STUDENT PHOTOGRAPHIC PROJECTS

14

Derral Cheatwood

Visual images and the tools for producing them are literally ubiquitous in our society, and the hand-held still camera has long been a staple of families in the broad middle class which populates most colleges. With a modicum of effort, successful social science photographic projects using this tool can be undertaken in situations where there is interest on the student's part, but in which neither the student nor the instructor has specialized knowledge or training beyond normal snapshot familiarity with a camera.

In the following pages I will examine still photographic formats in which such projects can be conducted and describe their relationship to modes of presentation. This discussion assumes very little knowledge on the part of an interested instructor, and those having wide experience in photography may already be familiar with much of what follows. The specific application of photography to student projects in the social sciences, however, does generate problems and possibilities all its own. At times these are purely conceptual, but in many cases they combine technical and conceptual issues. A choice of camera, for example, may determine the kind of phenomena we can most easily photograph, and, as such, influence our sense of what is visually interesting. That, in turn, may lead us to ask particular questions or outline distinctive categories for the analysis of our data. In this way whatever theory we develop is indebted to the technical capabilities of the camera with which we work.

The same can be said of presentation. In choosing to show color slides, arrange prints into a book, or display them on gallery walls, we are selecting a presentation format with distinctive advantages and disadvantages. In organizing our social science analysis within the context of such media, we have to work back and forth between what we want to say and what, in fact, can be said at all.

In the case of both camera and presentation, the format we choose influences the kinds of questions we raise and the kinds of answers we can propose. This is true as well for written materials. The tangible nature of camera equipment and the dramatic content of images produced with it, however, make choice of format a highly "visible" issue in designing and assessing photographic projects. In teaching social science, we have much to learn about these matters as well as a great deal to learn from them.

KINDS OF CAMERAS

In all likelihood the camera which the student will want to use will operate in one of five formats. Four of these are very similar and produce negatives which can be made into prints or slides; the fifth format is the instant or "Polaroid" type.

THE 110 FORMAT "POCKET CAMERA"

The smallest format cameras use film identified as 110. These produce a negative 12 mm by 16 mm and are generally identifiable as "pocket" cameras, small, rectangular, and usually less than two inches thick. In general use they have three major advantages: their small size, their ease to use, and their cost. Their major disadvantage is the size of the negative produced. Although slides can be made from these negatives, many commercial houses do so only through special orders. The resultant slides are much smaller than normal and are of lower quality than those of the larger formats. This same problem of image quality occurs in making enlargements from the small 110 negatives, particularly those greater than the standard three by five inch print. The three by five inch image itself may work moderately well in a book format—although it can become monotonous in that form—but the poor quality of 110 prints becomes distracting in a gallery format employing eight by ten inch, eleven by fourteen inch, or larger images.

The advantages of this format are the same for a social science student as they are for the general public. The cameras are generally inexpensive. For twenty five to seventy five dollars a camera can be bought which will have three "zones" for focusing and an automatic exposure eye. A camera such as this requires neither detailed focusing nor adjustment of the lens opening and shutter speed. As such it can be useful to a novice or to any student working in situations where more sophisticated adjustments are difficult or impossible to make. Thus, if the student's technical limitations or the limitations of the situation argue against more sophisticated equipment, one is better off with a fair pocket camera than none at all.

THE 120 "BOX" CAMERA

This is an older camera format, and the film it employs is much larger, producing negatives which measure 2¼ by 2¼ inches. In terms of ease of operation, cost, and lack of manual controls, the box camera is essentially the same as the 110 pocket camera, and its advantages and disadvantages for students are similar. The larger size of the 120 format, however, is both an asset and a liability. The box camera will produce larger negatives; and even though the lens and technical capability of most of these cameras are not the best, most enlargements up to eight by ten inches will be satisfactory. On the other hand, the camera is large and conspicuous, and it may be difficult to handle, focus, and shoot under awkward or trying circumstances. The 120 box camera also suffers from a lack of popularity, and its availability is much more limited than that of the pocket camera.

THE 35mm CAMERA

Because of its technical sophistication, high optical quality, relatively small size and great flexibility of operation, the 35mm camera is the chosen equipment of many serious photographers. The production of top quality Japanese models in recent years has made cameras of this format available to a much broader spectrum of the population, and it is quite common for students to either own or have access to one.

Cameras using 35mm film are generally divided into two broad types depending on the manner in which they focus: the Single Lens Reflex (SLR) and the Rangefinder (RF). Within the viewfinder of an SLR camera, a complex of mirrors enables you to look directly through the lens to focus and compose the picture. In short, what you see will be the image the lens transmits to the film. At the moment of taking the picture, the mirror in front of the film flips out of the way, and the mechanism for moving the mirror is responsible for two disadvantages of the SLR models. In order to accommodate the mirror and its mechanism, an SLR is usually larger and heavier than an RF camera. In addition, mirror movement produces a very noticeable noise when the shutter is tripped and the picture taken. The SLR is thus at a disadvantage in situations where this noise may be disruptive.

There are, however, substantial advantages to the SLR format, the most notable of which is the camera's adaptability to a wide range of different lenses. Because viewing is through the lens itself, framing and focusing adjust automatically for a change in lenses. The same camera body can accommodate normal, wide angle, and telephoto lenses without modification, and the ability to use these lenses well and at the proper time—without becoming too enraptured in the technological fallacy (see Chapter 18)—represents a real resource to students of society.

In the RF camera, the viewfinder makes use of a separate and secondary lens arrangement for focusing and framing, and the photographer cannot see through the "taking" lens of the camera itself. As a result, interchanging lenses is much more complicated than for the SLR, and most RFs do not have this capability. Without the need for mirror moving mechanisms, however, the RF's size and weight are usually less than that of the SLR, and the camera is dramatically quieter in operation. Due to this difference in engineering, RF 35's also tend to be less expensive than their SLR cousins.

The major advantages of both the 35mm cameras are their flexibility, good image quality, and relatively small size. This latter feature is a real asset in terms of convenience and the potential for nonobtrusive picture taking. Contrary to most persons' beliefs, however, it is not necessary for every photograph to be candid and taken without the subject's knowledge. It is both possible and reasonable for the subject and the photographer to be fully aware of their special encounter; and in introductory level projects, it is highly advisable that they be. Students attempting to take pictures of persons without their knowledge may engage in activities which violate the rights of confidentiality of the subject. On the other hand, people who know their picture is being taken usually learn to go about their business in a normal fashion after the first few clicks of the camera's shutter. The discovery of this fact constitutes one of the most valuable learning experiences generated by projects of this sort.

THE 2¼ FORMAT

For many professionals this is the ideal format, for it can combine the large film size of the box camera with the flexibility and optical quality of the 35mm camera. In addition to SLR and RF models, there is a "Twin Lens" version, and all of these produce a large 2¼ by 2¼ inch negative which makes superlative enlargements. These cameras can be complex, sophisticated, and expensive. They are invariably larger than 35mm cameras, and in some areas it may be difficult to find a wide range of film and accessories. To obtain a 2¼ camera which has the full flexibility of a 35mm SLR may be prohibitively expensive, but the less expensive RF and Twin Lens models can produce images of high quality for display in a gallery format or in a book. Its larger film size makes the camera inappropriate for producing normally dimensioned color slides, and so it is not recommended for that use. Overall, the camera is probably less suited to most student projects—because of its expense and more cumbersome dimensions—than are cameras of other formats.

THE INSTANT PICTURE POLAROID FORMAT

"Instant Picture" cameras are those which produce the finished picture by themselves, usually within a few seconds. *Polaroid* is a commercial trade name; the company led the development of this format, and its virtual monopoly on such cameras—until recently—has led many to identify the product brand with its generic type.

The one great advantage of this format is that it allows the photographer to see the product of his activity within seconds after the picture has been taken. As a result, errors can be identified and corrected on the spot. If the photograph is badly composed, poorly exposed, or uninformative; then additional photographs can be taken until the photographer's aims are achieved.

A major disadvantage peculiar to this format, however, is that most of these cameras produce only one print and no negative. As a result, some other kind of camera must be used in making copies (if more than one print is needed) or slides from the original Polaroid picture.

Any of these formats can be used to advantage in student projects, but it is important to keep the distinctions between them well in mind (see Consumer Reports, 1976, for their comparative costs). Some cameras are clearly more suited to different picture-taking strategies and situations than others, and the focus of such a project will in part determine which format is most appropriate. An additional factor to be considered, however, is the manner in which the completed project will be presented. To understand the connections between camera equipment and the photographs they produce, it is important to examine the variety of contexts in which photographs can be displayed, viewed, and commented on.

PHOTOGRAPHIC PRESENTATIONS

Photographs are commonly presented in three different formats, and with obvious modifications these can be used by students as the final form for their course work: the slide presentation, the "book", and the mounted show or gallery display.

Each has distinctive strengths and weaknesses, and both students and instructor should be aware of these in choosing between them. First, one must consider what is being done and for what purpose. Different projects within a classroom setting will demand different formats. Second, the student's resources have to be considered; his or her economic means, familiarity with the subject matter and camera technique have to be taken into account. Finally, one must keep in mind the intended audience of the final product, whether it is to be the instructor, the class as a whole, or a large audience outside the classroom.

THE SLIDE PRESENTATION

Presenting the final project as a slide show has two major advantages over the other formats. The first is the potential control over audience response which the slide show can engender, a characteristic which makes this format useful to the expression of conceptual arguments and explicit analysis. Such presentations can be quite impressive simply in terms of the size and color of the images displayed, and the format is familiar. Most students have seen slide shows before and are accustomed to viewing them as pedagogical or entertainment "events." The second advantage may almost dictate its use in certain situations, for the slide show is the only means whereby an entire class or other large group can view the same work at the same time. If a project is designed for such an audience, the slide presentation may be the only answer.

In most situations the student whose slides are being shown should handle the presentation and exercise control over both audio and visual material. The student thus decides which slides—and how many—are to be shown; the order in which they will be presented by one, two, or more projectors; how long each will remain before the audience; and what spoken or written explanation will accompany the images.

In editing such a show, students have in mind what they want to communicate and how much time they have in which to do it. The editor must remember that this will be the first time the audience has seen the slides, and try to avoid the tendency to move through them too quickly. I have found that in a normal presentation organized around a conceptual point, it takes about ten seconds for viewers to begin to feel comfortable with the information they gather from a slide. I am sure that the time varies with content (ten seconds per slide for fifty slides of the neighbor's new baby is anguish) and with the perceived need for detailed understanding (Are you going to be tested on this stuff?), but ten seconds per slide is a useful rule of thumb. In a fifteen minute presentation—allowing five minutes for setting up, preliminary explanations, and removing the equipment when finished—one is left with ten minutes of "showing" time, or time for a *maximum* of sixty evenly paced slides.

There are, of course, exceptions, and individuals who are more sophisticated or innovative can develop numerous variations. Rather than talking along with the slides, for example, the student can prepare a timed, tape-recorded text to accompany the showing. Multiple projectors, dissolve units— which allow the slide projected on the screen to fade and dissolve into the next image to be projected—and many other technical products can greatly improve the quality and effect of a presentation. Such refinements, however, involve advanced technical knowledge on the part of either the student or the instructor—or the willingness and desire to seek it out—and should be attempted only if one of those conditions is met.

If a projector is available through the school, the actual cost per slide makes this format relatively inexpensive; and for purposes of working with color, slides are less expensive to have prepared commercially than prints. Although commercially processed color slides are the most commonly used, it is relatively easy for a student familiar with developing black and white negatives to produce black and white slides as well.

The disadvantages of the format are the "other side of the coin" of its advantages. Because the student controls the presentation, there is no chance for the viewer to pause, reflect, perceive, or comment at his or her own pace. There is no chance to spend as much time as one would want on aspects which are of personal interest, nor is there a chance to return at will to earlier images. As a result the order and structure of the slide presentation is more demanding than that of other formats, for there is no opportunity for viewers to reorder the images to please their own preference.

In sum, the slide presentation is best used when it is necessary to present images to a large group at the same time. It lends itself to a high level of formality and control of the audience's response to each image and the written or spoken text which can accompany it. It is a familiar and easily understood format; and, if a projector is readily available, it is relatively inexpensive to produce.

THE GALLERY FORMAT

The "Gallery Format" involves hanging photographic prints on the walls of a designated "gallery" setting. The setting itself may be the classroom, but an energetic student might be able to find a regular art gallery or showing room suitable for an exhibition.

Exhibitions of photographs have characteristics—some explicit, some implicit—which reflect immutably on the content of the show. In the first place, the gallery, by implication and association, tends to raise issues of "aesthetics" more than do the other formats. It is also the format least familiar to students and others; almost everyone sees slide sets and photography books, but few make their way to art galleries to view displays on photographs. Combined with the colloquial association of the gallery with very high culture, these factors create a situation in which exhibited photographs are expected not only to carry social scientific content, but also to meet higher standards of visual and technical excellence.

Although materials required for printing and mounting photographs are not "objectively" expensive—twenty dollars would be a minimum budget for supplies for a small exhibition—it may be prohibitively so for an undergraduate preparing such an exhibition solely as a class project. The matted or mounted print is a relatively permanent item; the matte cannot be rented, and schools do not regularly supply matting materials. Because schools do supply slide projectors, as a rule, an exhibition may cost the student more than a slide show.

The gallery exhibition makes two demands which should be remembered when considering this format. First, is image size and quality, and, as a result, neither the 110 nor the Polaroid format lend themselves particularly well to such shows. Second, to work in this format, students may need to know how to develop their own negatives, make enlarged prints, crop and mount their work, and perform the variety of other tasks regularly associated with preparation of an exhibition quality print. Students unskilled in these tasks could, of course, pay for such work to be done commercially, but to do so would cost a great deal. For students competent in photographic technique and focused on an appropriate topic, a gallery show can be an interesting and valuable approach. Because the student has less control over how people will respond to the photographs themselves, this format may require a great deal of attention to details, order, and conceptual focus. As such, the gallery exhibition makes its special demands. In many ways, however, it offers as well the most intriguing possibilities.

THE BOOK FORMAT

The "book" format is based on organization of the traditional written essay, paper or book. Photographs can be mounted or pasted on regular paper, or plastic overlay sheets can be used to hold them in place. The format allows for varied numbers of photographs to be arranged, ordered, and accompanied by text or titles.

In the preparation of a paper of this sort—as with the other presentation formats as well—it is important to identify at the beginning whether the project is intended to be photojournalistic, photodocumentary, or visual-anthropological in style. It is additionally necessary to keep in mind some of the important characteristics of each approach, and to design the presentation to highlight those characteristics. With photojournalism as the model, for example, the student should concentrate on ordering the prints, making sure that the work starts somewhere, moves in the direction of the story to be told, and ends with the completion of the idea or point to be made. With photodocumentary work, it is important to see that the subject has been accounted for adequately, that there are no extraneous nor unnecessary prints, but that no information essential to the topic is left out. In a more anthropological approach, the student should be sure that the prints presented are adequate to illuminate, elaborate, or explain selected aspects of the group or culture being studied.

The book format is inexpensive and suitable to any of the camera formats previously discussed. Beyond the costs of film and development, the only additional expenses a student need bear are those of paper, overlays or mounts, and a cover, scarcely more than what is needed for a regular term paper. With reasonable effort, patience, and imagination, a beginning social science student with minimal experience and some interest in photography should be able to produce an interesting visual essay of high quality.

One very real advantage of the photo book or essay is that it is the only format for which Polaroid cameras are really well suited. For students working with other camera formats, the book presents the possibility of using prints of various sizes to suggest the relative importance of different photographs. By enlarging some prints to four by five inches, five by seven, or eight by ten, a student is able to vary the visual rhythm of the work and selectively draw attention to certain crucial images.

Most students will find it easier to compose their final work with an accompanying text. As a term paper it is reasonable to expect something between five and fifteen pages of written material—either in a separate section or interspersed with the prints—and some ten to twenty prints. These are only rough guidelines, however, and the dimensions of the book or paper format is less bounded by external factors (such as audience, viewing time, or display area) than are those of the slide show or gallery exhibition.

GENERAL RECOMMENDATIONS

Table 1 summarizes recommendations we would make regarding project presentation and camera format. Selection of both, of course, will represent a compromise between the camera the student owns or can secure, the subject to be covered, and the type of format which can best do that job, as well as available presentation equipment and facilities, potential audiences, and the purposes of the presentation itself.

In completing a successful project, there are at least five initial questions which must be answered. First, what is it in specific that the student is going to study? Second, what features of this inquiry lend

Table 1: Recommendations on cameras and formats

Camera format	Slide show	Book format	Matted show	Beginners ease of general use	Equipment cost	Range of uses and techniques
110	Poor	Acceptable	Poor	Excellent	Low	Fair
120	Poor	Acceptable	Fair	Good	Low	Fair
35mm.	Excell.	Acceptable[a]	Good	Poor to Good	High	Excellent
2¼	Poor	Acceptable[b]	Excellent	Poor to Fair	High	Excellent
Polaroid	Poor	Acceptable	Poor	Excellent	Low to High	Poor

(a) For sophisticated students, the 2¼ format allows for maximum enlargement, which might be a factor in this decision.

(b) For beginners who need to see their work "on the spot" to ensure that they have photographed what they wanted to photograph in the manner they wanted it photographed the "instant picture" cameras are a must. Their prints are best used in a book format, and are excellent for such a use.

themselves uniquely to the use of photographic methods or techniques, and how can these features be best presented? Third, which of the camera formats available to the student is best suited to undertaking this project? Fourth, what will be the final format for the presentation of this project, and how well does it correspond to appropriate and available camera equipment? And finally, by what critical vocabulary and by the tenets of which discipline will the final project be evaluated?

(1) Focus. Generally the same basic guidelines apply to a photographic term project as apply to more traditional papers. The first item of importance is the topic itself. To the greatest degree possible, there should be a clear idea of precisely what is to be examined, and how it will be done. In photographic projects, the topic should be *very* specific, for with broader topics there is a tendency to use cliché images and to include nonessential pictures. A basic rule is to start small, and start specific, with a clear idea of the phenomenon to be investigated. Another rule is to develop and print photographs as they are taken— so that they can be examined as field notes—to constantly refine the topic and its scope and suggest areas in which supplementary work is necessary.

(2) Visual Features. With a topic clearly in mind it is necessary to identify which of its aspects or characteristics lend themselves to photographic study and presentation. What is there about the topic that photography can reveal and that other methods cannot reveal quite as well? Further, how can these revelations best be presented? Are there particular features of the groups or concepts being studied that *should* be presented visually? The photograph is a "frozen image," a concretely captured moment of time and space. If there are aspects of that space— its appearance, movement within it, size, color, shape, physical relationships, and the like—that can be "shown," as well as talked about, then these are proper subjects for photographic technique.

(3) Camera Format. The instructor and student should discuss and decide on both camera and presentation format at the initial stages of the project. The student's means and expertise, the design or intent for the final project, the place of the project in the larger business of the course, and the relationship of format to topic must all be considered, and all elements brought into reasonable correspondence with each other. A student who wants to photograph violence at sporting events, for example, is setting out on an almost impossible task unless equipped with telephoto lenses and a sophisticated camera.

(4) Presentation Format. In terms of presentation, the final editing process on any project should work in two directions. First, every photograph presented should have a distinct purpose, and the student

should be able to explain that purpose in concrete terms. Second, there should be enough photographs to explain or cover the topic, or there should be good explanations as to why no such photographs exist. The latter may occur, given the problems of technology, time, and limitations of knowledge. In some classes I allowed students to use slips of paper describing what they would have taken if they had been able to. In other instances I have required students to edit their prints down to the single most important photograph, then rebuild the set by adding the smallest number of prints required to explain the theme of that one print.

(5) Evaluation Criteria. Finally, a decision must be made about criteria for evaluating the student's work. The project is, it should be remembered, first and foremost an exercise in social science. As a result, the critical orientation within which it will be assessed should respect social science as its primary source, and the central concern should be how well the project has realized the social science objectives for which it was intended.

Other critical vocabularies, however, should not be totally ignored. Questions of composition, lighting, focus, and image quality are quite revelant to a visual project; just as questions of spelling, grammar, and style are relevant to written work. Each of these bases for criticism are exercised to ensure that material is presented in the best possible format and style, and good photographs can convey the information of a social scientific statement better than can bad photographs. The ability to take technically excellent pictures is not enough, of course, for a technically perfect photograph may be of no social scientific value, and, as such, inappropriate for inclusion in the project. By the same token, aesthetically effective photographs can help to do the job of the project, but are insufficient in themselves as statements of social scientific import.

An almost classic difficulty encountered in encouraging visual projects in social science arises from these varied critical contexts. Although most students can work within the context of social science, those with training in photography frequently want to produce images which are first evaluated technically and aesthetically, and only then assessed for their social scientific value. At its worst this latter orientation can lead students to present landscapes and cloud scenes as a final project in visual sociology or anthropology.

This problem can be avoided in part by requiring students to have at least two or three people in every photograph they present. No matter who the people are, nor how instant their connection, discussion of possible relationships between them makes the variety of interactions in society more "real" to student photographers. Ideally, (as Howard Becker has suggested to me) the student would develop from exercises of this kind the ability to conceptualize such relationships prior to taking photographs, and to frame and shoot so that resultant images express an understanding of social phenomena. In fact, however, it may not matter whether this process occurs before or after the photographs are made. If understanding social phenomena is the central objective in teaching visual social science, it should be recognized that it can be apprehended by looking at photographs which "fail" as well as those which "succeed".

When the topic has been clearly identified, the camera and presentation format chosen, and the criteria for evaluation established and agreed on, the instructor's teaching is hardly over, for it is the rare student who will not need careful guidance in the completion of the project. Unless the student has done this kind of work before, he or she will need helpful feedback on the direction and progress of the visual enterprise; and in providing guidance, the instructor can begin by asking the sort of questions asked of any term paper: Does it seem to be covering the topic? Does it have a direction or consistent theme? Is it including everything that needs to be included? Is it excluding those things that do not need to be included?

It may well be that both instructor and the student are relatively new to this kind of work, but that fact alone should deter neither from working in this media, for the use of still photographs in a term project can be quite enjoyable and informative for both. It is certainly not the only way to proceed, of course, but the incorporation of photography in student projects in the social sciences can generate a remarkable amount of enthusiasm and intellectual concern. After teaching students to use appropriate photographs in their course work, it has become difficult for me to imagine not doing so, and, perhaps, rightly so.

PART IV

TEACHING APPLICATIONS

Introduction

Earlier chapters in this volume have illustrated or examined the application of photography to social science research and teaching. The three chapters in this section continue that theme but illustrate "application" in yet another sense: the use of social science itself by other disciplines and professions. The first two chapters by Lifchez and Ellis describe photographic efforts to teach social science to students of architecture and environmental design. The third is a report of Krieger's use of photography in teaching social science to students of public policy.

The "social science" in these courses is neither comprehensive nor all of a piece. In that respect it is probably representative of most extradisciplinary applications. Reduced to their simplest ingredients, however, each of the three courses described in these chapters calls attention to a distinctive order of social phenomena. Lifchez, for example, concentrates his work with students in the social-psychological terrain of perception, interpersonal process, and visualization. Ellis, on the other hand, focuses on the explication of implicit social theory and encourages students to increase their sensitivity to the details of behavior in physical settings. In the third selection Krieger attends to yet another area of inquiry, the visual coefficients of social values and the processes by which they emerge and guide social policy.

Taken together, these three chapters illustrate the potential of photography to serve as a bridge between a number of disciplines and professions. They also give an account of some of the social scientific "traffic" which the bridge can support, and, in doing so, call attention to teaching questions of presentation, interpretation, and the formation of visual imagery. For social scientists who want to share their work with those outside their disciplines—whether they be beginning students or mature colleagues in related fields—these chapters describe a variety of useful heuristic formats.

SEEING THROUGH PHOTOGRAPHS
Projection and Simulation

Raymond Lifchez

15

People quickly discovered that nobody takes the same picture of the same thing, the supposition that cameras furnish an impersonal, objective image yielded to the fact that photographs are evidence of not only what's there but of what an individual sees, not just a record but an evaluation of the world [Susan Sontag, 1977: 88].

So as not to appear a lesser profession, architecture has always considered itself the "mother art," bringing under her mantle all the others. Originally, there were only drawing, painting, and sculpture, then history and philosophy were added. In recent years we have quite nicely nested even more arts—psychology, social psychology, sociology, and even anthropology—that is, the social sciences. One has only to look at the curriculum of a prestigous architecture school to see the rationale behind each incorporation.

Usually, what students learn about social science in an architecture curriculum they learn outside the design studio. A sociologist or psychologist gives a kind of "environmentally slanted" course, and students take it. Once in a great while some connection is made with studio work through a variety of ambitious assignments—identification of "user needs"—for which students go out and interview people or groups of people to find out what they want from a designed environment; the assignment of studio problems relating to the houses of exotic cultures beyond their real-life experience, assignments of designing for the city and its special populations (e.g., minorities, institutional residents, and the like), and so on.

The assumption behind all of these arrangements is that the studio is a setting for design simulation at low risk, through which students learn the routines and technical skills of professional work. The tacked-on social science courses and assignments are supposed to ensure that when students leave they are capable not only of dealing with the hardware of architecture, but also with the software—what people want, need, and desire.

It is unclear how well this arrangement works. When I began teaching an introductory design studio some years ago—a course intended to deal explicitly with social, psychological, and cultural dynamics in architectural practice—I shied away from this short but well-accepted tradition. I wanted to teach both design skills and content—and I wanted the content to be the social, cultural, and psychological dynamics of people alive and acting in the world—but I wanted to teach them in a way that was both integrated and grounded in detail. To do so, I developed a number of strategies addressed to a special population which students had not yet carefully assessed and for which they had not thoughtfully designed—themselves. Several of these strategies hinged around the use of photographed images of either my own or the students choice.

REVEALING THE COMMUNITY OF STUDENTS

When I first met the studio class I looked out over a sea of eighty to ninety students, and I noticed that the group I was facing was not homogeneous at all but very mixed. They were all somewhere between the ages of eighteen and thirty (most in their early twenties), but they were male and female of all races and, I think, social statuses. There were Chinese, American-Chinese, Japanese, American-Japanese, Chicano, black, white, and many groupings in-between. They represented an enormous variety of sexual interests and attitudes and an even greater variety of processes for working out life as they wanted to live it—living communally, monogamously, as single parents, working at various jobs—and with an astonishing range of political, social, and spiritual commitments. It occurred to me that in that room alone there was an enormous vitality and rich resources for examining the content of the course. I decided to try and tap what was available and work from their experiential knowledge as a base. Rather than have them run around the country—or the library stacks—making superficial studies of different "peoples," why not engage them in an in-depth study of themselves, as social, psychological, and cultural actors?

TOOLS FOR INDIVIDUAL AND COLLECTIVE INQUIRY

In order to use the class as a community—and to generate social scientific statements about it—we needed to develop tools and techniques suited to that purpose. It would not do to simply insist that social and psychological factors are crucial to intelligently shaping the environment—although we did so insist—and then let the students run free. We needed exercises, assignments, and methods of inquiry which would allow the students to reveal to themselves and to each other that for which they would be the best informants—the social structure of their own lives. And to have this happen in the most unself-conscious way possible.

WORK GROUPS

Working in groups is a common feature of many design studios. In this course, however, we took groups seriously not only as "task forces" to complete design projects, but also as a microsetting in which students would learn social science content. We started using photographs immediately, and our hope was that the students in work groups —and in the class as a whole—would derive some sort of detailed, precise, and yet experiential understanding of others taking the course. To do so, of course, required the use of exercises which both revealed students as exemplars and yet protected them as individuals within the setting of the studio.

We began with an exercise in which students brought in ten photographs of the environments that meant something to them, pictures which ideally contained images of the people who use those places. At first we had the students bring these photographs from books and magazines. After one quarter, however, I realized that it was important to the long-range goal of the class—to design something—that students actually make the photographs from scratch. This meant that they had to look for something in the world and catch it at a moment when it was working in a way they considered to be important.

This catching the place while it is "working" is a lot like architectural design itself. Designing places is really designing settings for life activity, and you have to have that activity in your minds eye as an ongoing situation in order to design the setting. For the designer the setting must not be a passive receptacle waiting to be filled; it must be conceived of in response to an ongoing act.

As a result of these concerns, we quickly had students switch to making photographs themselves, color slides, and showing them in groups. The picture shows which emerged from this assignment were wonderful, and at times they took up an entire week—of our ten-week quarter—during which I spent my time with 5 or 6 groups of fifteen students and looked at all their photographs. The photographs were not only interesting, but also productive of a lot of spin-offs. People began to talk to each other about the photographs, for example, and when the design work of the class really got underway, the photographs remained for the group as a sort of shared life experience. A student would say, for example, "Well, I can't tell you exactly how this is going to look, but I want it to be like John's photograph of the attic when there was sun late in the afternoon, and we all were in the attic playing checkers." When we looked back to the 150 pictures that the 15 people in the group had shown, we could see that they spanned years of experience, and contained images of every ethnic, cultural, and individual setting. They were a remarkable collection of images brought together in one room over a period of a few days and a good collective base from which to work.

After a few years of this assignment, however, I dropped it, mainly because I wanted to try something else, an exercise that would actually get people into the work groups as well as give them access to each other once they were together.

The most extravagant exercise involved sixty pairs of photographs and a computer program. The exercise had three parts: In the beginning students viewed each pair (as color slides) and scored them as to their preferences (most preferred, preferred, least preferred). These data were fed into a program which worked something like "The Dating Game," but using a graded scale; those with similar preferences were shown to have a higher affinity for one another than those with dissimilar preferences.

Then we placed the same pictures in the studio as full-blown color photocopies in the same pairs. Students had to write a statement about their preferences for one image or another, and the statements and photographs stayed up for the first week of the term. We also structured some discussion and interaction around the photographs so that people could argue for or against pictures. In these discussions a rich range of attitudes about life, self, work, and architecture were revealed or at least suggested by the students' comments. There was one very important lesson in this for the students: the disparities between the personal reasons for having preferred the same photographs.

This process worked well for the purposes we had in mind, and students formed themselves into groups after having had this rather revealing encounter with each other through the photographs.

VISUALIZATION

Photographs were thus used to generate a common starting point for the course, to represent cultural and physical settings and interactions, and to introduce students to each other in terms of the social science design content of the course. As the class progressed we also called on photographic assignments to help students visualize a design problem or to resolve an ambiguity within their work groups.

For example, four or five people working as a team inevitably reach the point where they have to conceptualize three-dimensionally, taking their project beyond a written agreement about what it should be or a functional diagram of how it might work. This is a very difficult moment for the team because verbal agreements and flow diagrams are not very explicit. Bill says that he likes a green lawn and a house in the country and Mary agrees, but if they try to build this house together Bill discovers and labels Mary a hippie because she likes old sawed lumber and she doesn't mind a broken car in the front yard, whereas he . . . and so on.

To turn the ambiguity of a design program and group agreement into the reality of individual differences requires a vehicle for developing finely detailed visualizations. Students have to make a conceptual leap from agreements about how life should be and what the environment should be like to something into which they would actually walk and hang their hat inside the door. Therefore, before they started working three-dimensionally, we asked them to bring in pictures of the kind of architecture each would like the design to resemble. These were useful in revealing both areas of agreement and disagreement between members of the group, and they clarified positions enough so that the group could proceed.

THE PHOTOGRAPHIC FIGURES

In some sense the use of work groups to explore the social and psychological dynamics of those within it only dealt with part of the problem of teaching social science to design students. There are other difficulties to be encountered, and some of them are closely tied to the professional practice of architecture, notably, the conventional presentation drawing. There is a remarkable incongruity between the detail and precision with which physical structures are drawn and the ambiguity and clumsiness with which human figures are sketched into the setting. Many human figures in architectural drawings look comical or grotesque: people walking dogs and pushing baby carriages all look square-headed, incredibly skinny, and unreal. I have always had an unpleasant feeling that those distorted images of human beings make their way into the students' mind, and become the people for whom the place is really designed. Furthermore, I suspect that the grotesque figure is only the tip of an iceberg of disdain which lies underneath. These drawing conventions suggest that the building is something very superior to the people. Architects would never make their buildings look comical, but they make people look absolutely ridiculous. This is problematic in the profession in general and especially so in a course on social, psychological, and cultural dynamics.

At first I worked at this "disdain" for the human form and human activity by asking students to draw their figures very carefully, asking them to be quite precise, and suggesting that the scale of the building is really jeopardized if the scale of the figures is not correct. From the first we had worked with both drawings and models—always at a very large scale (one-half inch equaling one foot)—and I insisted that students try to draw the people and what they were doing as well as they drew the building.

One day we had a guest in the studio and I was showing him around, discussing the students' models. He commented on the precise way students were drawing the figures, and in a brief flurry of comments I said, "Wait until next quarter, because then all the little people are going to be photographs of the students themselves and of those they call their clients." It was an idea that stuck. I was trying to get students to respect the process of putting themselves into the environment. I had talked to them about this and we had discussed it many times, but here was a technical vehicle by which we could actually do it. The photographs of students—which they made to the same scale as they had made the drawings—became for me an assurance that they were imagining themselves to be inside the environments they designed.

The implications of this decision were almost overwhelming to the process of the class. To this day I will never know what students are really thinking when they use the photographic figures. Both in conversation and in the way they use the figures, however, they reveal an immense amount of information about their own understanding of social life and the social order. When these individual relations are brought together within the course, the little photographic figures appear almost as a simulation of the community of the class, a representation of what goes on and what students think ought to go on in the world. It is a community one step removed from the students themselves, and that makes it a bit safe. It is a community so deeply grounded in their own experience, however, that it gets to the heart of what they know and want to be true.

For example, on the architectural side the figures are very helpful because the photograph is absolutely precise and very real looking, appropriately shaded, and with all body features in perfect balance. Gestures are genuine and explicit. In contrast, the modeling materials for the structures are quite crude: cardboard walls and blocks of wood for furniture, pieces of cloth for carpeting, and so on. When these explicit human images are juxtaposed with the fairly crude environment, however, everything takes on a heightened realism.

"**You could look** at the design and feel good that a part of you was in it, that your identity was respected by the others and you could get pleasure from having been a part of the group process."

"**We wanted to prove** that people should live closer together, share more things and in doing so, gain from each other, give and take, save energy, enrich their minds and bodies. All in all, live, not just vegetate."

In terms of a projective device, the figures contribute immensely to work in the studio. Through their presence you step into the simulated world they occupy. In this way, as an outsider, one comes closer to entering the world as the students had projected it in the design they had made. Students use the figures ingeniously. And the arrangement and disposition of the figures can tell you a great deal about what the students are thinking as to the appropriateness of the design for certain human conditions: ethnicity, sexuality, age, ways of being alone, and the interactions of people. For example, if a student says, "This is a good place for my grandmother who's elderly," and you look in the model and see a photographic figure of a person forty years old, you get the sense that the student has had a somewhat limited experience with older people. But this can then help you to broaden the student's point of view about the elderly. Or if you see a group of students designing an environment for elderly people, and they have installed photographic figures of only elderly women, you then have a basis of inquiry with the group. In finding out what they know, you learn a great deal about what they don't know: "Are there no elderly men in the world?" you may ask, and by their responses uncover the attitudes about elderly men underlying the design they have made.

Projective statements made with the figures are not restricted to student images of the social world, however, and the photographic figures also reveal something of what is going on with individuals in their own lives. For example, a student might be designing a house in which she says she's thirty-four years old and living with an older man who has two children by a former wife. According to her they are going to try and make a go of it, and she's making a place for them in a rich communal environment. She's doing beautifully, and then one day you come over and discover she's added an older woman to the household. When you ask how this changes things—without being too personal (this is a design class, not a therapy group)—the student says that she's at that age now where she's really interested in the lives of older women. And then the next time you come by you discover she's torn up the whole thing. She's thrown out the man and his two children and left the older woman, who she's now decided is really more her mother than "an older woman." She tells you that she's now at a point in her life when she's interested in finding out something about her relationship to the man she was living with and feels her mother can be helpful to her in working the issue through.

In addition to images of social reality and the lives of individual students, the photographic figures also suggest some of the social life of the studio itself. There might be seventy to eighty students in the

Acting out senarios

The proposed environment

course working in twenty groups of four and five. Each group is responsible for designing accommodations for twenty-five or thirty people. So, we have now several hundred to a couple of thousand photographed figures in the studio at one time. Because the students are asked to live in the things that they're making, you can see reflected in their work some of the realities as well as their fantasies about life with their classmates: who's looking after whom, who's in charge, and who's not joining in too well. If they designed for a family, who did they pick to be mother, father, and the children and in what relationships do they appear?

In some other kinds of courses, these personal projections of the students and their work groups might be less important, but in the design studio—particularly one in which social and psychological issues are a major theme—they are serious business. In some sense the images which students have of the world are the primary information they use in their design process. In order to refine and inform that image, it is important to know what it is to begin with, and the manner in which they manipulate the photographic figures can provide important clues. Because the students have photographed themselves as residents of their structures, the design process is additionally clarified, for they have to act both as "architect" and as "clients" for the structures they design.

SOCIAL EXPERIMENTATION

There is an additional feature of these scaled-down "people" that makes them an essential contribution to the student's learning process—their participation in social experiments.

A student might say, "I don't really know how large this room should be," and you could ask, "Well, what's the largest function that's going to take place in it?" Let's say the student tells you that it's a fairly intimate space, one that would have at the most fifteen or twenty people in it. You can tell the student to collect fifteen or twenty photographic figures of people he or she would like to have in that space at one time in the postures or poses in which they would most likely be engaged. The student collects a set: some sitting, some standing, some eating, or playing the guitar. And then you ask him or her to get the furnishings together that are needed for the gathering and to arrange it. After all this is in place the student can begin to construct or manipulate walls and roofs and other architectural elements.

What is important about this process is that the "building"—in this case a model—goes up *after* the student has taken a look at the social activity characteristic of the setting; the student starts with the people

"**Through much discussion** I think we began to realize that changing our whole lifestyles 180° from that whole American ideal of the single family dwelling to the loosely defined 'what's mine is yours' was going to be much more difficult than just picturing it in our minds."

"**Basically, I'm saying** that what hindered us was a lack of a different basic viewpoint within the group. Of course, this is not the answer to a successful group, since this having someone from a different background usually results in communication problems."

and then designs a structure to house and facilitate what they are inclined to do.

A second feature of this "social experimentation" is generated by
moving the figures around, having them try out the physical structure.
As a teacher you can say, "O.K., this looks good, but now suppose these
three women decide to leave or this man begins to play the guitar. What
then? How's the structure going to work under that rearrangement of
activity?" You can actually move the figures to the new position,
manipulate them, let them age or become sick and infirm, take them
through changes of lifestyle, economic hardship, energy crises, diet,
or even remove them from the setting altogether. And by asking what
difference this imposed change makes to the design of the setting the
student is more likely able to clarify those attitudes and assumptions
about the person which helped shape the setting as a design.

These experiments in the simulation of activity do not give us back
empirical evidence revealing how people actually would act in the setting, but they do demand that the student clarify his or her own understanding of the phenomena. And, if there is activity about which the
student simply does not know enough, we can then begin to talk about
how to find it out.

REINFORCING THE PROFESSIONAL ROLE

There is one additional use to which we put photography in this
course, and that is, to take pictures of the models and the scale figures in
process and on completion of the projects. These photographs have
proved to be invaluable in teaching subsequent courses, for they give
students images of a variety of ways in which the figures and models can
be used. In addition, the practice of photographing the models is seen
to pay a certain kind of professional attention to the students' work.
This attention is enlarged on when photographs of one class's projects
are shown to other students during the following term.

Taken together these aspects of photographing the students work
have contributed a sense of continuity to the studio course. Former
students come back to see what their successors are doing, and there
is a wonderful sense in which the figures and models and students
themselves are affirmed through photographic documentation of what
they have done. The kind of studio culture which this course has built
generates a lot of enthusiasm and interest among entering students,
and makes them a rather nice group to begin to teach.

"**We simply began** to see the necessity of privacy . . . 'communalism' in the terms we had been picturing it . . . demanded things from us that we simply were not willing to give."

"**It is interesting** to note that at the end of the quarter he admitted that he may have done certain things to maintain a leadership image through his actions in the project. A good example of this is his use of the crumpled paper for the representation of the bushes on the site. It was something he did and left for the rest of us to comment on or to follow."

CAUTIONS AND CONCLUSIONS

The use of the photographic figures to simulate activity and life processes is a powerful vehicle for classroom teaching. The power of these figures, images, and models, however, is not necessarily contained within the academic process of the course. As a result, I think it is important to exercise a certain caution, not so much in directing how the figures are to be used by the students, but more in creating an appropriate context in which the figures and models can be interpreted and assessed.

For example, when commenting on a student's use of the figures, I think that teachers ought to restrict their remarks to what is appropriate to the academic goals of the class. The figures themselves and the projections they make possible are very potent and they provide a palpable—but dangerous—vehicle for psychoanalysis or therapy. Students are not in the class to be psychoanalyzed, however, and it seems to me that the teachers ought to be clear that they are not there for that either.

Caution also should be exercised in critiquing the production of the figures. For example, one day I looked into a student's model environment and saw that the heads on all the figures he had photographed had been cut off. I was really distressed by seeing that, but was even more alarmed when the student told me that this particular setting being made was one in which to go mad. This was the first time that I'd seen something other than a desire to make something good or nice or beautiful with the figures and models, and I didn't know how to respond. The student's work really contradicted my own religiosity about architecture—that it is a positive thing.

The more I talked with the student and a colleague, Suzanne Crowhurst Lennard, who was working with me at that time, the clearer it became that the thing he was making was to his mind beautiful, but that it was also frightening. Work with the figures is one way of encouraging students to be a little more open, but if you choose this route you then have to be prepared to be surprised. Students have conflicts which will emerge if given the chance, and one way for them to emerge is through their treatment of the figures. Or, they will design places in which to experience feelings other than happiness—feelings of grief, depression, despair, and the like. Using the figures and simulations brings a whole range of experience into the classroom which might otherwise be kept out. This is one of the most important values of the approach, but it also represents a major liability. The simulations should not be taken lightly, and the teacher has to remain sensitive and thoughtful in working through their meanings with the class.

In my own teaching the photographic figures and models have made a real contribution. Together they have allowed students to experience the importance of social, psychological, and cultural dynamics to the design process. Through the use of these simulations I have been able to underline the important wisdom that architecture is in no way value-free and that there is no such thing as "pure design" in environments designed for people. Everything we make has significance for social life and cultural processes. Whatever we design for someone else can be no better than our understanding of that person.

These are lessons of especial importance to design students. They have to know themselves, and they have to make a significant effort to know the selves of those for whom they design. In applying knowledge about human activity to the design process, architects must learn to recognize their own projections. If social science is going to contribute to design, it must make its way into the very language by which architects and planners talk about the world. For those of us who teach, the language can be found with much of its complexity and power intact in photographic figures, scale models, and studio simulations.

HUMAN/ENVIRONMENT ENCOUNTERS

16

ENCOUNTERS

W. Russell Ellis

If it is true that each of us carries around an implicit theory of human personality or behavior based on continuing experiences . . . it is probably no less true that architects, designers, and planners have built into this theory something about people in relation to places and spaces. . . . [A] process of 'exposure' would in all probability reveal the implicit assumptions about people and their behavior that underlie the architect or designer's approach to designing space [Harold Proshansky, 1974: 80].

Designers have good eyes. They have the talent or wind up with the skill to *see* their conceptual problems and visually represent them to each other in very efficient forms. The graphic conventions—especially in architecture—are quite old and stable, and a great deal of information about proposed or existing buildings is readily communicated through them. Among the stuff the designer's seeing gathers and rearrays for graphic presentation are elements of style, manner, mass, material, order, and form. Because his or her recognized task is also to create enclosures which facilitate life conduct, however, this vision must include some active pictures or outlines of what it is that people do at work, play, dwelling, worship and in all the little suboccasions of which housed social life is comprised.

Architecture is not itself a discipline, but it takes advantage of the method, theory, and practice of other endeavors which are. It is a business, and, when good, a humane craft. Many of its practitioners and commentators have thought of it as art. The inevitable content of its practice includes people, but—save for anthropometric calculations of technicians and wide-ranging speculation by those architects most admired in the profession—there have been no consistently explored or explicit images of human action in built things. Great American architects like Louis Sullivan and Frank Lloyd Wright have held out the prospect of a socially informed architecture. Sullivan argued that "to discuss architecture and to ignore life is frivolous." Wright went so far as to describe the architect in such a way that we could "expect of him a system of philosophy and ethics which is a synthesis of society and civilization." Generally, the right to an audience for such social speculation has had little to do with an architect's base of social knowledge. Rather, it has reflected the esteem in which an architect's artistic work is held. What is more, such reflections seem most palatable to the architectural community when reduced to aphoristic formulae. At least since Sir Henry Wooten ("Well building hath three Conditions, Commodite, Firmeness, and Delight.") these formulae have either hidden, or, at best, only indirectly implied actors and action in relation to built form. We can guess that delight is someone's experience, but where, for example, is the human encounter in Le Corbusier's "house" which "is a machine for living"? (See Jeanneret-Gris 1960).

IMPLICIT SOCIAL THEORY IN THE PRACTICE
OF ARCHITECTURE

Eight years ago, when I first began working with architectural designers and students, I noticed a seeing-linked ability I call "imaginative self-projection" which seemed to get architects visually in touch with what the human experience of a proposed design might be. I was especially stimulated by an observation of Robert Maxwell's

> We look at plans and we imagine doors swinging, drawers being pulled, corridors full of racing feet, people falling down unexpected steps or jamming on landings. We compare the drawing with similar drawings or with actual building in our memory store and we say, with considerable confidence, it wouldn't work, the circulations would cross, the corridor is too narrow, the room is claustrophobic, the wc's are too far away, the waiting space is intimidating, and so on.

> In other words, we attribute to the drawings or models operational qualities based on our own experience, and assess the performance which we would expect, imagining the building built and us in it [Perin, 1970: 116].

Over and over again in design sessions or studio "crits" I heard designs referred to as if they were occupied. The traditional architectural program encourages this tendency through articulation of the prospective design's using clients and their activities: a family of five, "low cost housing," a day care center, a factory for the production of electronic equipment, and the like. For some experienced architects such a program will prod their visual imagination beyond the mere square footages or equipment specified. In greatest measure, however, the "occupants" which architects project into their designs and plans are quite abstract, and design education itself has only recently begun to address in any immediate detail the *content* of human activity.

One can easily understand the necessary abstractness of actors and action in the frequent instances where the using clients of a proposed building are in large measure anonymous, e.g.; a public bureaucracy. What has come to interest me, however, are the features of the implicit actor who lurks in the designer's imputations. What is this model actor like who falls down steps, for whom drawers jam, who has the experience of claustrophobia, and the like?

It is a question I have been exploring in various ways. My effort has been to encourage architects and designers to make explicit their models of social activity and human behavior so that these might be tested out against the real world of the people for whom they presume to design. To do so in the classroom, I recently designed a number of exercises. These were developed to better understand student modes of expression —to meet them half-way—and better communicate my own version of a relevant sociology.

The exercises themselves are lodged within the context of a more general question: How is it that we organize our various understandings of social life? I have found in my work with architects and designers that Alfred Schutz's formulation—directed toward social science itself —is remarkably applicable.

Schutz (1962) contended that the peculiar stance of the scientist of society is that of having no "Here"—no living locus—around which the meaningful social life she or he attempts to understand can be spread. Even the participant-observer in the field setting, he contended, only temporarily drops the "scientific attitude" in order to make close experiential contact with the group being studied. Presumably, this temporary adoption of a position in the field gives the participant some advantages in understanding the subjective meaning to actors of their observed social behavior. But, ultimately, the scientific attitude requires not only understanding, but the actual "construction of some model of the social world and the actors in it." To make sense of observed behavior, the scientist invents an actor with features related to the phenomenon under investigation (e.g., status occupancy, family life, power, and the like). The scientist supplies the invented actor with a "fictitious consciousness." Schutz imagines this invented actor as a kind of puppet or "homunculus" and, in a critique of the social sciences, says,

> these models of actors are not human beings living within their biographical situation in the social world of everyday life. Strictly speaking, they do not have any biography or any history, and the situation into which they are placed is not a situation defined by them but by their creator, the social scientist. He has created these puppets or homunculi to manipulate them for his purpose. A merely specious consciousness is imputed to them . . . which is constructed in such a way that its presupposed stock of knowledge at hand . . . would make actions originating

from it subjectively understandable, provided that these actions were performed by real actors within the social world. But the puppet and his artificial consciousness is not subjected to the ontological conditions of human beings. The homunculus was not born, he does not grow up, and he will not die. He has no hopes and no fears; he does not know anxiety as the chief motive of all his deeds. He is not free in the sense that his acting could transgress the limits his creator, the social scientist, has predetermined. He cannot, therefore, have other conflicts or interests and motives than those the social scientist has imputed to him. He cannot err, if to err is not his typical destiny. He cannot choose, except among the alternatives the social scientist has put before him [1962: 41].

What is interesting about Schutz's observations—aside from its critique—is his speculative examination of a way of working by which students of society "model" a real phenomenon in order to understand it. Architects, I have discovered, because they have focused on building, have a distinctive set of tendencies in their modelling of users. They differ greatly from Schutz's characterization of the social scientist.

ARCHITECTS' HOMUNCULI

Architects characteristically assume meaning and potential action to reside in things. They do not usually make a clear connection between human interchange and the resultant *deposit* of meaning in "mere" things. The architect's homunculus, is often featureless and emerges first as disembodied actions interlarded among a design's details. Actions float free. As in Maxwell's comment, there are "doors swinging, drawers being pulled, corridors full of racing feet." There are "circulations" which cross. Unlike the social scientist's invented actor, consciousness does not appear to be a common feature of architects' homunculi. Indeed, in imaginatively moving through designs with some architects you get the impression that an indistinctly motivated lump of somatic stuff—born in and taking the shape of bubbles in a bubble diagram—is being conducted, via arrows, along paths and loci of "circulation," "living," "eating," and so on. It is not extreme to say that, for many designers, the architecture *creates* the homunculus. The emergent plan generates the action of the somatic lump, and, as the design takes on added features, so does the puppet. But this little being, though animated by the designer, tends to remain passive, decorative, and unobtrusive of the design's flow. The plan is the puppeteer.

THE COURSE

It was in response to this severe abstraction of imagined human form and activity and against hard architectural determinism, rampant even among students, that the following lower-division undergraduate course was offered:

The Built Environment in Use

Buildings and clusters of buildings are often seen as forms, sequences of spaces, objects inventively arranged in space, etc. The aim of this course is to help beginning students of environmental design (and other lower-division students with a general interest) to develop an orientation to the built environment which includes attention *to both buildings and the personal and social worlds* which surround and infuse them. The goal, concretely, is to elevate the patterned varieties of human association in groups, families, at work, play, celebration, residence, etc., to an equal level with the things of the environment.

The medium of this effort will be the camera. It will be used to consciously frame and "capture" units of human-environmental association from the level of the room through the dwellings, public areas, offices, etc.

Basically, the goals of the course were:

—To woo the student away from inclinations toward an environmental deterministic conception of the built environment and toward an interactionist one (Ellis, 1974).

—To develop an ethnographic attitude toward the camera as a tool; to get the student to move, as it were, empathetically through the lens toward the scenes framed and captured employing some sense of self-experience.

—To get students visually to play with a literal physical model of a person in a way which might highlight the relationship between meaning in things and meaning in human interaction.

The selection of the camera as an instrument for class exercises came from the fact that the camera has become the recording instrument-of-choice for design students. It has replaced the traditional sketchbook in capturing everything from corners of rooms to an array of people seated on a ledge. The haptic empathy which is part of drawing is not a necessary feature of photography. Indeed, the simplicity, elegance, and speed of current inexpensive photographic equipment may make it particularly easy *not* to attend to the human experience in scenes captured on film. The course was structured to at least bring such matters to the attention of the students and have them individually and collectively approach the world of built things-in-use with these issues in mind.

These goals and issues were built into the course through discussions of topics such as: observing the environment of human relations; seeing things and people simultaneously; the social nature of the self and others; accurate and inaccurate imputations of actions, meaning, and subjective states; and issues of the looking, seeing, observing, framing and capturing characteristic of photographic work. These topics were further elaborated through examination of a simple and relevant text: Ashcraft and Scheflen's *People Space: The Making and Breaking of Human Boundaries.* In addition, I led the class on an excursion through a set of sociospatial concepts from the social science literature. A final feature of the course was a series of presentations by visiting lecturers of slides they had taken themselves and were prepared to talk about in terms of framing and intent.

THE EXERCISES

Some developments in the design instruction "culture" of my department provided the opportunity to begin primitive play with models of people in relation to the physical environment and to insinuate some sociological ideas into that relationship during the play. One instructor found inventive ways to use scale-model, cut-out photographic images of people—usually the students themselves—in the act of using the spaces they had collaboratively designed. (See Lifchez Chapter 15 in this volume). Other faculty used this device as well, but it achieved interesting proportions when a colleague developed, in the basic graphics course, a series of exercises dealing with light and shade. One of these required individual students to project a photographic slide of themselves onto a cardboard surface, and draw in, with various techniques, the features and textures of face, clothing, and so on, then cut the life-sized figure out and place it somewhere in the departmental environment. These figures, scattered throughout the building, were sometimes astonishing for the life-like feeling they gave to those coming on them all-of-a-sudden or who caught them in peripheral vision. The cardboard cut-outs were also recognizable individuals whose alter-images could be seen walking around the building (photos 1 and 2). Early in the course I used these figures, stored from a previous academic quarter, to generate the following exercise:

ASSIGNMENT #1

This assignment involves your interpretation of "normal" and unusual relationships between life and things of life. A CONGRUENT ("normal") relationship between people and things is one which does not surprise the eye or the mind of an average member of the society.

The goal of this assignment is to have you investigate congruence and incongruence between people and human-made things.

(A) In Tom Stone's office (Wurster Hall, Room 103) you will find several **life-sized cardboard figures of people. Take one of these figures**

Photo 1

Photo 2

(overnight only, please). Submit *one* photograph of the figure in the most CONGRUENT relationship to a setting of physical things.

(B) Submit *one* photograph of two (real) people involved in an activity **as INCONGRUENT as possible with the physical things in, on or** around which the activity is being conducted. (This photograph may be either posed or natural).

(C) Submit *one* photograph of a thing in which a great amount of human activity has been deposited.

You may use any camera you can find for this assignment, but do not edit the photographs in the darkroom or with scissors.

Mount each photo separately on a four by six (inch) card.

The very simple definition of "congruence" was recommended by the early stage in the course at which the assignment was given. That is, students had not been exposed to any social science literature at the time. The strategy of the exercise was twofold: to put unreal people in a situation which produced the illusion of greatest reality; to put real people in the most unreal situations. The first notion was intended to heighten the understanding of the physical setting's contribution to the social meaning of situations. The second was to heighten the students' understanding of the physical setting's connection to the meaning of gatherings, and so on, by dislodging "normal" human gatherings and occasions (Ellis, 1971) from their expected settings, thereby enhancing the sense of their normal connectedness.

The third part of the exercise was intended to have a physical thing "speak back" the human activity and relations with which it was associated and from which it derived its meaning. The language "life" and "things of life" derived from an unplanned doubling back in the course which I had to undertake in order to show graphically how certain themes hung together.

THE PHOTOGRAPHS

Part three of the exercise elicited photographs of small items such as an old shoe, a coffee cup, an unmade bed, and the like. In general, the students were inclined to deal with very small objects throughout the exercise rather than with larger architectural elments.

The second part of the exercise produced fascinating photographs, e.g., two well-dressed women having tea seated on a cyclone fence! (sic), a card game in a bathtub, and so on, and in subsequent class discussion it emerged that students were surprised by the radically different ways they had of achieving relevant results.

The first part of the exercise, however, proved most difficult for the students to understand and execute. Simultaneously, it was most effec-

Photo 3a

Photo 3b

Photo 4a

Photo 4b

tive in highlighting connections between thing, person, patterned association, meaning, and so on. Keep in mind that the cardboard people were not created by members of the class who used them. Whatever gestural animation they contained was placed there by others at a prior time and for other purposes. Also, the students were to make the implied animation "unsurprising" to the "ordinary" eye by finding a "setting of physical things" with which it was congruent. In the final photographs students were outstanding at finding physical settings which absorbed the figures into unsurprising normalcy—even if they occasionally appeared silly—and they found a wide variety of ways to accomplish this goal (see photos 3-6).

Three major devices were used: (1) Making the gesture and the set of physical props *narrowly* related, emphasizing the limited range of meanings normally associated with the physical props (see photos 3 and 4). The narrowness of the connection resides in the fact that we cannot read the recent interactional histories or likely social destinations of the woman in photos 3a and 3b. That is, we do not know from the scenes depicted what she has recently been doing, with whom or why. Nor do we know the role the surrounding physical environment plays in these doings. By contrast, in photos 4a and 4b the students' use of meaningfully loaded physical props, especially the police car, allows us more confidently to invent a recent past and, in photo 4a future interactional scenes for the person depicted. There is a somewhat more expansive meaning deposited in the gesture, the prop and, thus, the encounter between both.

(2) Using live people to pull out and connect the gestural aspects of the cardboard models to the physical setting. This device missed the point of the assignment by the widest mark. Examples are photos 5b and 6c. If we compare photos 5a and 5b, for example, it is clear in photo 5a how the physical link to the model tells a story dependent on that link alone, whereas, in photo 5b, the story of the scene points to or emanates from the social link *rather than pointing to the social as suggested by the supportive physical setting,* which was the goal of the assignment.

(3) Having the meaningful load carried by both the gesture of the model and the prop in such a way as to suggest a wide complex of interactional relations beyond the scene. This was the best response to the assignment, but was infrequent. An excellent example is in photo 6a. The student had, without doubt, the advantage of a clear and normatively delimited world of social rules to work with—the game of soccer. But the desired link is made more effectively than in photos 6b and 6c where, respectively, another person is employed or the residue of

Photo 5a

Photo 5b

Photo 6a

Photo 6b

Photo 6c

another's action, in the form of a flying football, is used to animate the gesture and give the setting meaning.

The course ended with a second major exercise which attempted to benefit from the earlier explorations. Students formed into groups of five or more. I asked them to go out, find and photographically "capture" *Ecotopia: The Notebooks and Reports of Wilson Weston* (Callenbach). This novel is a description of a secessionist nation comprised of northern California, Oregon, and Washington. What is especially interesting about the novel is that the author, a resident of Berkeley, has nested his utopia in things, values, and activities visible and visibly acted out in (at the time) contemporary northwest styles in housing, clothing, demeanor, belief, and the like, clearly associated with a sort of "responsible" countercultural and environmentalist ethic. Lovemaking, technology, governance, sport, and so on, all operate in a systematic relationship contributing to the ecologically balanced and stable state: Ecotopia.

In reading the novel—which I assigned for the course—it became clear to me that Callenbach had intended to make the described utopia accessible by beginning with familiar and visible social scenes and tendencies: the world of Ecotopia begins with scenes discoverable in the Bay Area. Human actions are extensively described and the Ecotopian values associated with them are thoroughly articulated. The novel provided an excellent opportunity to have students attempt to visualize, through photography, the sociophysical world presented, indeed, to bring some representative concreteness to the novelist's humunculi.

Photos 7 and 8 are examples of some of the photographic results. The assignment required that the assembled scenes be associated with relevant quotes from the novel and that these, in turn, be assembled into a slide show. Prints from the slides were submitted to the author who then selected those (nearly half) which came closest to what he imagined his world to look like. Having given his fictional world features, his selected images were displayed for student inspection and discussion. They could see the author's image of his world as rendered by them.

CONCLUSION

Simulating or inventing worlds, novels, new towns, buildings and the like requires, at some minimal level of consciousness, that the inventor have an image of how things might be, might look, might work. Designers, in their purely inventive modes, must certainly be allowed their

Photo 7

Photo 8

physical selves in which the flow and cascade of novel ideas is not encumbered by the requirements of function, budgets, and the like. But, ultimately, the simulation and construction of the built environment involves practical imagination and the sources of designers' human imagery becomes crucial for the qualities of that environment. Even if a small percentage of our buildings are architect-designed, architects are still the fount and conduit of a great deal of our popular built-environmental imagery. Thus, in ways which are still unclear, the motivations and action animating the people in architects' heads give shape to the envelopes of our living.

The course I have described emerged from my conclusion that the design enterprise had become "bookish" with respect to human affairs. As the settings in which human enclosures are designed and executed become removed from the direct cultural experience of use, the content of "use" itself becomes similarly abstract and distant. The loss of this ethnographic closeness is critical for environmental design. When a culture's "voice" is muted on the meaning of forms such as houses, living rooms, schools, and the like, people have fewer resources for making clear and regular reports on what is or is not working for them, or at the least, such messages are slow to accumulate and difficult to read. At the same time, competing architectural versions of the human/environment encounter easily lead to a dominance of formal issues over human concerns. Herein lies the danger at which the exercises were aimed: a circumstance in which human beings become ornamental ciphers, cartoons to be colored with content by those interested in no more than design aesthetics and mere shelter. There is some urgency here, because the commodification of all life is being advanced by the cameras of commercial advertising (Ellis, 1976). In life as "advertised," our immediate environmental histories and futures imply acts of purchase, and human actions are parlayed as acts of consumption. For all these reasons, the battle for the content of the popular honunculus is very well advanced.

Static cardboard figures are not life, but by directing students to work photographically with small scenes—and with models of people in meaningful relation to these scenes—I was attempting to teach at that pivot peculiar to the designer's way of seeing. In imagined human encounters with the intended physical world, prospective designers might learn to see synthetically, to see the social in the physical and bring valuation to their interchange. Working to enliven this frozen place is a critical cultural task, and the camera is a principal tool for facing its challenge.

TRUTH AND PICTURES
"Fetishes," "Goodness," and "Clarity"

Martin H. Krieger

Truth and clarity are totalitarian notions if they are taken to imply a single vision of our world. But lying is not an acceptable alternative to truth, for systematic falsehood, as Hannah Arendt argues, would make it impossible for us to carry on our political lives. A vision of our lives, a picture of what is good and proper and just, and a way of conducting ourselves so that the vision is achievable, is also required.

Clarity and truth are dominant notions in the critical tradition of photography. Sometimes they have been signified by sharpness, at other times by showing the less pleasant sides of a society, and at others by emphasizing the spiritual. When photography is directed towards investigation, documentary, and social research, then clarity and truth have to be used carefully if they are not to end up reproducing structures of hierarchy and domination already embedded in our visual world. The meaning of "clarity" should not be restricted to modes of discourse and picturing characteristic of the most powerful in a society. And clarity may differ from truth, for the clear may well be false and the true may not be clear.

These theoretical ideas have important implications for applying social research, and they arise out of concrete problems. I teach courses in the foundations of public policy in a school of public affairs, planning, and administration. After having done a good deal of teaching about methodology, I felt the need for more substantive discussions with my students, most of whom were to become bureaucrats. In their future vocational roles, they would have to exercise judgment according to what they thought was "good" within a situation. I decided to study "goodness" with them for a quarter. We read Nietzsche's marvelous dissection of the idea in *The Genealogy of Morals* and *Beyond Good and Evil*. My interest in photography and social research—derived in part from a course with Paul Byers at Columbia more than ten years ago —led me to incorporate photography into the courses as well.

As an experiment I asked students to examine goodness visually: by finding pictures about which they had strong feelings; by finding pictures of good things, persons, places; and then by taking pictures of what they thought was good. They were trained neither in photography nor in other visual arts. I expected them to be somewhat less sophisticated in visual media than in writing and verbal argumentation, but it seemed worth trying. If they were unsophisticated they would have a lot to learn, and the course would be especially valuable for them.

Nietzsche showed how very particular qualities became associated with the abstract notion of goodness. He argued that this is an historical process and represents a political triumph of certain values over others. Hence, picturing goodness is a political activity, a study in the particular signs of value (which we might call fetishes) in a society. And it turned out that the students in the class reproduced, through their photographs, dominant values (such as ecological quality or modernity in architecture) in highly stylized ways, often depending on small, almost invisible cues to signal what they meant. In our discussions two questions became intertwined: how do the particular signifiers of goodness or value dominate what we think of as good; and, how can we be visually "articulate" and effective.

HOW THE COURSE WAS TAUGHT

The course was taught in a ten-week quarter, meeting twice a week. One meeting was devoted to discussing the reading from Nietzsche. At first I was mainly concerned with explaining his aims and modes of argument. Later in the quarter I spent more time on the connections between what we had been reading and the issues that came up in discussing the photographs. What might have seemed like disparate material began to come together. We also read Hannah Arendt's *Eichmann in Jerusalem: A Report on the Banality of Evil.* This reading encouraged us to return to some very concrete issues, now illuminated by the theoretical work we had been doing.

Our other meeting each week concerned photography. At first I lectured a bit about photography and showed lots of pictures I liked. I said very little, however, about photographic theory, such as about how the camera differs from the eye. I showed many books and collections of photographs, not just individual pictures which might be taken as precious artworks. I told students to purchase and read either Ralph Hattersley's *Discover Yourself Through Photography* or Charles Gatewood's *People in Focus.* And I mentioned Hine's (1932) and Winogrand's (1979, 1977) work because they happened to be getting a lot of coverage in the popular press.

Fortunately, just as the course began, the Walker Art Center opened a show of Photojournalism in Minnesota over the past forty years. We met at the show and I analyzed various pictures, how they worked, just what made them effective. The large exhibition prints were useful for noting details and for a discussion of the peculiar demands of newspaper reproduction compared to the capabilities of photographic papers. I could talk about how goodness worked in photographs and about some of the technical problems in conveying it.

I did not train students in taking pictures, and they used whatever cameras they had. I recommended commercial processing because they had limited time for the course and I did not want to get them involved with darkroom techniques just then. They could crop (cut up) a snapshot to have some control over composition, and I pointed out some of the problems of the small size of their pictures so they could appreciate what could be done in a darkroom.

I asked students to keep diaries of their intentions before they obtained or took photographs so that they might compare those intentions with the images they made or found. I encouraged them to think ahead of time about what they wanted to photograph. Because most people in the university think verbally and not pictorially, it might have been better to encourage students to do a lot more looking (and picture taking) before the diary work. Experienced photographers, on the other hand, might be able to think about a story ahead of time with greater benefit.

The initial exercises, as I mentioned above, were to find pictures about which they had strong feelings. I did not specify whether the strong feelings concerned the picture or the subject matter or both. As a result, some pictures were chosen because they were beautiful or ugly, and some because of what they showed about the world. The sentiments might be abstract yet about poverty, or quite concrete and centered on the idea of the American family.

In a second exercise, students brought in their own pictures of what they had thought was good. It was more difficult for them to distance themselves from these, to examine them as cultural artifacts reflecting particular styles and fashions about goodness. I found that I had to allow lots of time for looking at pictures, being quiet, letting the class discover things among themselves. Telling is not enough. They have to learn to rely on their own eyes.

At this point in the course I assigned further reading. I had them look at Wilson Hicks' article on photojournalism in R. S. Schuneman, *Photographic Communication,* John Szarkowski's discussions in *Looking at Photographs*, his introductory remarks in *The Photographer's Eye,* and some of Howard Becker's sociological articles in *Afterimage,* and in the *American Sociological Review* (1974). I could have assigned James Agee on Walker Evans or Helen Levitt, or something by Wright Morris, Ken Heyman, or Margaret Mead. I wanted to hint at some of the standard ways we think about photographs without giving students a course in theory.

In the rest of the course students took photographs, essentially on their own assignment. They had to take pictures of something that had become a fetish, something that preoccupies and obsesses them. How did alternative meanings slip in? They also had to do two small picture stories about things that were good and had value for them. They had to rely on pictures, not text, to do most of the work. How do pictures add up to make a story? How do you control the viewer and manage his or her possible interpretations of a set of photographs?

I had a great deal of trouble effectively demonstrating to students how the photographs worked and did not work. As I will discuss below, my critical method defeated my own theory. Our conflicts and disagreements took many forms. One student wanted to make artistically effective photographs. Another, in architecture, and much more visually aware than anyone else in the class, let his taste for design overtake the story he wanted to tell. And, teaching in Minnesota, I had many students who irrationally valued rural life as much as I irrationally valued urban life. Overwhelming all these differences, however, was the pervasive power of currently popular styles of photography. What magazines featured deeply influenced what people thought was the proper way to photograph.

The students sometimes wanted to know what I was looking for. What would satisfy me? I was not sure. I was hunting for certain kinds of photographs and certain kinds of concerns. I thought I had made clear by the kinds of photographs—documentary, photojournalism, social reform, people—I showed them and the reading I assigned. But I could not clearly articulate my expectations, and they could not read my mind, in part because they could not read pictures very well. Only now am I capable of saying more about what I was up to.

ISSUES ABOUT ULTIMATE VALUES

I wanted to explore the role of ultimate values such as goodness or justice in social research and public policy. Photographs are not only used as illustrations of concepts and as expressions of these ultimate values, but ground our understanding of them. Our discussions focused on the manner in which concepts were pictured, and on how the detail of a particular photograph related to more general notions, that is, on how concepts are developed.

I was interested in the relationship of words to actual pictures, and the manner in which these come to be known together. Nietzsche argued that this was true even for abstract notions such as goodness. In this context, the idea that concepts are subsequently *illustrated*—as if first there are concepts and then illustrations—is misleading, for we always draw on a set of prior pictures of a concept rather than starting with nothing. To some extent we are trapped, yet also rooted by the images which originally "came" with our concepts.

Particular illustrations of a valued concept will give power to certain political constellations. My criticism of student assignments appears as a process of political reeducation, one in which each of the following issues play a central role:

Goodness and the Documentary Image. The social and documentary tradition provides us with some of our most powerful images of what is good and what is not so good. Farm Security Administration (FSA) photographs of the thirties, and *Life* of the forties and fifties are prototypical recent sources; food, fashion, and home advertising represent another. Even Eliot Porter and Duane Michals are influential here. Whether or not we approve of those values as they are presented, the pictures can be analyzed to determine which of their features indicate that "this is good." Regardless of whether one is sympathetic to Arthur Rothstein's FSA photographs, for example, one needs to be aware of how they were made to convey a particular set of feelings, and how certain of his photographs became famous because they fit our notions of what the Depression "really" means.

Goodness and Capitalism. John Berger, following Walter Benjamin, has argued in *Ways of Seeing* (1973) that the rise of the market and industrial capitalism—and the breakdown of traditional society—led to treating material signs of value and wealth as indicators of intrinsic goodness and virtue. A portrait of a nobleman is surrounded by the material signs of his wealth and being. Marx called this a *commodity fetish,* treating a product of commerce as if it had intrinsic value as an object rather than as a part of a social-economic complex.

Superimposed on fetishization is the issue concerning words and pictures. We have separated the two from each other, treating one or the other as a secondary activity filled with the possibility of deception. Pictures have been seen as feminine, deceptive, and irrational when compared to words, which are male, truthful, and rational. *Showing* (which is actually kinesthetic but we take to be pictorial), however, is often seen as more effective and less subject to misinterpretation than *telling* (which is oral but we take to be verbal and written).

The reduction of our complex interactive lives to a set of hierarchical values and signifiers of those values has profound consequences. Our problem becomes one of "processing" the fetishized "messages" which call our attention to the attractiveness of objects "in and of" themselves.

Equating Clarity with Truth. Nietzsche argued that our conception of goodness is an attempt to give an otherworldly imprimatur to certain values. It becomes no longer a matter of good versus bad, what I desire versus what you desire, but good versus evil and a matter of avoiding the absolutely forbidden. We manufacture our ideals and then try to find a means of selling them that hides their mundane and dirty origins. The ideals of truth and clarity share the same fate. They too have had social and political functions, controlling what was so and how it was to be expressed. Nietzsche's argument does not destroy truth as a reasonable goal, but it does displace it from its supermundane position. We can treat truth as important insofar as it actually is useful for us, and contrast this to its absolute value for the philosophers.

We believe that truth should be pure and simple and clear, even if our path to it is complicated. But "Supposing truth is a woman—what then?" Nietzsche asks. What if truth fulfils the (male) image of woman as deceptive, impure, misleading, contradictory? Or, what if our notion of the way of the world, the true, is in fact just a very sophisticated projection of what men have come to believe themselves to be? Our Western photographs feature heads and peaks in the action, but perhaps the truth lies in the feet and in the peeks behind the action.

To be scientific has come to mean a claim about being clear, pure, and nonrhetorical. But that ideal requires a rhetoric (a set of tropes and forms) and a means of realizing it. Everyone who does social science is aware of that, and knows that there are built-in biases in any scheme of analysis. But when we enter the world of the visual we are more willing to believe we can actually read a photograph and make it clear in a way that we would never do for a painting or a poem. As I have said, this our self-mystification, and I believe it is a result of our marvel and Augustinian temptation at the *presence* produced by the sharp lens and fast fine-grained films.

Clarity as an Obsession. One explanation for our obsession with clarity is that we have a notion that fundamental units of knowledge are small and isolated bits rather than ongoing patterns of life and interaction. We might call this a fetishization of facts, a treatment of what we have made *(facta)* outside of the complex of circumstances of its origins. While this can be liberating for a while, it is ultimately a destruction of our historical grounding.

To be in command of something, whether it be a photograph or a situation, we believe it must be "factorial," a simple pure unit, available to our knowledge "at once." Or, particulars or units of photographs must represent the general in an almost miniature way (the microcosm of the macrocosm). Or, the general must be simply composed of particulars, say by averaging. There can be no emergence of new properties. There can be no "hidden" processes—such as market economies, evolution, pregnancy, or historical forces—that work their way into something surprising—such as the efficient market, new species, a baby, or the next historical period—which we only recognize after it has appeared. While men may be surprised, women bear these "children."

Whatever the reasons for it, the obsession itself takes two forms, so different that each would seem to exclude the other. The first form of being clear is familiar. It is a matter of being sharp, full of information, having good contrast. Documentary records often fulfill these aims, although much of documentary photography may be grainy and muddy for technical and aesthetic reasons. This kind of clarity fixes things, sets them into an archive, produces evidence useful for further generalizations, or social action, or essays. Now that you have this picture in front of you, you can see, obviously, what is so.

A second kind of clarity is that of "being clear" in the mystical sense. Clarity is here a matter of a whole vision of the world. What is true appears to us as unified, comfortably holding together what we had previously seen as contradictory. We have these moments of clarity when we "understand," and then say, "Aha!" We often treat works of art including photographs in this way. Our vision of them is whole and they appear to us as masterpieces possessing an aura, sitting outside of space and time.

There is something "true" to each of these conceptions of clarity, and yet we cannot rely on them. The power each has over us comes not only from its usefulness, but from our obsession with the simplification of our relationship to the world, which each implies.

Conventions for Establishing Clarity. Even though we might appreciate that "absolute" clarity is a deceit, we persist in searching for it, and we find it—again and again. The obsession is not a madness, but is actually grounded in satisfying experiences of comprehension, understanding, presence, and obviousness. Sometimes this is almost immediate. For other cases, say the most difficult or ambiguous of photographs, it takes years to develop a more settled sense of their meanings. We find an interpretation that is stable for a while and we are satisfied. We have found a way of being with the photograph so that it is clear.

If we understand clarity to be a modal form of interpretation located within a particular tradition, it loses its claim to be a universal value or style. Clarity remains an important way of being with a photograph, for within it the photograph is easier to read, has a more general appreciation, and lets contemporaries use it for documentary purposes. Clarity becomes no longer a matter of avoiding deception or of claiming dominance. It is rather one of the most effective rhetorics for certain populations. The question of whether we are more likely to reflect the truth if we are "clear" remains open.

Fetishes about Truth. If we operate within a particular convention or tradition, then truth and goodness are signified by certain objects, in a way almost independent of what they accompany: jewels and a crest-of-arms, sometimes; small error bars at others. There are distinctive criteria for evidence and value under each regime. And if we are given the mode of thought of the regime—whether it be paternity or science, for example—then those signifiers are rational and true and justifiable. They are not merely fetishes inauthentically linked to a person or situation. As the times change, the reasons we offer for why a particular thing means goodness or virtue may become less believable—for the way our social or political lives work may change. So what was once a sensible indicator of goodness or truth may no longer be. And if we shift our frame of reference, the signifier potentially becomes "an object of extreme irrational reverence of devotion" as Webster's New International Dictionary defines a fetish.

Those who believe there is an absolute truth would also believe there is a "point of view" from which we are not only viewing the world, but from which we actually "have" the world. Under such conditions, we would not have the danger of a fetish, for our pictures would in fact be true. While on alternate days I go along with this position, on the other days I am less sure. Then I think, for example, that even if we are always subject to being shown up—even if our notions of clarity will succeed and overturn each other—we might as well be clear for now, and laugh when we are exposed. We can hope that the next generation will find a way to give meaning to what we do, a meaning that will not be so exalted as the one we would like for ourselves, but still one that places us comfortably in history.

A LESSON FROM TEACHING

At the end of the course I realized that my pedagogical style in raising these issues undermined what I was trying to teach. I took an olympian critical stance, showing how goodness and truth were fetishized and became inauthentic in the work of the students, in photojournalism, and in classical photographs. I thought I was pointing out degrees of quality in different work: how some ways of indicating goodness actually were genuine and effective, and how others were comparatively sham and cheap. The essential theme was deception and its unrooting. But as I have pointed out, we cannot root out deception, but only learn to live with it laughingly and do the best we can. "Could we lie and tell the truth with the same relish?" I should have asked.

I had criticized fetishization in its own terms; I had treated the photographs as if they were made up of features. This was just the position I was trying to question, and it contradicted my more humanistic sensibilities, those which lead me to think that photographs "work" when they permit us to carry on our lives with them in a way that we find satisfactory and virtuous.

While I would not want to argue that photographs succeed or fail independent of their more particular features, I do want to suggest that these features explain quality only within a particular interaction. Within another pattern of interaction, the previously failed photograph might work very well.

None of these issues would have come up obviously and poignantly if I had not used photographic assignments in a course on goodness and Nietzsche. I am much more skilled at avoiding the hardest problems if I talk and write essays, rather than if I use visual material. My students and I confronted issues through the photographs which would have been glossed over without them.

SOCIAL RESEARCH AND ULTIMATE VALUES

One of the goals of teaching public policy is to help students increase their sophistication about the relationship between our understanding of society and political values. But how? Work with photographs in my course suggests at least one model that may be used for thinking about these more general issues.

The meaning of photographs, whether it is particular or general, is not a problem about photographs—except that we sometimes are quite sure that a photograph is a veridical report of what there is. Rather the problem lies in our confusion about the relationship of words to pictures, as if they had never had the most intimate of connections. We need to know more about the rhetoric of words *and* pictures, so that the mystifications we get ourselves into will at least be new ones and not ones we could otherwise avoid.

So too, the meaning of "information," whether it is particular or general, is not a problem about facts or data, but a problem in our understanding of their relationship to ideals and action. In educating our students, it is that relationship which needs to be explored, a relationship in which features of social phenomena are carefully distinguished and just as carefully protected from becoming fetishes in a pursuit for knowledge.

PART V

PROBLEMS AND PROSPECTS

VISUAL SOCIOLOGY 18

*Derral Cheatwood
and Clarice Stasz*

During the nineteenth century Western culture produced two disciplines which later grew to serve as revolutionary actors in our understanding of culture and society. Both sociology and photography trace their origins to the period between 1835 and 1850. Between 1850 and 1870, both experienced an explosion of use, a period of development, sophistication of technique and formalization.

Photography and the social sciences have had periodic attempts at integration, and the techniques of one have been used by the other with various degrees of success. From the start, photography was seen as a tool in anthropology and archeology, with a growing precision of application as these fields themselves developed more fully.

In the United States during the beginning of the twentieth century both photography and sociology entered new eras, becoming accepted features in the American landscape and vocabulary. Kodak introduced the first point-and-shoot camera for widespread popular consumption ("You push the button, we do the rest," was their slogan), and the *American Journal of Sociology* published a series of articles with accompanying photographs representing the work of some twenty-five sociologists between 1896 and 1916 (see Chapter 8). This early courtship between the fields was brief, but around 1970, a new courtship began. In his introduction to *The Human Image: Sociology and Photography,* Irving Louis Horowitz observed that both disciplines were then going through a troublesome, posthoneymoon phase. Others, however, could find no record of the original wedding, and this left visual sociology with very real questions about its legitimacy in terms of either parent, sociology or photography. Most practitioners in both fields treat it with the disdain illegitimate children face in traditional communities, and the difficulty of finding its proper place is compounded by the fact that the parents are unsure of their own identities.

THE PROBLEMS OF HERITAGE

Both photography and sociology are troubled with self-definition. The dominant figures in each field, or certainly major figures in each field (Sontag, 1977; Davis, 1959), would argue that their profession is some unified phenomenon of singular characteristics which is moving in an identifiable, essentially correct, direction. In spite of such claims, honest examination of the fields discloses serious internal questioning and doubt. Is either discipline art, science, journalism, documentation, propaganda, or disguised ideology? Naturally, photographic sociology inherits these questions of identity and adds a few synergistic elements of its own.

At the very foundation of this confusion is the lack of a coherent critical vocabulary for the field. A vocabulary or language is not just a common set of words; it is a foundation for talking about a subject which preestablishes what one is going to look at, what will then be seen, and what one will be able to say about it. When we look at documentary photography, we find three distinct critical vocabularies that direct the construction and evaluation of images: sociological, technical, and aesthetic. For example, in discussing his documentary film *Rain*, Joris Ivens (1969: 40) says:

> The most serious criticism against the film was its lack of "content." In a certain way this was an exact criticism. I failed to emphasize sufficiently *human beings' reactions* to rain in a big city. Everything was subordinated to the *esthetic* approach. In a way I am glad that I laid a foundation of *technical* and creative perfection before working on other more important elements [emphasis added].

Here, Ivens indicates that he was willing to forego sociological content for aesthetic and technical effects. He is aware that there are separate vocabularies of criticism, that his dispute with the critics is a matter of preferring to operate with one vocabulary rather than another.

Each of these approaches or vocabularies has legitimate claims in visual sociology as well. The impact, importance, and priority of each varies, however, and attempts to integrate them produce additional problems for coherent analysis. Each vocabulary carries a set of evaluative procedures and measures. As such, each holds certain criteria to be essential and prior in evaluation, and each produces a fallacy of belief when seen as the only context in which to evaluate a process as socially complex as photography. In addition, specialization in any one of them contributes to little more than a layperson's understanding of the others.

Consider first the relationship of each discipline to its techniques. Sociologists continually encounter the lay view that because everyone lives in social groups, everyone understands society. Lay cynics define sociology as common sense disguised with big words. Similarly, photographers hear that anyone can take a photograph and that " . . . the line between between professional and amateur is not just harder to draw in photography . . . it has little meaning" (Sontag, 1977). Applying these from each discipline to the other, we find a photojournalism fallacy in photography and a snapshot mentality in sociology. Professionals in both fields tend to believe that their own work is difficult and requires a lengthy apprenticeship, but that work in the other profession is simple, requiring mastery of only a few techniques.

THE TECHNICAL FALLACY

Every field is characterized by a set of technical skills which one may reasonably expect the practitioner to have mastered. The belief that the mere ability to perform these skills with precision will bring required professional results is the technical fallacy, a phenomenon closely related to the inversion of means and ends which one finds in bureaucracy.

The technical fallacy is rampant in modern sociology. It is characteristic of the researcher whose only concern is that the proper steps be taken in the proper order, as in reified research processes and statistical analysis. As sociologists, it is too easy to forget that a level of significance is merely a conventional abstraction and not reality, truth, or fact. Similarly, visual sociologists can be lured into believing that precision prints taken with the finest lens and camera and developed in the finest grain developer will produce the best product. It may be that for much useful work sociologists need considerable photographic competence. This is an issue to be discussed, however, not presumed through belief in the power of equipment.

Our experience suggests that technical skill does increase the sociological usefulness of photographic work through improving the chances that images will be well exposed and through control of printing to heighten interpretations and focus. Concern with such proficiency becomes counterproductive, however, when it takes priority over sociological subject matter. In general, photographic sociologists have been too conservative in imitating the technical competencies of professional photographers, and too timid as well (perhaps because they model themselves after documentary photographers, the least manipulative practitioners in the field). Thus, they rely on the 35mm camera, head-on shots, and straight printing.

THE AESTHETIC FALLACY

On the other hand, we confront an aesthetic fallacy which suggests that the primary questions to ask of any work have to do with composition, shading, color, and beauty. But photography is a medium of communication which may or may not be used as an art form, and there is no reason not to use it in sociology, regardless of the form it takes elsewhere. Photographs, for example, are used in chemistry, meteorology, physics, and other sciences without anyone arguing that they are art, hence inappropriate to the field. One does not find chemists rejecting photographs of compounds because the sodium grains are not balanced or because the composition is poor, for the photograph is used for other obvious purposes. Yet, in fact, some of these scientific photographs have found their way into exhibits in art galleries.

This suggests that the art/science categories are false polarities for analysis within visual sociology. An emphasis on producing only that which is aesthetically correct—in terms of a set of formal conventions—constitutes the aesthetic fallacy, and photographic sociologists need worry themselves less than they have with the artistic qualities of their work. On the other hand, aesthetic conventions of presentation, taste, and statement find their way into society as a whole and frame the way in which others perceive photographs in general. To the degree that our prints or visual images conform to these aesthetic tastes, we will increase our ability to reach a broad audience. To the degree that we are aware of these aesthetic conventions and employ them, change them, or contradict them to our own ends, we will increase our resources for communicating through this medium.

THE SOCIOLOGICAL FALLACY

The first criterion for evaluation of visual sociology must be sociological. If we are to speak to a sociological audience, then our capacity to communicate in an adequate language must be our first concern. Too often, however, we find among sociologists avoidance and dismissal of more aesthetic or technically innovative styles involving unusual camera angles, multiple image printing, print manipulation, posed shots with large format cameras, and so on. It is implied that these manipulations are proper to photography as an art form, thus inappropriate to science and to sociology. Further, such a choice presumes that one format and one procedure used in a standardized manner are the means by which to secure "objective" data. To do anything else is to appear subjective, and therefore incorrect. This simplistic belief produces stilted, hackneyed shots with an implicit but unstated ideological stance. There is a definite use for each form of photographic technique and manipulation. The misuse of a technique or the manipulation of data or procedure to produce biased results for unstated reasons is as immoral and unprofessional in visual sociology as in any other field. Sociologists should avail themselves, however, of the whole range of techniques for working with and presenting photographs.

The belief that only one process and one product is correct is the sociological fallacy. Given that both photography and sociology have long histories of involvement in social reform, one finds a bias toward shooting particular subjects rather than others: bums rather than insurance agents, portraits of old people rather than the middle aged, prison or hospital activities rather than church activities. Just before her death, Dorothea Lange observed similarly that photographers of urban life were relying on trite or cliché-ridden images, such as drunks, when they should be taking the mundane features of city life that are more telling, those less expected by the viewer, such as shoppers and office workers.

THE REALITY FALLACY

Underlying the problems in both parent disciplines and visual sociology is the belief that sociology studies real things and that photographs are valid images of reality. In fact, what the sociologist or photographer sees as real comes from unstated assumptions about the nature of social life derived from his or her general culture and the culture of the discipline involved. The act of photography is itself a social process, and its practice changes slightly the culture of the photographer and the subject. The "reality" involved, then, is the created nature of the social world. The belief that there is an external, constant and absolute reality which can be recorded, measured, or analyzed with photography or sociology—and is thus independent of the activity of the two fields—constitutes the reality fallacy.

Consider the reality vocabulary. One can show people snapshots that are technically terrible—a man's forehead cut off, his face in shadows, eyes red from flash flare, and someone will say, "That's Uncle George, that looks just like him." In fact, Uncle George has a complete head, a contoured face and clear eyes. Embarrassed, Uncle George might respond that it in no way resembles him. The reality mythology dominates much everyday use of snapshots, and the deficiencies with it are clear from this illustration.

In social science this fallacy can take a parallel form. For example, some anthropologists argue whether certain turn-of-the-century portraits are any good, because the subjects are not dressed in authentic costume but in garb that reflects the portraitist's view of how Indians should dress. This invocation of the reality principle seems proper on the surface if one is studying Indians. It does say something about Indians, however, that they would allow themselves to be posed in inappropriate garb. At the least, it leads us to wonder if costumes held the meanings for Indians that anthropologists attribute to them.

The point here is not that any evaluative vocabularies are necessarily wrong, but that we must be more cognizant from the start as to which one is being given priority. As a photographer, one should understand ahead of time which vocabularies are going to guide the work. To take naively a set of pictures and then represent them as an aesthetic experience or a scientific study is analogous to forcing or fudging data once it's collected. Sometimes something useful emerges serendipitously, but the productiveness of the set will be enhanced by knowing from the start the limitations under which one chooses to operate.

Each of the three vocabularies has utility, particularly if one is aware of its potential fallacy. When taking and looking at photographs, one can use them productively singly or in any combination. Still one problem remains—for the vocabularies are like lemmings, and they have a drive to purity. As each develops and becomes more refined, it enables us to be more specific and precise. This purity comes at a cost—a loss of the range, the flavor and the coloring that flowed from its initial ambiguity.

For example, the technical vocabulary is now so elaborate that one can sit down at a machine which will register the exact contrast between the blacks and whites of a print, and hence determine whether contrast is within a desirable range. This is analogous to the use of statistical tests in sociology which allows one to judge with a probability of .05 that a relationship is valid. In both cases, the technical criterion can lead us away from contemplating the meanings and implications of what we have before us.

THE PROBLEMS SHARED WITH SOCIOLOGY

A common myth held by many sociologists concerning visual sociology is that it is not "scientific." This is probably no more nor less true for visual methods than for any other. Most sociologists contend that "science" is a method of regular observation and analysis making use of appropriate checks for reliability and validity, and there is nothing in this definition which rules out visual methods.

What makes visual methods more difficult to handle—at this point in time—is that we have not yet elaborated our critical and procedural methods and vocabularies. Certainly, insofar as we are seeking regular and direct observation, visual procedures are among the most viable to use. Most of what is regarded as "observation" is visual, and the ability to establish a visual record is an obvious advantage to science. What poses problems is the need to establish measures whereby we can assure reliability and validity, and two comments are called for here: Part of the difficulty with setting up such procedures is the vague, amorphous, and undefined use of "reliable" and "valid" within sociology itself. In general, these concepts themselves are circularly defined—through attention to "indicators" and measures of significance—within the reified process or research. If, however, we return to the underlying meaning of the terms, then they too become viable in visual methods. They require, of course, that the procedures under which we take photographs are clearly and honestly put forth (no matter how "subjective" they may be). Theoretically, this practice allows other observers to compare our results with theirs and with other known aspects of the phenomena under study, and implies that other researchers using the same methods in the same or similar situations might be expected to reach similar conclusions.

Another criticism about the use of visual sociology emerges from a lack of knowledge within sociology on the possibilities of photographic work. These criticisms have to do with the need for light, the interference of flash in dark situations, the need to ensure that the photographs are candid, the inability to control for subjects desiring to be or not to be photographed and the like. Most of these are invalid or beside the point. It is possible, for example, to take regular photographs in very low light situations: with the use of special films, photographs can be taken in "total" darkness. As such, it is seldom necessary to use flash. Further, these criticisms ignore selection of sociology as the primary evaluative vocabulary, for photographs which would be far from acceptable on aesthetic or technical ground may be completely adequate as data for sociological analysis.

An additional misconception is that shots must be candid to be meaningful. In fact, we find that when we photograph people in most situations over a long period of time, they react to the camera much as the animals in game preserves do, by ignoring it. People engaged in some work activity, those who know you and what you're doing, and those engaged in activities in which they expect to be photographed, can all be studied photographically without having to be candid.

This is not to suggest, however, that the camera is not an intrusion in some situations, nor that intrusion and reactivity are not real problems. In discussing his photographs of hobos, Douglas Harper (Chapter 2) observes that as his attachment to the culture and particular men developed, his feeling increased that photographing them was an intrusion. It is interesting to note, however, that he did not feel that the type of shots he was able to secure or their quality differed over this period of time. His experience suggests that the main concern of the visual sociologists doing research in the field must be a sensitive and sincere concern for his or her subjects.

PROBLEMS IN THE CULTURE

There are three fundamental and very general problems related to the assumptions of our own society about the nature of photography.

First, no clear understanding exists yet of the social nature of picture taking, production, distribution, and use. Barbara Rosenblum's study of photographers (1978) and Howard Becker's (1975) article on photography have attempted to discuss this relationship, but there is no conceptualization of the complex network of persons, position, expectancies, and conventions which make up photography within the society. Until this is formulated in more detail, it will be difficult for sociologists to clarify either their role as visual sociologists or the impact of their photography on the subject.

Second, there are a variety of common sense/common sight meanings within the society, visual clichés if you will. These underlie the usual and unstated principles we regularly use to look at and interpret the images we see. We employ these to understand the narrative flow of movies, for example, and through them are able to see actions presented to us in sequential fashion as occurring simultaneously within the plot. We must be aware of these conventions for paradoxical reasons: first, to be able to use them in the presentation of our material; and second, to be able to avoid them and thus eschew the trap of cliché.

Finally, as we have said before, visual sociology exhibits confusion about its critical vocabularly. Some clarity may be achieved by simply determining which critical context should take precedence. However, before the field can fully mature there must develop a set of evaluative procedures distinctly appropriate to its purpose.

There are, of course, real limits to the use of visual methods in sociology, at least two of which are so important as to deserve consideration even at this early stage in the development of the field.

Visual sociology requires technical items for securing, preparing, and displaying images. These can produce problems at any stage. In the first place, the equipment is expensive, and unless the practitioner is working within the aegis of a well-financed institution, costs may inhibit the development of visual work. Second, equipment needs may confound research or presentation. At some professional meetings sociologists have been unable to present findings because the necessary projectors or monitors were unavailable; in the field some have been unable to photograph needed information because of equipment failure; accidents in the darkroom or lab have destroyed irreplaceable data, and so on. These are of course, the plagues of anyone working with mechanical equipment. However, because technical items are essential to visual sociology, the plagues will be visited on professionals in direct proportion to their involvement in the field.

Finally, visual sociology relies on one sense—sight. Although most persons think of sight as their primary sense—and this may in fact be true—it is certainly not the only constituent of social reality, and attention to sight alone may produce bias as substantial as that produced by those who use only numerical data or census information. If we are to study social life in all its complexity, we must attend to all the senses employed by social creatures in the setting. This orientation is both essential to the empirical study of social behavior and the reason for visual sociology.

VISUAL ANTHROPOLOGY 19

John Collier

Visual anthropology and the camera's eye can extend and refine scientific description by including detail and nuance presently lacking from the written field records of sociology and anthropology. These are in part missing because the general discipline of scientific work rejects impressions and insights that are not derived from tangible evidence. Records and descriptions of behavior are no more deep nor expansive than are methods of gathering this tangible evidence and, as behavioral science has no effective verbal or mathematical techniques for recording qualified visual detail, much subtlety is left out of the scientific record.

A similar taboo against investigating the unmeasurable was held by Ernest Hubert, my professor of gross anatomy at Johns Hopkins Medical School in 1935. During a casual conversation, this Swiss scientist informed me that he could not discuss matters that could not be proven! Certainly this was the voice of the European rationalist tradition, yet Hubert was also an artist. He made drawings of the dissected facial musculature of monkeys with the sensitivity and beauty of a da Vinci anatomical sketch.

Throughout the fields of psychology, sociology, and anthropology today, there are men and women who work creatively beyond the limitations of their disciplines. This chapter is directed to those scientific artists, who, each in his or her own way, attempt to assemble structural understanding that is artistically whole.

VISUAL OBSERVATION AND DESCRIPTION

Visual anthropology is based on the photographic record, and in significant ways camera vision is very different from observing human eyes, which are narrow of field and capable of witnessing whole actions only by constantly shifting their focus. As a result, visual comprehension through direct sight is consciously and unconsciously selective, and elements which are disturbing or irrelevant to the observer can be conveniently edited out. In contrast, the camera eye (depending on lens focal length) has an optically wide field and sharp focus; it mechanically records all circumstances within its field of vision. As a result, the camera image can be the least disturbed visual record we have.

271

With scientifically disciplined selectivity, the camera can even gather a contextual record, a larger view of what is there.

As research objectives in modern social science become more specialized the *whole* of environmental relationships is frequently lost. Further, in field situations the restraints of scientific discipline inhibit the rapid sensory responses needed to comprehend the enveloping character of cultural circumstance. The recordings of disciplined science gather factual elements but are a poor descriptive resource for capturing overtones necessary to complete the human portrait. Field notes too often describe faceless men and women void of emotions or refinements. The logistics *are* gathered. But in many anthropologies people are described mostly in terms of their clothes or other material possessions. This may not be the intent, but it is a default of discipline, for scientific description is based on elements that are measurable, computable, and verbally defined. The promise of photography is not only that it can gather valuable research tangibles, but that the detail of the visual evidence it provides can preserve a constantly "present" context for subsequent analysis.

TANGIBLE DETAIL AND SUBJECTIVE MEANING

Without tangibility no record can be scientifically studied, and behavioral research seeks various ways to validate evidence. Psychology often validates the evidence of emotion (conscious or subconscious) through a variety of tests that "materialize" it. As with so many abstracted uses of statistics and graphs, however, human feelings come to be seen as *test scores*. There are ways of observing emotional expressions directly in human behavior, and psychologists, like all of us, *do* respond to these direct signals of behavior. In company with anthropologists, however, they do not record these responsive insights into behavior, for they lack both criteria and methods for incorporating them into their professional work.

Insights into nonverbal communication developed through visual anthropology, however, *can* be used to reliably and directly read human emotions as they are signaled by facial expressions, movement of the extremities and body posture. Through photographic studies, Paul Ekman (1972) of the Langley Porter Clinic, a psychologist by discipline, has established an index of the emotional expressions of the face. Ray Birdwhistell (1970) of the University of Pennsylvania has codified the messages of body language. The anthropologist Edward T. Hall (1959, 1966, 1977) has interpreted the cultural significance of spatial positioning. All of these studies are based on the tangible detail provided by photographs! And yet photography has been historically neglected as scientific method in both sociology and anthropology, largely because these fields have had no means to unlock the rich information available in photographic images.

Novelists work with meaning. They use all their available sensory insights in order to realize full-dimensional characters in their writing. But because their information processes are overtly *subjective*, intuitive, and creative, they are free to respond with all their intelligence. These writers compound reflections of reality by filtering them through their own sensitivity. Obviously, such responses cannot be used directly by the social scientist who, by discipline, must refine the cultural record as matter, that is, as evidence, of proven existence and shape. Unfortunately, emotions and the refinements of personality are ephemeral and difficult to define as matter. They remain undefined impressions unless ways can be found to record them tangibly, and in general, they have remained unrecognized in the descriptive processes of science.

Photography can broaden our powers of scientific description to include some of these neglected elements. In doing so, it offers much of the tangible detail which the novelist transcribes from subjective reflection. A photographic document of a man and woman resting in their environment, for instance, may contain many of the complex elements of the novel; the stage setting, material possessions, and the psychological projections of the actors. If such a photograph were studied meticulously the analyst could inventory directly a large part of the novelist's description. The photographic record of a home setting would reflect religiosity, ethnicity, and elements of history; and it might provide insights into psychological processes by revealing order, disorder, or the symbolism of artifacts and their arrangement. Photographic details of its inhabitants would yield information about age and passage of life, as seen in face, hands, and posture. A study of clothing might reveal profession, taste and economic well-being. The manner in which the clothing was worn might, along with posture, reveal psychological states and emotional welfare. These are all elements which can be responsibly identified through the analysis of kinesics (body language), proxemics (significance of space), and the cultural symbolism of artifacts.

Visual anthropology's major discipline thus lies in reading the photographic evidence with accuracy, and this reading can extend this credibility and scope of the descriptive records of behavioral science.

Visual imagery becomes increasingly important to anthropology as the search for significance shifts from *how* people behave to *why*, for insights that may not be revealed in material observation can be found in subliminal messages surrounding the artifact, in technology and in ceremony. Traditionally, beyond the interpretation of verbal interviews, there are few responible ways of studying the psychic fulfillment of otherwise pragmatic activity. Visual anthropology makes possible a shift in focus from descriptive analysis of artifacts and behavioral process to the emotional overtones and fulfillments of culture.

A great many overtones of culture and personality *can* be read directly from photographs, but all this evidence is often no more than a clue to the unseen. To go further, we can investigate this inner domain by projective interviewing with photographs, an approach that can reveal the significance of unseen emotional functions in what seems to be a practical routine activity. Why do the modern Hopi Indians really farm? For subsistence or for ceremonial reward? Why do the Navajos have such need for a flock of sheep? For mutton or wool? Or is the process of tending sheep one that holds together family and child development as well? Of course, these areas can be probed verbally. Verbal revelations without the clarity and support of photographic imagery, however, can often be deceptive, for the communication barrier of specialized language twists questions and confuses answers. Statements of value about the concrete evidence in photographs can stabilize such projective response.

Photographs as probes in interviewing *ask their own questions* which often yield unpredictable answers. The imagery dredges the consciousness (and subconsciousness) of the informant, and in an exploratory fashion reveals significance triggered by the photographic subject matter. The content of the imagery which photographically is an *outside* view is used projectively with the informant to give us an *inside* view of our research territory.

When we were tracking the migration of French farmers to English mill towns in the Maritimes of Canada (The Stirling County Study, Cornell University, 1953, reported in C. Hughes, 1960), we used photographs to probe attitudes about this migratory change. I photographed a mill where French migrants worked amid conditions of poor industrial safety and dangerous housekeeping of lumber and machinery. We wanted to know whether this shift from farming to congested industry was a stressful experience for the French Acadians. We showed the mill photographs to a French husband and wife who both worked in this plant. To our surprise the couple looked over the pictures with pleasure, remarking what a happy place it was to work. Then two weeks later we returned to this family with bucolic pictures of their farm. They shuffled through these pictures with apparently low interest and then burst out emotionally about how much they hated working in the mill. They were so upset they suggested quitting the mill and returning to agriculture. This contradictory reaction uncovered the information that their way of surviving the industrial stress was to anesthetize themselves to the mill's existence. It appeared that they had literally never seen the mill until studying the photographs. Over the two weeks of our absence the photographs had been eating at their consciousness until finally they became aware of how deeply disturbed they were by the move into industry.

THE DEVELOPMENT OF VISUAL ANTHROPOLOGY

Over thirty years ago Gregory Bateson and Margaret Mead (1942) carried out the first visual research in anthropology. Their measuring of Balinese child-rearing practices was so persuasive that anthropology generally accepted their photographs as a reliable tool for the measurement of child development.

But Bateson and Mead were not the first behavioral scientists to use the reliable eye of the camera. In the 1920s and 1930s Dr. Arnold Gesell assembled his classic *Atlas of Infant Behaviour* with stills from motion picture film. Long before Gesell, Eadweard Muybridge (1957) seized upon the camera to win a bet for Leland Stanford that a horse gets all four feet off the ground at once while galloping. This was truly the *first* responsible use of the camera to analyze *motion*. Considering how easy it is to motion study today with frame-for-frame analysis, Muybridge's experiment was a miracle of ingenuity and validity. A line of eight by ten cameras were set up along a racetrack and a running horse tripped each shutter by hitting a string with his hoofs in passing. This was the first *time-and-motion* study ever made.

But it was Bateson and Mead who applied the camera record to anthropology. Considering how enthusiastically the anthropological field accepted the Balinese study it is amazing and significant that it was thirty years before a second study was made that compared with this pioneer method. In 1976 Richard Sorenson published a depth study of ecology and child development in New Guinea titled, *The Edge of the Forest: Land, Childhood and Change in a New Guinea Proto-agricultural Society*. It too was illustrated with stills from 16mm film. Symbolically, it was Margaret Mead who wrote the introduction to this study that carried child development photographically into the ethnography of culture and its natural environment. Sorenson not only carried out his research on film but did a thorough documentation of the geographic environment with still imagery.

Bateson and Mead experimented with diverse ways to get the richness of information from their data in both film and stills. Their approach to studying photographs was directly judgmental: look at the photographs and write down what you see! At times teams of observers worked over the images together and separately. They were primarily enthusiastic about employing the image for direct insights and informally used all the approaches now common in film and photo analysis. But Mead did not develop a formal language with which to research their imagery, and it is certainly possible that the free and creative way in which these pioneers used the evidence of the image bewildered other anthropologists and inhibited them from pursuing the uses of photography in research.

In 1952 when I was hired by Alexander H. Leighton of Cornell University to use photography in his social psychiatric research, I found no anthropologists at Cornell who ever used photographs, except for occasional illustration. To my further bewilderment, Leighton and my supportive colleagues confessed that they had no insights or methodologies for evaluating the voluminous file of still camera records that I had made in the Maritimes of Canada. It was only then that Dr. Leighton informed me that I had been hired to show anthropologists *how* to use photography in research. I launched my own investigation but refined only one research use of the camera record, the use of community-based photographs in informational and projective interviewing.

While I was submerged in this experiment in the Canadian Maritimes —and on the Navajo reservation—Edward T. Hall was director-anthropologist for the Foreign Service Institute, an orientation school for the State Department in Washington, D.C. Hall's assignment was to train State Department personnel to work overseas. As a scientist, he followed his students into the field observing them succeed and fail in alien cultural circumstance.

Dr. Hall found major human relations disasters took place *in time and space*, both of which are used differently in various cross-cultural circumstances. In his research, Hall developed the science of human relations in space, which he called *proxemics*. This was the first step in formalizing nonverbal observation.

Ray Birdwhistell, researching nonverbal behavior in this same period, developed and defined the measure of body language, which he called *kinesics*. The precision of Birdwhistell's observations were demonstrated when, on viewing only two minutes of film of a mentally ill mother and her child, and after studying the footage frame for frame, he was able to diagnose their illness as the *double bind*. These observations were reviewed by a group of psychiatrists who decided Birdwhistell had made a more accurate diagnosis than the family's own psychiatrist.

With these two approaches, proxemics and kinesics, anthropology now had both formal language and method for researching film and still photography.

In 1968 Paul Byers and Margaret Mead published a text entitled *The Small Conference*, an account of a university meeting of Fulbright scholars, for which Byers' contribution was a description of the phenomenon of socially and culturally programmed behavior. Byers tracked the action of the scholars with a 35mm camera from their first interaction to final socialization. He found total congruence of group behavior as contained and structured by rooms and events, especially proximity. Byers' study demonstrated that it was possible to capture precisely the shape of behavior with a camera as well as tangibly measure social space and analyze the exacting relationships of interaction.

A few years earlier Edward T. Hall had observed this same phenomenon when filming a fiesta at San Juan Pueblo. When a fifty-foot reel of Super eight film was screened in slow motion, an Indian family, a Spanish-American family, and an Anglo family were seen moving across the plaza, each according to a distinct pattern, each responding to its cultural programming. The Indian family *drifted* through space, the Anglo men, women, and children *marched* through space, swinging arms, hurrying forward!

Through the 1970s Paul Ekman refined his photographic research of the emotional signals of the human face at the Langley Porter Psychiatric Clinic. This research on facial kinesics continues to offer diagnostic insights into nonverbal behavior that could be valuable to psychotherapists. But some medical colleagues questioned whether this study had value only in Western society.

Ekman doubted this and later put this question to a test in a series of systematic observations in the highlands of New Guinea. What he found seemed to make sense biologically but was revolutionary in the development of visual anthropology, for New Guinean aborigines interpreted his photographs of facial expressions in appreciably the same way as they were read by Westerners in the Langley Porter Clinic. When a second group was asked to express a series of messages through facial gestures—such as "I am hungry," "I am unhappy," "I am very happy"—they signaled meanings in much the same way as did the patients in Ekman's San Francisco laboratory.

In his writings Ekman points out that such universal signaling might be observed openly only in childhhod, and that later, these universal responses may be obscured by the curtain of behavioral protocol. Each culture has its own system of responses to emotional circumstances.

In 1965 Alan Lomax began a film investigation of the syntax of
world dance. There were other visualists studying film at this time,
but Lomax was faced with a peculiar challenge in comparing and
investigating dance as a cultural reflection. Dance is choreography,
a projective pattern moving through time, and in recording and studying
this flow, Lomax established a new dimension of visual research:
choreometrics. Hall had already observed time-oriented body language
in his spontaneous study at San Juan Pueblo, and I had been influenced
by Hall in my own film research of behavior patterns displayed by
Eskimo children as they move through schools of white culture (1973).

The concept of *choreometric movement through time* is at the heart
of most film research in which patterns of activity can be studied as
a graph line, rising and falling with the dynamics of behavior. With
still photography this flow of behavior is recorded by time sampling.
Photographs made of a bus stop every half hour, for example, from
early morning to evening, can gather evidence of the rhythms of transportation. A time study of a bus or streetcar stop not only records
the ebb and flow of commuters but yields a detailed pattern of the
movement out and into an urban community from dawn to dusk.

In my six years of collaborative film research on the welfare of
culturally different students in white/Anglo schools, we have found that
we can responsibly identify the major interaction dynamics of a classroom. We have witnessed teachers fearful of children, the absence
or presence of a cultural chasm between teachers and students, emotional involvement being turned on and off, concentration, reception,
well-being, or stressfulness. We have tracked these states by using all
the developments of methods for the study of nonverbal language:
proxemics, kinesics, and choreometrics, and we have found that visual
anthropology can record and reveal behavior often sensed but not
otherwise validated. In educational research, for example, we need
not rely on test scores alone for evaluation, but can study directly
patterns of success or failure in the process of learning.

But to do this we have used motion picture studies, and this raises
another question: can still imagery reveal the culture of a classroom?
Our research suggests that the still image can approximate the film
record, but it cannot offer as high a level of tangibility. One would
need hundreds of photographs to compete with film; this would be a
laborious way of documenting, and later research through such masses
of images would prove tedious. To be profitable, still photography
in educational research should limit itself to recording informational
peaks in specialized learning circumstances. For example, a teacher in
a predominantly Spanish-speaking school used his still camera to

convince his principal that bilingual instructions would increase the participation of Mexican children. This man set up a quick experiment of differential responsiveness to English and Spanish. A colleague presented a learning problem in English and then repeated the presentation in Spanish. The investigator shot a dozen stills of first the English and then the Spanish communication. When these pictures were enlarged to five by seven the principal agreed that they should incorporate bilingualism. The sequence showed Mexican children sitting back, slouching, with wandering eye focus, rarely looking at the English-speaking teacher. When the lesson shifted to Spanish the student posture changed; they leaned forward with kinesic intensity, their eyes all focused on the teacher. Using the same criteria we used in analyzing film, the still record demonstrated increased attention, facial focus on the teacher, and alertness in body posture.

INVESTIGATING SENSITIVITY AND INTELLIGENCE IN MOTION PICTURES

In an introductory anthropology seminar in which *Learning from Film* is examined, we discuss the question: *What is the curve of sensitivity and intelligence in the rise of civilization?* What is the correlation between material culture, high technology, and human sensitivity? This is a difficult question to explore through library research. Generally, builders of great temples and producers of complex technology are seen to represent the highest evolution of human refinement, leading ever upward to the "good life" of modern society. Certainly this is the message of the written record.

But what if this question were examined in terms of first hand observation of a living society of primitive people? In the seminar we attempted this at second hand by studying a film account of a group of ancient migratory hunters (with a low material culture) in order to establish a base line for civilized evolution.

The visual record we used was *The Hunters*, filmed by John Marshall, and released by the Peabody Museum of Harvard University. The students observed naked hunters, wanderers, gathering food from the Kalihari desert of Africa, hunting game with poisoned arrows, killing a porcupine with sticks and spears, throwing the carcass into a fire for immediate appeasement of hunger. But after the violence of the hunt, we see the men relax with their families, play with their children, mingle together with gentleness, communicating with their fellows.

This is the visual challenge: Are these primitive hunters and gatherers insensitive people? Or are they thoughtful and considerate of one another, gentle, and loving of their families? Do they appear to have intelligence comparable to people today who live in complex urban societies?

The general response to this field-film opportunity might be considered surprising, for students found the Kalahari hunters intelligent through the reading of faces, gestures, and strategies. The hunters appear considerate of each other, gentle in their interaction (seen in their body signals and kinesics of communication). They are affectionate with their families, show delight in their children (kinesics of group relations and kinesics of body contact). Based on these observations where do the Kalahari people fit in the curve of civilized behavior?

Anthropologically, this describes the value of film to the humanism of behavioral science. Photography and film offer a primary exposure to cultural contrasts, images of primitive cultures, and the activities of modern society, as well as contemporary poverty and affluence. Photographic exposure to human diversity can balance the scales of human refinement which have been obscured by the abstractions of written records. Visual anthropology offers a holistic record of human circumstance that can give depth and qualification to written ethnographies which too often view humankind through Western eyes alone.

THE CONTRIBUTIONS OF STILL PHOTOGRAPHY

The still photograph can be used to *count, measure*, and *record* infallibly all *stationary evidence*. As a mapping tool, the camera can record all precise topological relationships. The photograph can also be an encyclopedic recorder of information when details are validated by the native specialist. As an interview probe, the photograph helps the informant recover memory and express sentiments. Finally, the photograph is a key that can open the door into otherwise closed circumstances.

The photographer's first practical contribution to regional and community studies is in the mapping of spatial and ecological relationships. The second, and maybe the *most* valuable contribution, is found in the camera's ability to gather swiftly and clearly the *cultural inventory*. Photography's ability to record artifacts and possessions systematically offers support to countless surveys that are made in social science.

One example of such a survey is the San Francisco State University study of the *mental health and adjustment of native Americans relocated into cities*. The visual anthropology of this study was carried out by a cultural inventory of a sample of twenty-four Indian homes. As the photographer and visual anthropologist for this project, I visited each home once in company with the area field worker. I photographed the living room, kitchen, and one bedroom in each dwelling. Based on the rapid inventory, we concluded reliably (correlated with the psychological study on each family) that success of relocation could be measured by the style and order of each home. We were able to describe ethnographically the home culture of Indians who would fail in relocation as well as those most likely to succeed.

Beyond the cultural inventory, the photograph as a probe and stimulus to interviewing has proven to be consistently invaluable. In tests carried out for Cornell University we compared the value of interviewing with and without photographs and discovered that the picture interviewer could continue his interrogations indefinitely, as long as he continued to bring in fresh photographs. In contrast, the exclusively verbal interviews became unproductive far more quickly. In terms of subsequent content analysis, picture interviews were flooded with encyclopedic community information, whereas in the exclusively verbal interview, communication difficulties and memory blocks inhibited the flow of information. As suggested earlier, memory trauma can obscure interview content. The farmers with whom we were collaborating had lived on the same acres often since their childhood, and because of this unbroken continuity had short memory spans. When they were probed to go behind this memory curtain, they became frustrated and their verbal recall could be exhausted in one interview visit. When questioned further, they could become angry and break off the interviews. In contrast, photographs appeared to offer them a doorway to lost memory.

In all this work we found photographs of community process to be highly volatile, releasing expressions of values and previously submerged emotional feelings. As this suggests, with creative and consistent methodology many forms of human interaction can be responsibly researched through still images alone. But when the data of visual anthropology shifts from still photography to moving images the additional possibility of direct recognition of emotional overtones greatly increases. Film *can* reveal the process of psychological involvement, and it is the character of *motion* that qualifies and gives nuance to behavior.

PHOTOGRAPHY AND SOCIAL SCIENCE PROCESS

20

Jon Wagner

This book has reported on the use of still photography in two areas of social science activity: research and teaching. In reviewing its various chapters, we can begin by asking what they imply. Taken as a whole does the volume suggest anything which is not already stated by one or more of its authors? We can also look at the book as a sort of benchmark—a description of current efforts—and ask as well what more we can expect from this line of teaching and research. A third order of questions can be raised about the book as a product of social phenomena itself, an expression of social scientific inquiry. What can we learn about these more general matters from a close look at the particulars before us?

One thing we might note about the chapters in this book is that they deal with phenomena which are profoundly interdependent. This is true not only in the sense that "applications" always involve "issues"—and vice versa—but also that research and teaching are both implicated in any discussion of scientific discovery and presentation.

The interdependence of the phenomena described in this volume is particularly salient in the context of presentation. Jay Ruby has argued (1976) that there presently exists no context appropriate to the "ethnographic" viewing of visual imagery. Formally, he may be quite right, and in and of itself, this book is no exception. The images we have been able to include, for example, are but a very small sample of a much larger body of prints prepared by each author-photographer. Compared to all the images each of these individuals has taken, they represent an even smaller sample. To do justice to the subtleties and complexities of their photographic work, we would need a great deal more space for each.

There is more than space at issue, however, for the book format requires linearity of its research presentations. Schatzman and Strauss (1973) have argued that research practice itself is never really linear, but that it is all right to translate such practice into linear presentations. That will certainly work for some of the contributions—Ervin Zube's work on pedestrians, for example—but something is also lost and something gained when a "set" of images is ordered into an arbitrary sequence. The sequence may be something other than arbitrary, of

course—and those of our contributors are hopefully good examples—
but the matter is never settled. As Cheatwood has described elsewhere
in this volume (Chapter 14), presentation format has a great deal to
do with the kinds of content that can be conveyed.

We should remember, however, that "context" means something
more than physical setting, and Ruby's observation covers more ground
than questions of limited space and the organization of images. To
examine the "context of presentation," for example, we have to look
as well at what people bring to the setting in which the images will be
viewed. What are their assumptions about the meaning and significance
of the photographs they might see? What images do they already have
which serve as the standards against which new photographs are
judged? By what processes will they look, and what questions will
they ask?

There is something said in the book about these questions within
the context of the classroom, and I encourage readers to ask them as
well. "Are these photographs being presented or viewed as background
information, data, or illustrations?" "According to what critical vocabularies should we evaluate these photographs?" "What social theory
has informed these images?" "How can these photographs be used to
ask questions?" and "What does response to these images indicate about
visual literacy?"

The interdependence of the phenomena reported on in the book
extends much further, of course, and we could productively examine
each chapter in the terms of the questions raised by others. What does
Musello's work with family photographs suggest to us, for example,
about the images of Harper, Ewen, and Aron? What are the implications for Zube's research of the ideas expressed by Shanklin or Collier?
Are the photographs in the volume examples of "goodness" as discussed
by Krieger?

From this interdependence we must conclude that photography and
visual imagery is something more than a "method" in the social sciences.
As a technology it may play an important role in social research, but
the attention given to it within this volume is that given to visual and
visible social phenomena. The camera can be used as a tool for generating representations of these, but the images it produces become
part of the phenomena themselves. This characterization of visual
social science raises far more questions than it answers, and it also
shifts the focus from the emphasis on "methods" with which we began—
in introducing the volume I outlined five different "modes" of visual
research—to substantive areas of social science investigation.

PHOTOGRAPHY IN SOCIAL RESEARCH

Application of photography to social research shows the potential for making significant contributions in at least three areas of inquiry: behavior of the human "organism," the meaning and structure of situated action, and the nature of visual imagery and imaging.

STUDIES OF THE ORGANISM

Ethnologists have studied animal behavior in other species in greater detail than it has been studied in our own, frequently by making use of photographic observation and recording. These techniques can be applied as well to the study of human behavior in physical settings, and Ervin Zube's chapter on pedestrians is a rare and well-conceived example of this approach. Good systematic visual studies of people in public places, waiting in lines, crossing streets, moving in crowds, responding to presentations, engaging in conversation, interacting with each other, enforcing rules, presenting themselves, and so on are far too few. We might think that from the attention Edward Hall's work (1959) received several years ago, social researchers would see cameras as standard equipment for systematically recording human behavior, but not many have done so.

There are problems with this kind or work, of course, and these may have discouraged some. Covert observation—whether through photographs or not—raises a host of ethical and political issues (see Diener and Crandall, 1978 and Douglas, 1976 for contrasting points of view). There is as well a healthy reluctance by people to have their privacy invaded and to participate in activities which portray them as simple organisms. A conceptual problem is related to these matters of method, however, and it takes shape within the limitations of remote systematic observation to deal with questions of meaning, regardless of techniques employed. As a result, we have a great deal to learn about human behavior through these rather distant photographic research strategies, but these strategies alone will never allow us to account for the meaning of behavior to actors themselves.

STUDIES OF SITUATED ACTION

Photography can be used to study behavior and its meaning, however, if we focus on actors, the structure of their action, and their comments about what they do. This line of inquiry draws heavily upon the traditional fields of ethnography and ethnology, disciplines in which the camera is already a somewhat familiar piece of field equipment. Field studies themselves, however, are rarely as complete or

as varied as we would like, and this has important implications for
how photography can best be used.

In this "visual ethnography" we find a double inadequacy of existing
studies (similar and almost parallel to the "double inadequacy" Becker
[1963] has found in studies of deviance). In the first place, there are
too few visual studies of people acting in natural settings. We simply
have not seen enough of what people do and the physical contexts in
which it is done. In the second place, we know too little about how
people themselves see the settings and their activities. Even when we
have images of people in the setting, we have little sense of what they
make of it all or of the images themselves.

The first of these inadequacies is more characteristic of social science
literature than it is of the literature of professonal photography. For
decades photographers have been making their way into obscure,
exotic, and unfamiliar locales to bring back photographs of things
other people normally do not see. Some of these photographers have
produced work characterized by at least an implicit analytical focus
as well as explicit attention to visual impact. Danny Lyon (1971) and
Bruce Jackson (1977) have both made strong visual statements—
records of a sort—about prison life. Geoffrey Winningham has done
the same for professional wrestling (1971), and the Texas State Fair
(1972). Bill Owens has worked in the "documentary" tradition in photographing people at home in the suburbs (1973) and at work (1977).
Casting a long shadow over these more recent efforts is the large body
of work produced in the 1930s and 1940s by photographers under
auspices of the Farm Security Administration.

There are two problems with this photographic literature for social
scientists. The first is that the themes examined are frequently more
general and diffuse than those of contemporary social science research.
"Life in a Prison," for example is an appropriate title for a photography
essay, but professional research is typically far more narrow and
specialized. As a result, social scientists looking at the work of these
photographers will not necessarily find answers to, illustrations of,
or information about the specific research questions they have pursued
themselves. To correct this lack of correspondence would require
either that social scientists address broader questions in their research
or that photograhic studies become more specialized. I recommend
both.

A second problem with the work of most photographers is that they
give visual detail and form priority over concepts and analytical categories. In making photographs, for example, they typically begin by
"looking," not by designing a scheme for visual analysis. In contrast,

most social scientists give concepts and analytical categories priority over visual details. As Becker has observed (1975), this is not necessarily a virtue, and a better balance between the two would probably increase the value of both social science and photography.

There is yet a third problem characteristic of this line of work, one which is as true for photographers as it is for social scientists, and that is the externality of information generated through observation alone. As I mentioned above, we need to know not only more about how situated action looks and takes shape, but also how it appears to those engaged in it. One way into these questions is through questioning people about the meaning of their activity. As I described in Chapter 6, such questions can make good use of photographs. It may be particularly important to encourage such reflexivity in studies where information about the setting is also visual, as Ewen describes in her work on the beauty ritual. Our understanding of social activity would be greatly enhanced by this dual attention to how it looks from the outside and how it looks from within.

STUDIES OF VISUAL IMAGERY

By combining questions about the meaning of activity with questions about imagery—as I suggested above—we could study imagery phenomena itself. Sol Worth and John Adair (1972) pioneered inquiry into these matters, and Richard Chalfen (1975), Jay Ruby (1975, 1976), and others have continued that tradition. In his essay on family photographs (Chapter 7), for example, Musello has examined the use of images as well as the kinds of meaning attached to them. As he indicates, we need drastically to enlarge the sample of families—and kinds of families—in which we examine these processes.

In addition, we need drastically to enlarge the sample of social settings in which the same questions are asked. We might begin, for example, by attending to some of the issues Ewen and Ellis (1976; 1978) raise about the "fictionalized" images of advertisements. How do these images relate to our developing sense of what it means to be an adult? A success? A good child? A competent member of the culture? Or, what about the use of images in "journalism" and "news" (see Barthes, 1961). How do we process such photographs? How do we use them in our everyday life? What differences can we find in the ways different people or groups of people attach meaning to them?

What Musello has observed about family photographs may be true for some of these other "modes," but then again it may not. At the least, however, we must remember that photographic images are deeply grounded in visual detail at the same time that they are dependent in interpretation on information and context to which they can only obliquely refer. As social scientists studying visual imagery, we could profitably explore this theme in our own use of the medium. According to what patterns are photographs interpreted by members of different professional disciplines? What kinds of supplementary information are required for us to feel we understand a photograph? What meanings do we attach to different kinds of images?

PHOTOGRAPHY IN SOCIAL SCIENCE TEACHING

In all three areas of inquiry—behavior of the human organism, situated action, and the meaning of visual imagery—the reports in this volume suggest a largely untapped potential for photography in social science research. The same can be said for its potential contribution to teaching. The classroom combination of visual and verbal media, for example, can encourage students to think critically as well as to pay attention to detail. Photographs can enliven classroom process and course work whether they take the form of student projects (Cheatwood), exercises (Curry and Clarke), or projections of the students themselves (Lifchez). Attention to photographs can also bring both observational detail and conceptual imagery to more traditional examinations of social theory (Krieger). Additionally, through experiments and manipulations, we can use them to reveal and explicate implicit social theory and the structure of social awareness (Ellis).

In all of these ways, photographs can contribute not only to teaching but to presentation in general. They can play an additional and valuable role, however, in teaching students to make informed field observations. As records of what students have seen in the field—at least what they have seen through the view-finder of a camera—photographs can be used by the social science teacher to comment on the process of observation itself. Such comments can be made about written field notes as well, but there is an immediate and "inclusive" quality to the photographic images that is uncharacteristic of written work. By attending to the images which students bring to class, teachers can attend as well to development of skills in direct observation and the conceptual sensitivity in which they participate.

Photographs also offer the potential for a wide range of interdisciplinary applications. Because they do not as yet take form within different professional vocabularies, these images are available for analysis within a variety of social science disciplines. This does not mean that they are a universal language or that they convey the same information to all who view them. What it does mean, however, is that we might find discussions of images a good vehicle for teaching each other about what we do.

This accessibility and availability applies as well to those whose major business is something other than scientific inquiry. As the articles of Lifchez, Ellis, and Krieger illustrate, photographs can be used to explore social science with members—in these cases, members to be—of applied professions. Once again, as a vehicle for stimulating communication across disciplinary lines—and perhaps across subcultural lines as well—photographs can be used to good effect. They never tell us all that we want to know, of course, but they can provide an excellent vehicle for asking important questions.

UNREALIZED POTENTIAL

We might ask why, if photographs could play such an illuminating role in the social sciences, have they not yet done so? It is a good question, one carefully addressed by Cheatwood and Stasz in a preceding chapter. In addition to their analysis, however, I would like to suggest that in the most general sense, photographs have indeed already played such a role and informed the sense we have of the world in an almost overwhelming way (see Sontag, 1977). It is through photographs that we have seen and shared the sights of war and birth, visualized our history, identified our families, and become aware of the richness and complexity of our culture. These heuristic functions of photographs, however, have taken place outside rather than within the social sciences. The potential contribution of photography is thus not something which is totally unrealized in the culture, but rather something which is not yet fully realized in the disciplines themselves. What remains is for social scientists to understand this medium in such a way that they feel comfortable using it, analyzing and evaluating the images produced through it, and building space for it within existing conventions for presentation and communication.

This is no small matter, of course. Economic and technological factors, as well as professional conventions, limit what accommodations can be made. In addition, social scientists typically have better preparation in manipulating data than they have in obtaining it or presenting it. Statistics courses, for example, are almost universally required of students in graduate social science programs. It is much less common to find offered—let alone required, though I by no means recommend more requirements—courses in direct observation, photography, tape recording, and writing. To learn about photography, social scientists have had to look outside their own professions. For many, becoming competent in yet another approach to inquiry has not seemed worth the effort. As Becker (1975) observed some years ago, however, there is certainly something to be gained from trying.

VISUAL SOCIAL SCIENCE

There are other factors which may help explain why the potential contributions of photography to social science are poorly realized. Some of these are central to what we have been calling visual social science and they describe a more particular orientation to the study of social phenomena. To the extent that other social researchers have this orientation, they may find photography an attractive medium in which to work. To the extent to which they do not, it may seem to have little value.

CLOSE WORK WITH RESEARCH SUBJECTS

To make photographs of people, you have to see them, even if from a distance. For most people and in most situations, it is unlikely that you can do so without being seen yourself. As a result, visual social science—as a form of "field" inquiry—ties into most of the dynamics of participant observation. Not everyone is comfortable working this closely with research subjects—particularly in uncontrolled and open research settings—and the underutilization of photography in social research may in part reflect a more general neglect and avoidance of field settings per se.

There are things to be gained from this close work, however, and its contributions should not be dismissed, even if there are those who prefer to work in other contexts. Close work increases the communication between subjects and researcher, and in so doing, it increases the amount of information obtained. If the focus of study is quite narrow, this may not be much of an advantage. On the other hand, in exploring the meaning of situated action, it is almost essential. In fact, the narrowness of much social research may stem in part from the great remove at which the researcher seeks to understand the subjects of his inquiry.

Close work—with or without photographs—also lends itself to interdisciplinary efforts. When the details of the social phenomena are concrete and palpable, a variety of questions can be asked about them. It is when such details have been reified and classified under more abstract categories that they lose their general significance. Close work thus makes possible a continuing discussion among scientists from a variety of disciplines, each of whom can examine the activity about which different questions can be asked.

CLOSE WORK WITH AUDIENCES

Photography brings many of the features of direct field research to presentation as well. This generates problems for those who want more control over audience response, and it does so in a couple of ways. In the first place, using photographs in presenting an analysis gives the audience access to at least some of the original data, as it is portrayed in the images. As in the classroom, the retention of detail in presentation data makes any particular analysis vulnerable to critique and counter-analysis. This is of course true for all studies, but the particulars which are preserved in photographic images—combined with their power to undermine the traditional verbal authority of presentation settings—make for a lively counterpoint to what the researcher intends to say.

Research presented through photographs as well as verbal text seems to take a different form from that presented by text alone. The context of presentation becomes in fact another context of discovery. Much more information may be "generated" than is "passed on," and the distance between presenter and audience seems reduced by an appreciable factor.

This close work with audiences offers many of the rewards of close work in the field, however, and has provided some of the best moments at meetings of professional societies and associations. The discussions at sessions in which images are shown—with or without text—generate a different kind of enthusiasm and energy among the audience. Indeed they might, for rather than listening to social science in these settings, audience members are in a position to participate in it themselves.

EXPANDING THE MORAL COMMUNITY

Not all social scientists think that there is value in increasing access to their work and their concerns to those outside the profession. For those so inclined, however, photographs can provide an important vehicle for beginning communications. The professional boundaries which help to keep social scientists ignorant of each other's work are permeable to images in a way that they are impermeable to professional rhetoric. Commenting on making social science accessible to those in other disciplines as well as subjects of study, Dell Hymes (1974) has encouraged expansion of the "moral community," and suggested that this is, after all, what social science ought to be about. For those who agree, photography is a rich resource. For those who disagree, it probably represents a threat to long-established traditions of scholarship and presentation.

Disagreement about these matters receives a high charge in discussions of applications of science to human affairs and social problems. It is here however, that photography has been used most ingeniously in processes of inquiry. In designing literacy programs for peasants in Latin American, for example, Paolo Friere (1973) found it essential to understand their social and phenomenal worlds. In order to investigate these, he adopted the research strategy of taking photographs of the people in their settings and having these same people respond to the photographs in group showings. On the basis of this research, Friere was able to design literacy programs which tied the peasants' consciousness of the structure of their lives to the vehicle of written language.

Other examples of the use of photography in applied research are perhaps less dramatic or famous than Friere's work, but are important in their own right. The Slide Tape Collective (see Lewis, 1976), for example, has used slide shows to assess residents consciousness about community issues and immediate, small-scale social change. As in any process of inquiry, the residents' consciousness of the issues is increased by asking them questions about it, and this serves important political functions as well. Individual and family therapists have worked in a similar fashion. Using family photographs to ask questions about their clients' lives, they generate both information and interest in patterns of social interaction.

There are those who feel that social science should not lend itself so easily to politics and practice, and those who feel it cannot even if it tried. The use of photographs to investigate social phenomena for purposes of changing it has probably been subject to less abuse than other modes of inquiry—surveys, polls, and analyses of aggregate data—but there is no guarantee that this will remain the case. Nothing is simply settled about this business any more, and that is probably a good sign. On the other hand, there are those, such as Friere, who have been using photographs as an indirect vehicle of political and personal liberation for some time. There are good grounds for being cautious, but few to defend restricting access to social science from those it is practiced on.

RECOMMENDATIONS

For all these reasons, the potential use of photography in social science is problematic. It does not answer questions which have already been asked—although it can be used to examine them in different ways—and it raises several questions of its own. It can lead to less rather than more control over research practice and presentation. It can make accessible to a wider range of people the images and implicit theory with which social scientists busy themselves. And, finally, it can raise methodological questions about language, science, data, and observation, questions which reflect back on the practice of social science itself (see Percy, 1975, for an intriguing look at these as problems of "language phenomena"). To embrace this mode of inquiry is both to lose and to gain; to broaden the range of phenomena for which we hope to account; and to complicate dialectically the means we have at our disposal for doing so.

What guidelines can we follow in taking on these mixed assignments? What advice can we tease out from the experience of those who have contributed to this book? What can we leave with you to assist in this peculiar and fascinating business?

I would place at the top of the list encouragement to make and view photographs within a framework of social scientific analysis. For example, in what is perhaps the most provocative series of essays written about photography in recent years, Susan Sontag (1977) has called the medium to task on a wide range of counts. Many of her comments are lucid, telling and insightful, but much of what she has written confuses photographic technology with contemporary photographic practice. She cites Brecht's comment that a photograph of the Krupp works "reveals virtually nothing about that organization" as an indication of the limits of the medium, but it is a limit transcended by many of the selections in this book. Obviously, such uninformative photographs could be taken, but substantive and telling visual accounts are possible as well. To make these more useful portraits, however, photographers and those who view photographs will have to work within the disciplines of social science, whether or not they are of the profession.

To work analytically with photographs means that we resist the temptation to equate a building with a social, economic, and political organization. It means as well that we move beyond the identification of power with the faces of those who occupy powerful positions, and the simple conceit of showing what happens at a particular place at a particular time. To show what is essential to the Krupp works—or any other large and complex organization—we would have to photograph the conditions in which its owners and employees live out their lives, and something of the other organizations with which the one in question "does its business." We would have to photograph the products of such an organization, whether they be direct and material or indirect, manifested largely as changed social or environmental conditions. The subject of our photographs would thus not be a building, but a set of social relationships, a network of economic transactions, and wide-ranging social and environmental impacts of a particular organization.

Within the context of militarism and fascist Germany, it is ironic that Sontag has called on Brecht to affirm the critical primacy of words over photographs. For many Americans—perhaps for many Europeans as well—the essentials of the Krupp works and the Germany in which it thrived were not to be found in all the words that were written about the war, but rather in photographs of lifeless emaciated civilians piled unceremoniously into open trenches. An analytical social scientist, however, would settle neither for a photograph of an arms factory nor a photograph of victims of mass genocide. Rather, tenets of the discipline would suggest questions about the connections between the two. A commitment to critical inquiry would lead such a social scientist to examine the articulations between ideology, economics, social structure, and collective experience. A sense of humanity would encourage this scientist to identify the mechanisms by which individuals are robbed of their dignity, and a sense of political purpose would lead him or her to resist such mechanisms wherever they are found.

Second on my list of recommendations would be an admonition to resist letting analysis deteriorate into the two poles of the positivist romance, that "all photographs are lies" or that "photographs tell the truth." Rather than play around in this conceptual hurdy-gurdy, it makes more sense to ask about the kinds of truths and the kinds of lies which photographs might contain. Howard Becker has proposed such an orientation to photographic imagery (1978a), and his suggestion—that we ask ourselves what kinds of questions a given photograph might be able to answer—seems a good place to begin.

Third on my list of recommendations for work within this area is that the dialectic between use of photographs to study human activity and the study of photographic imagery itself be kept alive. This involves a commitment on the part of those involved—and to the present day, it has been largely found—that they will use images as well as entertain questions about what they mean.

Keeping this dialectic and reflexive orientation alive, however, is not a simple matter. It thrived for a while, for example, around the use of mathematics in social science. While some have continued to examine the media (e.g., Cicourel, 1964, 1968), those working within it have largely kept right on plugging, hardly missing a step. The same is true for survey research. A large body of work has called the meaning of surveys into question (e.g., Deutscher, 1973; Phillips, 1971, 1973; and Rosenthal, 1966), but this has had little effect on the continued authority attributed to survey data. For both mathematics and surveys, the critiques emerged, were noted, and then isolated from the mainstream practice of most professionals.

Clearly, this could happen with photographs, but as yet it has not. While there is some segregation between those who examine the language itself and those who use the language to investigate human activity, they still show up at the same meetings (e.g., Conference on Visual Anthropology, Visual Sociology Sections), and they still read the same journals (e.g., *Afterimage*; *Studies in the Anthropology of Visual Communications*). This is all for the best. At the moment, this area is not only vital but an excellent context in which to raise both big questions (e.g., the meaning of social science activity) and little ones (e.g., How do you prepare your cameras for a field trip to the tropics?).

The dialectic may make this area of inquiry appear less organized and more ambiguous than other modes of social research. In fact, it may be less so. On the other hand, commitment to the dialectic encourages a playfulness and humility towards the process of social science in general—both Phillips (1973) and Feyerabend (1975) seem to think this is a good thing—features which might well enhance the rest of the discipline. We might want to keep in mind, for example, that there are sometimes striking resemblances between the playfulness towards words practiced by linguists and that practiced by poets. With this in mind, it should come as no surprise that both artists and social scientists are to be found playing with cameras and photographs.

A FINAL NOTE

Jon Wagner

At heart, the best reasons for encouraging the development of visual social science lie within the disciplines themselves and the more general process of inquiry on which they are founded. It matters little to social science, for example, that some of us see photography to be fun, fascinating, and a good thing to do. What does matter is whether or not this mode of investigation can examine anything which is not already accounted for without it. Fortunately or unfortunately, the answer to that question is unequivocally yes, for social science has traditionally ignored visual dimensions of the phenomenal world.

As Stasz and Cheatwood indicate, we do not live by our eyes alone, and many live quite well without the use of sight at all. On the other hand, as members of the culture, we know from our everyday experience that much of what we do involves direct processing and interpreting of visual features of our world. We know that there is a difference between night and day, light and dark, and we know as well that seeing many people is different from seeing but a few, even if we talk to no one but ourselves. We know that when we enter buildings or exit buildings, meet friends, and go for walks we negotiate the physical and social terrain largely through attention to what we see. We know as well that we are at times surprised by how things look, and this implies that we have carried with us another image, one formed out of the past and serving as an expectation for the present. And, if we are attuned to these things, we may also notice that such images inform not only our actions and our ways of seeing, but our thought and ways of being.

Social science has not totally ignored these aspects of our experience, but it has been hard to investigate within it their shape and meaning. If nothing else, photography can make that easier, and in so doing, give us another set of clues about the business of our social lives. Fortunately, we are presently suspicious enough of this medium to examine such clues carefully, ever attentive to the complex contextual processes which have brought them our way. Photographic work in social science is thus doubly congruent with the details of life as lived. It both attends to the visual dimension of our knowing as well as provides truths which we appropriately take to be temporary and slightly ambiguous.

Such activity and its products fit well within a process of inquiry, but not so well within the more ambitious notion of social science as a "body of knowledge," and it is here that the lines will probably be drawn. Those who take heart from the process may well find photography a remarkable and welcome addition to social science practice. Those who hold to the body of knowledge may find it a complicating, at times bewildering, and inappropriately ambiguous mode of inquiry.

On the other hand, there is at least the chance that photography itself will prevail, its potency outside the discipline too great to ignore and too attractive to resist. If so, then we might look forward to a rather remarkable collaboration between art and science, one which respects the power of photographs as well as the questions which should be asked about their social scientific value. Through work with these images, we ought to be able to make our way well into the world and yet remember that the world itself only takes form within the frame of our perceptions.

PHOTO CREDITS

Cover: Jon Wagner
Chapter 2: All photographs by Doug Harper.
Chapter 3: All photographs by Phyllis Ewen.
Chapter 4: All photographs by Bill Aron.
Chapter 5: All photographs by William Newbold and Howie Cohen.
Chapter 6: Photographs 1, 2, 6, 7, 12, and 17 by Jon Wagner;
all others by Lynne Hollingsworth.
Chapter 7: All photographs in the collection of Christopher Musello.
Chapter 8: All photographs courtesy of the University of
Chicago Press.
Chapter 12: Photograph 6, p. 185 courtesy of the Walter C. Johnson
collection. All other photographs by Timothy J. Curry.
Chapter 15: All photographs by Raymond Lifchez.
Chapter 16: Photographs 1 and 2 courtesy of Anthony Dubovsky.
All other photographs in the collection of W. Russell Ellis.

REFERENCES

Abbott, B. (1975) The World of Atget. New York: Horizon.

Agee, J. and W. Evans (1960) Let Us Now Praise Famous Men. Boston: Houghton Mifflin.

Akeret, R. (1973) Photoanalysis. New York: Wyden.

American, S. (1898a) "The movement for small playgrounds." Amer. J. of Sociology 4: 159-170.

——— (1898b) "The movement for vacation schools." Amer. J. of Sociology 4: 309-325.

Antin, D. (1976) Talking at the Boundaries. New York: New Directions.

Arbus, D. (1972) Diane Arbus: An Aperture Monograph. Millerton, NY: Aperture.

Arendt, H. (1977) Eichmann in Jerusalem: A Report on the Banality of Evil. New York: Penguin.

Arnheim, R. (1969) Visual Thinking. Berkeley: Univ. of California Press.

Ashcraft, N. and A. Scheflen (1976) People Space: The Making and Breaking of Human Boundaries. Garden City, NY: Anchor/Doubleday.

Bahr, H. (1973a) Skid Row: An Introduction to Disaffiliation. New York: Oxford Univ. Press.

——— and T. Caplow (1973b) Old Men Drunk and Sober. New York: New York Univ. Press.

Banish, R. (1976) City Families. New York: Pantheon.

Barndt, D. (1974) "Toward a visual study of society." Technical Report. Lansing: Michigan State University College of Social Sciences.

Barthes, R. (1961) "The photographic message." Communications 1: 15-31.

——— (1964) "Rhetoric of the image." Communications 4: 32-51.

Bateson, G. and M. Mead (1942) Balinese Character. Special Publication of the New York Academy of Science, Vol. 2. New York: Academy of Science.

Becker, H. S. (1963) Outsiders. New York: Free Press.

——— (1974) "Art as collective action." Amer. Soc. Rev. 39 (December): 767-776.

——— (1975) "Photography and sociology." Afterimage 3 (May-June): 1 and 2.

——— (1978a) "Do photographs tell the truth?" Afterimage 5 (February): 9-13.

——— (1978b) "Arts and crafts." Amer. J. of Sociology 2: 485-500.

Bellman, B. L. and B. Jules-Rosette (1977) A Paradigm for Looking: Cross-cultural Research with Visual Media. Norwood, NJ: Ablex.

Bellocq, E. J. (1970) Storyville Portraits. New York: Museum of Modern Art.

Berger, J. (1973) Ways of Seeing. New York: Viking.

Birdwhistell, R. (1969) "Still photographs: interviews and filming." Kinesics and Context. New York: Ballantine.

——— (1970) Kinesics and Context: Essays on Body Motion Communication. Philadelphia: Univ. of Pennsylvania Press.

Blackmar, F. (1897) "The smoky pilgrims." Amer. J. of Sociology 2: 485-500.

Blumer, H. (1969) Symbolic Interactionism: Perspective and Method. Englewood Cliffs, NJ: Prentice-Hall.

Bogue, D. (1963) Skid Row in American Cities. Chicago: Community and Family Study Center.

Breckenridge, S. P. and E. Abbott (1910) "Chicago's housing problem: families in furnished rooms." Amer. J. of Sociology 16: 289-308.

——— (1911a) "Back of the yards." Amer. J. of Sociology 16: 433-468.

——— (1911b) "The west side revisited." Amer. J. of Sociology 17: 1-34.

——— (1911c) "South Chicago at the gates of the steel mills." Amer. J. of Sociology 17: 145-176.

Brush, R. O. and E. L. Shafer (1975) "Application of a landscape-preference model to land management," in E. Zube et al. (eds.) Landscape Assessment: Value Perceptions and Resources. Stroudsburg, PA: Dowden, Hutchinson and Ross.

Bushnell, C. (1901a) "Some social aspects of the Chicago stockyards, I." Amer. J. of Sociology 7: 145-170.

——— (1901b) "Some social aspects of the Chicago stockyards, II." Amer. J. of Sociology 7, 3: 289-330.

——— (1902) "Some social aspects of the Chicago stockyards, III." Amer. J. of Sociology 7, 4: 433-474.

Byers, P. (1964) "Still photography in the systematic recording and analysis of behavioral data." Human Organization 23: 78-84.

——— (1966) "Cameras don't take pictures." Columbia University Forum 9: 27-31.

——— and M. Mead (1968) The Small Conference. Paris: Mouton.

Callahan, H. (1967) Harry Callahan. New York: Museum of Modern Art.

Callenbach, E. (1975) Ecotopia: The Notebooks and Reports of William Weston. Berkeley, CA: Banyan Tree.

Chalfen, R. (1974a) "Film as visual communication: a sociovidistic study of filmmaking." Master's thesis, University of Pennsylvania Annenberg School of Communication.

——— (1974b) "Review of Photoanalysis." Studies in the Anthropology of Visual Communication 1 (Fall): 57-60.

——— (1975) "Cinema naivete: a study of home movie-making as visual communication." Studies in the Anthropology of Visual Communication 2: 87-103.

Chandler, K. (1903) "A new idea in social fraternity." Amer. J. of Sociology 8: 442-455.

Chapin, F. S. (1950) "Sociometric stars as isolates." Amer. J. of Sociology 56: 263-267.

Cheatwood, D. (1976) "Visual sociology." Paper presented at the State University of New York conference on "Photography among the Disciplines," at the Visual Studies Workshop, Rochester, NY, October 29-31.

——— and T. Lindquist (1976) The Human Image: Sociology and Photography. New Brunswick: Transaction.

Cicourel, A. (1964) Method and Measurement in Sociology. New York: Free Press.

——— (1968) The Social Organization of Juvenile Justice. New York: John Wiley.

Cloninger, S. J. (1974) "The sexually dimorphic image: the influence of gender differences on imagemaking." Ph.D. dissertation, Ohio State University.

Clynes, M. (1969) "Toward a theory of man: precision of essential form in living communications," in N. Leibovic and J. C. Eccles (eds.) Information Processing in the Nervous System. New York: Springer-Verlag.

Cohen, H., T. McLaren, S. Moss, R. Petyk, and E. Zube (1977) Pedestrians and Wind in the Urban Environment. Amherst: University of Massachusetts Institute for Man and Environment.

Collier, J. (1957) "Photography in anthropology: a report on two experiments." Amer. Anthropologist 59: 843-849.

——— (1967) Visual Anthropology: Photography as a Research Method. New York: Holt, Rinehart & Winston.

——— (1973) Alaskan Eskimo Education, A Film Analysis of Cultural Confrontation in the Schools. New York: Holt, Rinehart & Winston.

——— and A. Buitron (1949) The Awakening Valley. Chicago: Univ. of Chicago Press.

Commons, J. R. (1897) "The junior republic." Amer. J. of Sociology 3: 281-296.
——— (1898) "The junior republic: II." Amer. J. of Sociology 3: 433-448.
Comstock, A. P. (1912) "The problem of the Negro." Amer. J. of Sociology 18: 241-257.
Cooper, C. (1975) Easter Hill Village: Some Social Implications of Design. New York: Free Press.
Cornell Peru Project (1956) Ithaca, NY: Cornell University Department of Anthropology.
Cullen, G. (1961) The Concise Townscape. New York: Van Nostrand Reinhold Co.
Curry, T. J. and A. C. Clarke (1977) Introducing Visual Sociology. Dubuque: Kendall/ Hunt.
Davis, G. and V. Ayers (1975) "Photographic recording of environmental behavior, " pp. 235-279 in W. Michelson (ed.) Behavioral Research Methods in Environmental Design. New York: Dowden, Hutchinson and Ross.
Davis, K. (1959) "The myth of functional analysis as a special method in sociology and anthropology." Amer. Soc. Rev. 24 (December): 757-772.
Dent, E. (1937) "The Leica in visual education," pp. 275-294 in W. D. Morgan and H. M. Lester (eds.) The Leica Manual. New York: Morgan and Lester.
Deutscher, I. (1973) What We Say/What We Do: Sentiments and Acts. Glenview, IL: Scott, Foresman.
Dewey, J. (1957) Art as Experience. New York: Capricorn. (originally published 1934)
Diener, E. and R. Crandall (1978) Ethics in Social and Behavioral Research. Chicago: Univ. of Chicago Press.
Dobroszycki, L. and B. Kirshenblatt-Gimblett (1977) Image Before My Eyes. New York: Schocken.
Douglas, J. (1976) Investigative Social Research. Beverly Hills, CA: Sage.
Ekman, P., W. Friesen, and P. Ellsworth (1972) Emotion in the Human Face: Guidelines for Research and an Integration of Findings. New York: Pergamon.
Ellis, W. R. (1971) "Planning, design and black community style: the problem of occasion-adequate space," in W. Mitchell (ed.) Environmental Design: Research and Practice. Proceedings of the Environmental Design Research Association/Architectural Research Conference, Los Angeles.
——— (1974) "The environment of human relations: perspective and problems." J. of Architectural Education 27 (June) 2 and 3: 11-18, 54.
——— (1976) "Advertised life: dwelling, family and commercial culture in American habitat," pp. 103-118 in American Values and Habitat: A Research Agenda. Washington, DC: American Association for the Advancement of Science.
——— (1978) "Media, dwellings and public life." Presented at the Seventy-Third Annual Meeting of the American Sociological Association, San Francisco.
Erickson, E. (1935) Employment Conditions in Beauty Shops: A Study of Four Cities. U.S. Department of Labor Bulletin of the Women's Bureau, 133. Washington, DC: Government Printing Office.
Erikson, K. (1976) Everything in Its Path. New York: Simon and Schuster.
Fairchild, E. M. (1899) "Society's need of effective ethical instruction . . ." Amer. J. of Sociology 4: 443-447.
Feyerabend, P. (1975) Against Method. London: Verso.
Filstead, W. J. (1970) Qualitative Methodology: First Hand Involvement with the Social World. Chicago: Rand McNally.
Fitzgerald, F. S. (1959) Flappers and Philosophers. New York: Charles Scribner's.
Francis, R. G. (1971) "How to make an inexpensive commentary film." A report to the National Science Foundation. (mimeographed, revised edition)
Frank, R. (1969) The Americans. New York: Aperture. (original publication 1959)

Friere, P. (1973) Pedagogy of the Oppressed (Myra Bergman Ramos, trans.). New York: Seabury.

Gatewood, C. (1977) People in Focus. New York: Amphoto.

Gesell, A. (1934) An Atlas of Infant Behaviour. New Haven, CT: Yale Univ. Press.

————— (1943) "Cinemanalysis: a method of behavioural study." J. of General Psychology 47: 3.

Goffman, E. (1961) Asylums: Essays on the Social Situations of Mental Patients. Garden City, NY: Doubleday Anchor.

————— (1976) "Gender advertisements." Studies in the Anthropology of Visual Communications 3 (Fall): 69-154.

Gould, P. and R. White (1974) Mental Maps. Baltimore, MD: Penguin.

Greebie, B. (1975) "Problems of scale and context in assessing a generalized landscape for particular persons," pp. 65-91 in E. Zube, R. Brush, and J. Fabes (eds.) Landscape Assessment: Value Perceptions and Resources. Stroudsburg, PA: Dowden, Hutchinson and Ross.

Griffith, J. and L. E. Miner (1972) "Visual literacy research guides." Audiovisual Instruction (May): 30-35.

Hall, E. (1959) The Silent Language. Garden City, New York: Doubleday.

————— (1966) The Hidden Dimension. Garden City, New York: Doubleday.

————— (1977) Beyond Culture. Garden City, NY: Doubleday.

Hall, E. T. (1974) Handbook for Proxemic Research. Washington, DC: Society for the Anthropology of Visual Communication.

Harper, D. (1975) "The homeless man: an ethnography of work trains and booze." Ph.D. dissertation, University of Michigan.

————— (1978) "At home on the rails." Qualitative Sociology 1 (September).

Hattersly, R. (1976) Discover Yourself Through Photography. Dobbs Ferry, NY: Morgan and Morgan.

Hawkins, M. L. (1971) "A model for the effective use of pictures in teaching social studies." Audiovisual Instruction 16 (April): 46-48.

Heidegger, M. (1962) Being and Time. New York: Harper & Row.

Heider, K. (1976) Ethnographic Film. Austin: Univ. of Texas Press.

Heyman, K. and M. Mead (1965) Family. New York: Macmillan.

Hicks, W. (1972) pp. 19-56 in R. Smith Schuneman (ed.) Photographic Communication: The Principles, Problems and Challenges of Photojournalism. New York: Hastings House.

Hine, L. (1932) Men at Work. New York: Macmillan.

Hockings, P. [ed.] (1975) Principles of Visual Anthropology. Paris: Mouton.

Horowitz, I. L. (1976) "Pictures at an exhibition," pp. 7-11 in D. Cheatwood and T. Lindquist (eds.) In the Human Image: Sociology and Photography. Fredonia, NY: State University College of New York Press.

Howe, L. (1977) Pink Collar Workers. New York: Avon.

Hughes, C. (1960) People of Cove and Woodlot: Communities from the Viewpoint of Social Psychiatry. New York: Basic Books.

Hughes, E. (1914) "The Lithuanians in the fourth ward." Amer. J. of Sociology 20: 209-312.

Hughes, E. C. (1960) "Introduction," pp. iii-xiii in B. H. Junker (ed.) Fieldwork: An Introduction to the Social Sciences. Chicago: Univ. of Chicago Press.

Hunt, M. B. (1910) "The housing of non-family groups of men in Chicago." Amer. J. of Sociology 16: 145-170.

Hymes, D. [ed.] (1974) Reinventing Anthropology. New York: Vintage.

Isyumov, N. and A. G. Davenport (1975) "The ground level wind environment in built-up areas," in K. J. Eaton (ed.) Proceedings of the Fourth International Conference on Wind Effects on Buildings and Structures. London: Cambridge Univ. Press.

Ivens, J. (1969) The Camera and I. New York: International.

Jackson, B. (1977) Killing Time: Life in the Arkansas Penitentiary. Ithaca, NY: Cornell Univ. Press.

————— (1978) "Documentary truth: working notes." Afterimage 6 (Summer) 1 and 2.

Jay, R. (1969) "Personal and extra-personal vision in anthropology," pp. 367-381 in D. Hymes (ed.) Reinventing Anthropology. New York: Random House.

Jeanneret-Gris, C. E. (1970) Towards a New Architecture, by Le Corbusier (F. Etchells, trans.). New York: Praeger.

Kaplan, R. (1975) "Some methods and strategies in the prediction of preference," pp. 118-129 in E. Zube, R. Brush, and J. Fabes (eds.) Landscape Assessment: Value Perceptions and Resources. Stroudsburg, PA: Dowden, Hutchinson and Ross.

Kaplan, S. (1975) "An informal model for the prediction of preference," pp. 92-101 in E. Zube, R. Brush, and J. Fabes (eds.) Landscape Assessment: Value Perceptions and Resources. Stroudsburg, PA: Dowden, Hutchinson and Ross.

Keller, S. (1976) Twin Rivers: Study of a Planned Community. Washington, DC: National Technical Information Service (NSF/RA-760749).

Lange, D. and P. S. Taylor (1969) An American Exodus. New Haven, CT: Yale Univ. Press.

Larsen, O. and W. R. Catton, Jr. (1962) Conceptual Sociology: A Manual of Exercises Relating Concepts to Specimens, Principles and Definitions. New York: Harper.

Lesy, M. (1973) Wisconsin Death Trip. New York: Pantheon.

————— (1976) Real Times: Louisville in the Twenties. New York: Pantheon.

Levitt, H. (1965) A Way of Seeing: Photographs of New York, with an Essay by James Agee. New York: Viking.

Lewis, S. (1976) Producing Slide Tapes. Cambridge, MA: Slide Tape Collective.

Lipman, A. (1969) "The architectural belief system and social behavior." British J. of Sociology 22 (June) 2: 190-204.

Lynch, K. (1960) The Image of the City. Cambridge, MA: MIT Press.

Lyon, D. (1971) Conversations with the Dead. New York: Holt, Rinehart & Winston.

Lyons, N. (1966) Photographers on Photography. Englewood Cliffs, NJ: Prentice-Hall.

McClintock, S.S.A. (1901a) "Kentucky mountains and their feuds." Amer. J. of Sociology 7: 1-28.

————— (1901b) "A cause of feuds." Amer. J. of Sociology 7: 171-187.

————— (1903) "Around the island of Cebu on horseback." Amer. J. of Sociology 8: 433-441.

McLean, A. M. (1903) "The sweatshop in summer." Amer. J. of Sociology 8: 289-309.

McPhail, C. and R. T. Wohlstein (1978) "Judging the presence and extent of collective behavior: a method for producing and analyzing film records." Presented at the 1978 annual meeting of the American Sociological Association, San Francisco.

Mead, M. (1963) "Anthropology and the camera," pp. 166-184 in W. Morgan (ed.) The Encyclopedia of Photography. Vol. 1. New York: Greystone.

————— and Bateson, G. (1976) "For god's sake, Margaret." CoEvolution Q. 10 (June): 32-44.

Milgram, S. (1976) "The image-freezing machine." Transaction 14: 7-12. (also appears in Psychology Today [Jan.] 1977: 50 ff.)

————— (1978) The Individual in a Social World. Reading, MA: Addison-Wesley.

Milliken, O. J. (1898) "Chicago's vacation schools." Amer. J. of Sociology 4: 289-308.

Mills. C. W. (1959) The Sociological Imagination. New York: Oxford Univ. Press.

Monroe, P. (1898) "Possibilities of the present industrial system." Amer. J. of Sociology 3: 729-753.

Moore, D. (1897) "A day at Hull House." Amer. J. of Sociology 2: 629-641.

Moore, E. D. (1897) "The social value of the saloon." Amer. J. of Sociology 3: 1-12.

Morris, M. B. (1977) An Excursion into Creative Sociology. New York: Columbia Univ. Press.

Morris, W. (1968) The Home Place. Lincoln: Univ. of Nebraska Press.

Musello, C. (1977) "Home mode photography: a study of visual interaction and communication in everyday life." Master's thesis. University of Pennsylvania Annenberg School of Communication.

——— (in press) "Studying the home mode: an exploration of family photography and visual communication." Studies in the Anthropology of Visual Communication (Spring).

Muybridge, E. (1955) Human Figure in Motion. New York: Dover.

——— (1957) Animals in Motion (L. Brown, ed.). New York: Dover.

Neutra, R. (1954) Survival Through Design. New York: Oxford Univ. Press.

Nietzsche, F. (1967) On the Genealogy of Morals (Walker Kaufman, trans.). New York: Random House.

——— (1973) Beyond Good and Evil (R. J. Hollingdale, trans.). New York: Penguin.

Norton, G. P. (1913) "Two Italian districts." Amer. J. of Sociology 18: 509-542.

Ohrin, K. B. (1977) "What you see is what you get: Dorothea Lange and Ansel Adams at Manzanar." Journ. History 4 (Spring): 14-32.

Owens, B. (1973) Suburbia. San Francisco: Straight Arrow.

——— (1977) Working: I Do It for the Money. New York: Simon and Schuster.

Penwarden, A. D. and A.F.E. Wise (1975) Wind Environment Around Buildings. Building Research Establishment Report. London: HMSO.

Percy, W. (1975) The Message in the Bottle. New York: Farrar, Straus & Giroux.

Perin, C. (1970) With Man in Mind. Cambridge, MA: MIT Press.

Phillips, D. (1971) Knowledge From What? Theories and Methods in Social Research. Chicago: Rand McNally.

——— (1973) Abandoning Method. San Francisco: Jossey-Bass.

Platt, J. M. (1975) Visual Literacy. Washington, DC: National Education Association.

Proshansky, H. (1974) "Environmental psychology and the design profession," pp. 72-80 in J. Lang et al. (ed.) Designing for Human Behavior. Stroudsburg, PA: Dowden, Hutchinson and Ross.

Pushkarev, B. and J. M. Zupan (1975) Urban Space for Pedestrians. Cambridge, MA: MIT Press.

Redfield, R. (1960) The Little Community: View Points for the Study of a Human Whole. Chicago: Univ. of Chicago Press.

Riis, J. A. (1971) How the Other Half Lives. New York: Dover. (originally published in 1890)

Rosenblum, B. (1978) Photographers at Work. New York: Holmes and Meier.

Rosenthal, R. (1966) Experimenter Effects in Behavioral Research. New York: Appleton-Century-Crofts.

Ruby, J. (1973) "Up the Zambesi with notebook and camera or being an anthropolotist without doing anthropology . . . with pictures." SAVICOM Newsletter 4: 12-15.

——— (1975) "Is an ethnographic film a filmic ethnography?" Studies in the Anthropology of Visual Communications 2 (Fall): 104-111.

——— (1976) "In a pic's eye: interpretive strategies for deriving significance and meaning from photographs." Afterimage 3: 5-7.

Schatzman, L. and A. Strauss (1973) Field Research: Strategies for a Natural Sociology. Englewood Cliffs, NJ: Prentice-Hall.

Schutz, A. (1962) "Common-sense and scientific interpretation of human action," pp. 5-47 in M. Natanson (ed.) The Collected Papers: Volume 1 The Problem of Social Reality. The Hague: Nijhoff.

Seaford, H. (1971) The Southern Syndrome: A Regional Patterning of Facial Muscle Contraction. Ph.D. dissertation, Harvard University.

Sekula, A. (1975) "On the invention of photographic meaning." Artforum 13 (January): 36-45.

Shanas, E. (1945) "The American Journal of Sociology through fifty years." Amer. J. of Sociology 50: 522-533.

Shroder, D. (1973) Engagement in the Mirror. Ph.D. dissertation, Northwestern University.

Simmons, M. W. (1904) "Education in the South." Amer. J. of Sociology 10: 382-407.

Slavin, N. (1976) When Two or More Are Gathered Together. New York: Farrar, Straus & Giroux.

Small, A. (1905) "A decade of sociology." Amer. J. of Sociology 9: 1-10.

——— (1907) "Points of agreement among sociologists." Amer. J. of Sociology 11: 633-649.

Smith, E. (1958) "Drama beneath a city window: sixth avenue photographs." Life 44 (March 10): 107-114.

Smith, W. E. and A. M. Smith (1975) Minimata. New York: Holt, Rinehart & Winston.

Sontag, S. (1977) On Photography. New York: Farrar, Straus & Giroux.

Sorenson, R. (1976) The Edge of the Forest: Land, Childhood and Change in a New Guinea Protoagricultural Society. Washington, DC: Smithsonian Institution Press.

Spindler, G. and L. Spindler (1965) "The instrumental activities inventory: a technique for the study of psychological acculturation." Southwestern J. of Anthropology 21: 1-23.

Spradley, J. (1970) You Owe Yourself a Drunk: An Ethnography of Urban Nomads. Boston: Little Brown.

Stack, R. (1975) Warriors. New York: Harper & Row.

Sudnow, D. [ed.] (1972) Studies in Social Interaction. New York: Free Press.

Suttles, G. (1972) The Social Construction of Communities. Chicago: Univ. of Chicago Press.

Szarkowski, J. (1966) The Photographer's Eye. New York: Museum of Modern Art.

——— (1973) Looking at Photographs. New York: Museum of Modern Art.

Thompson, K. S. and A. C. Clarke (1974) "Photographic imagery and the Viet Nam war: an unexamined perspective." J. of Psychology 87: 279-292.

——— and S. Dinitz (1974) "Reactions to My Lai: a visual-verbal comparison." Sociology and Social Research 58: 122-129.

Tinbergen, N. (1968) Curious Naturalists. New York: Natural History Press.

Trembley, M., J. Collier, Jr., and T. Sasaki (1954) "Navajo housing in transition." Amer. Indians 14 (3): 187-218.

Van Schelle, A. F. (1910) "A city of vagabonds." Amer. J. of Sociology 16: 1-20.

Vincent, G. E. (1898) "A retarded frontier." Amer. J. of Sociology 4: 1-20.

Vishniac, R. (1947) Polish Jews. New York: Schocken.

Walker, N. (1915) "Greeks and Italians in the neighborhood of Hull House." Amer. J. of Sociology 21: 285-316.

Weegee (1945) Naked City. New York: Essential.

Whyte, W. (1972) "Please just a nice place to sit." New York Times Magazine (December 3): pp. 20 ff.

Wilson, H. L. and E. W. Smith (1914) "Among the Slovaks in the twentieth ward." Amer. J. of Sociology 20: 145-169.

Winningham, G. (1971) Friday Night in the Coliseum. Rochester, NY: Allison.

——— (1972) Going Texan. Houston: Mavis P. Kelsey, Jr.

Winograd, G. (1977) Public Relations. New York: Museum of Modern Art.

——— and J. Szarkowski (1979) Animals. New York: Museum of Modern Art.

Wiseman, J. (1970) Stations of the Lost: The Treatment of Skid Row Alcoholics. Englewood Cliffs, NJ: Prentice-Hall.

Worth, S. (1974) "Pictures can't say ain't." In Proceedings of the International Conference on Semiotics, Milan.

——— and J. Adair (1972) Through Navajo Eyes: An Exploration in Film Communication and Anthropology. Bloomington: Indiana Univ. Press.

Yates, F. (1966) The Art of Memory. Chicago: Univ. of Chicago Press.

Zelditch, M. (1962) "Some methodological problems of field studies," Amer. J. of Sociology, 67: 566-576.

Zube, E. et al. (1975) "Perception and prediction of scenic resource values of the Northeast," pp. 151-167 in E. Zube et al. (eds.) Landscape Assessment: Value Perceptions and Resources. Stroudsburg, PA: Dowden, Hutchinson and Ross.

Zueblin, C. (1898) "Municipal playgrounds in Chicago." Amer. J. of Sociology 4: 144-158.

——— (1899) "The world's first sociological laboratory." Amer. J. of Sociology 4: 577-592.

ABOUT THE AUTHORS

BILL ARON is a free-lance photographer residing in Los Angeles, California. His photographic work has been widely exhibited (both in individual and museum thematic or group shows) and has appeared in a number of publications, including *Camera 35, The Village Voice, The New York Times Sunday Magazine, Moment Magazine*, and the *Baltimore Jewish Times*. Aron is represented by the Pucker/Safrai Gallery, which features his work both in Boston and as travelling exhibits.

HOWARD S. BECKER is Professor of Sociology at Northwestern University. He is the author of *Outsiders*. He is now completing a book on the arts, and has taught photography at the San Francisco Art Institute, Columbia College (Chicago), and the Visual Studies Workshop.

DERRAL CHEATWOOD is Assistant Professor of Criminal Justice at the University of Baltimore. He is the coeditor of *Qualitative Sociology* and author of *Restrictive Labels in a Juvenile Correctional Setting*. His many publications have appeared in *Teaching Sociology, Journal of Criminal Justice*, and *Sociological Focus*. His interests include the study of deviance and of visual sociology.

ALFRED C. CLARKE is Professor of Sociology at the Ohio State University. He is coauthor of *Introducing Visual Sociology*, and *Social Problems: Dissensus and Deviation in an Industrail Society*. His interests include the visual study of society, social organization, and the sociology of work and leisure.

JOHN COLLIER is Professor of Anthropology and Education at San Francisco State University. He associated with photographer Dorothea Lange as a member of the historical section of photography in the Farm Security Administration documenting the Great Depression. He is coauthor of *The Awakening Valley*, and author of *Visual Anthropology*, and *Alaskan Eskimo Education*.

TIMOTHY J. CURRY is Associate Professor of Sociology at the Ohio State University. He is coauthor of *Introducing Visual Sociology*. His articles have appeared in such journals as *Sociometry, The Geron-*

tologist, and *Pacific Sociological Review* His current research focuses on the impact of widely disseminated imagery in our society. He is also collaborating on a book regarding the sociology of sports.

W. RUSSELL ELLIS is Associate Professor of Behavioral Sciences in Architecture at the University of California, Berkeley. He has served as a design consultant to both the public and private sectors. His articles have appeared in *Architectural Student* and *Journal of Architectural Education.* He is the author of *Race, Change, and Urban Society* published in the *Urban Affairs Annual Review.*

PHYLLIS EWEN is Assistant Professor of Art Education at the Massachusetts College of Art. Her photographic work has been exhibited in New York, Portland, and Cambridge and in publications such as *Camera 35* and *Radical America.* And she is a contributor to *Our Bodies, Our Selves* and *Our Selves and Our Children.*

DOUG HARPER is Assistant Professor of Sociology at the State University of New York at Potsdam. He has done ethnographic field work in India, also among the police in Boston, and in freight trains, skid rows, and hobo jungles in many parts of America. His work is published in articles on tramp culture and the use of photography as sociological data. His photography has been shown in one-man and group exhibitions in Boston, Minneapolis, and New York.

MARTIN H. KRIEGER is a fellow of the National Humanities Center, Research Triangle Park, North Carolina during 1978-1979. He is Assistant Professor in the Hubert H. Humphrey Institute of Public Affairs at the University of Minnesota, Minneapolis. He works on the philosophical foundation of public affairs and design, as well as on environmental doom and on literary theory.

RAYMOND LIFCHEZ teaches in the Department of Architecture at the University of California, Berkeley. He is the coauthor of *Design for Independent Living: The Environment and Physically Disabled People,* a psychosocial study of handicapped people living on their own in Berkeley, California.

CHRISTOPHER MUSELLO is a research associate for the Center of Visual Communication, Inc. in Philadelphia. His photography has been shown at Colgate University, Tufts University, and the Boston

Museum of Fine Arts. He is currently engaged in research (at the University of Pennslyvania Annenberg School of Communications) concerned with house form, furnishings, and ornamentation as visually communicative events in addition to his continuing research on family photography.

EUGENIA SHANKLIN is Assistant Professor of Anthropology at Trenton State College. She is the author *Culture is As Culture Does: Informal Social Organization* (in preparation) and *Time's Bitter Flood: Tradition in Southwest Donegal*. Her field work includes the exploration of economic impact in the County Donegal, Ireland as well as studies of the Black community in Long Island and the South Bronx.

CLARICE STASZ teaches courses in documentary photography, documentary film, and ethnographic film in the Sociology Department at Sonoma State University. She has published numerous books and articles in the areas of simulation, sex roles, and social control. She is currently completing research reports based on her photodocumentary study of country fairs in Northern California and advertising signs in Los Angeles.

JON WAGNER is Director of the Field Studies Program at the University of California, Berkeley and the author of *Misfits and Missionaries: A School for Black Dropouts*. He has taught photography and sociology at Columbia College (Chicago), Trenton State College, and in the Architecture Department of the University of California, Berkeley. He is currently working on a book about the experiential connections between work culture and college student culture.

ERVIN ZUBE is Director of the School of Renewable Natural Resources at the University of Arizona. He is also a fellow of the American Academy in Rome. As a consultant, he has served public and private agencies in the United States and the Caribbean, including the National Park Service, Army Corps of Engineers, Nantucket Conservation Foundation and the governments of Puerto Rico, the Virgin Islands, and Jamaica.